Spenser and the Motives of Metaphor

Spenser and the Motives of Metaphor

A. LEIGH DENEEF

DUKE UNIVERSITY PRESS
Durham, N.C.   1982

Printed in the United States of
America on acid-free paper.

Library of Congress Cataloging in Publication Data

DeNeef, A. Leigh.
    Spenser and the motives of metaphor.

    Includes bibliographical references and index.
    1. Spenser, Edmund, 1552?–1599—Criticism and
interpretation.   2. Metaphor.   I. Title.
PR2364.D4   1982   821'.3   82-14737
ISBN 0-8223-0487-2

Contents

Acknowledgments

Anyone who chooses to write today on the poetry of Edmund Spenser must labor under the shadow and in the company of many who came before. The extent to which my own commentary has been guided by previous studies is only partially reflected in the notes, for it is impossible there to acknowledge my enormous debts to Paul Alpers, Harry Berger, A. Bartlett Giamatti, A. C. Hamilton, and Rosemond Tuve. I am sure that much of what I now take to be my own came originally from their provocative studies. I am particularly embarrassed by the fact that *The Structure of Allegory in The Faerie Queene* and *Allegorical Imagery* appear so infrequently in the notes, but I trust my general dependence upon both works is apparent throughout.

Also not acknowledged in the notes is my indebtedness to those students at Duke University who have sat patiently through my speculations over the past few years. Four of these students have helped in specific ways: John Skillen pushed me to clarify my notions about Spenser's poetic; David Estes taught me a mini-sequence in the *Amoretti*; Bernadette Bosky forced me to reexamine my earlier conclusions about *The Fowre Hymnes*; and John Morey led me to read "rede" in *The Faerie Queene*.

Robert Gleckner, A. C. Hamilton, Thomas Hester, Wallace Jackson, and Gerald Snare have affirmed for me all the blessings of the academic community by their willingness to read my work, to talk out problems with me, and to criticize in continually useful ways. Wally Jackson deserves more than the gratitude friendship owes, for he found in an earlier version the promise of a better book. If I have not delivered the book he saw, it is because my vision is not as keen as his.

Joanne Ferguson, Ed Haynes, and John Menapace graciously and skillfully guided the book through its stages of preparation, and the Duke University Research Council generously supported both its research and its publication.

I am grateful for permissions to publish in revised form work that earlier appeared in *Renaissance Papers*, *Studies in Philology*, and *English Literary History*.

My greatest debt, conventional though it sounds, is to my wife and colleague, Barbara J. Baines, whose constant faith, sanity, and encouragement made the writing of this book a genuine pleasure and an act of love. For her the work is made, "in lieu of many ornaments/With which my love should duly have been deckt."

Spenser and the Motives of Metaphor

Introduction

Edmund Spenser, like his modern critic, knows that the literary text is framed by two difficult tasks: the poet must express his meaning correctly, and the reader must interpret that meaning correctly. To write poetry and to read it are equal opportunities for proper or improper entry into that activity we call the *work* of art. In fact, "rightly to devise" and "to read aright" are not only artistic and ethical obligations but also literary and moral problems. Any poet who would address our profit and delight, as well as move us to virtuous action, must be alert to the abuses of the poetic word to which both he and we might fall prey. Such vigilance is particularly evident in Spenser's poetry. Throughout his literary career, he adopts a variety of defensive and self-defensive postures to protect his texts from potential misuse, from their being, in his words, either misconstrued or misconstructed. Indeed, it could be argued that the need to defend himself against detracting or distracting "wrong-speakers" and his verse against abusive "faultfinders"[1] threatens to overwhelm all of his other poetic intentions. Current criticism must attempt to understand the motivations and the manifestations of such defenses: why Spenser so constantly and conspicuously calls upon them, what dangers they bespeak in the poetic act, and what use Spenser makes of them in shaping his individual poems.

The literary threats posed by "wrong-speakers" and "faultfinders" are not only occasions for authorial defense. They are that, to be sure, but Spenser consistently draws the abuses of wrong writing and wrong reading into metaphoric relation, offering thereby to equate the two activities. It is easy enough to see one reason for such an equation: Spenser can treat two antagonists as one and ensure a right reading of his own text by assuring himself it has been rightly written. But his bolder scheme is to efface the rigid distinctions usually separating these two ways of entering a literary work. To Spenser, proper writing must remain conscious of, responsible to, and participating in, right reading; conversely, right reading is never merely an adjunct to but a necessary component of proper writing. The strategies by which Spenser yokes writing and reading, poet and audience, speaking and hearing, teaching and learning are many and complex. To follow them is to chart our way into the heart of some of his most difficult poetic challenges and to gain a better understanding of his artistic successes.

When Spenser published the initial installment of *The Faerie Queene*, he appended, as he had to his very first poem, an Argument of the whole book in order to guide the reader's "better vnderstanding." Obviously, Spenser felt in

1590, as E. K. had in 1579, that there was considerable risk in "labouring to conceale" the "generall dryft and purpose" of his work. Why, we might ask, is the meaning of the poems so difficult to discern? The usual answer would be: because both poems are allegories in which Spenser can only hint or "shadow" historical, moral, and religious realities. Spenser himself seems to concur:

> Sir knowing how doubtfully all Allegories may be construed, and this booke of mine, which I haue entituled the *Faery Queene*, being a continued Allegory, or darke conceit, I haue thought good aswell for auoyding of gealous opinions and misconstructions, as also for your better light in reading thereof . . . to discouer vnto you the generall intention and meaning, which in the whole course thereof I haue fashioned. . . .[2]

This description should remind us of Fidelia's sacred Book, "wherein darke things were writt, hard to be vnderstood," and which "none could read, except she did them teach" (*FQ* I.x.13, 19). The analogue might be taken as implying that Spenser has momentarily lost faith in Raleigh's abilities as a right reader. Indeed, Spenser frequently loses faith in his readers, especially when, like Redcross, he begins to doubt. One of our tasks, therefore, will be to mark the occasions of the poet's doubt and to watch how he "adds faith" in order to combat it. At the moment, however, the analogy between Spenser's book and Fidelia's offers a different clue, for it suggests that poetic instruction is not only, or even preeminently, a moral teaching but also education in the elementary task of faithful reading.

If this subject is at least part of Spenser's point in the Argument, we must not allow the vexed and specialized notion of allegory to divert our attention from the problems of right reading. Poetry would be "hard to be vnderstood" even if it were not allegorical. E. K. suggests this is so because verse unfolds its matter covertly rather than openly and because the poet labors to conceal as much as he wishes to reveal. Poetry, in short, says one thing to mean another. We might call this fact allegory, or we might argue that it is simply a consequence of the truth that poetry speaks by means of metaphors. Allegory, from this perspective, is merely the most blatant example of the way a poet devises his metaphors and the way a reader interprets them. Allegory is a metaphoric poetry that continuously announces itself as such.

Somewhat surprisingly, neither E. K.'s epistle to *The Shepheardes Calender* nor any of the Commendatory Verses affixed to *The Faerie Queene* once mentions Spenser's allegories or his metaphors. Instead, the poet is praised for his *conceits*. E. K. distinguishes the "uncouthe, unkiste" Colin Clout from that "rakehellye route of our ragged rymers" who seem, in the very midst of their poems, suddenly to forget "theyr former conceipt." The first of the seven

Commendatory poems is entitled "A Vision upon this conceipt of the *Faery Queene*." The third wishes grace to the Queen, who has infused "such high conceites" into her humble poet's wits; and the fourth contrasts Spenser's earlier pastorals with the "deepe conceits" he "now singes in Faeries deedes." Spenser himself twice alludes to the term in the letter to Raleigh: he opens his summary by referring to his "darke conceit," and he closes by suggesting that now Raleigh can gather "the whole intention of the conceit."

As a theoretical beginning, we might ask what relation the term conceit bears to either allegory or metaphor, and whether it clarifies the interpretive difficulties inherent in a poem which says one thing to mean another. To answer these questions, we need to turn momentarily to Spenser's friend and fellow poet, Sir Philip Sidney. In a critical paragraph of the *Apology for Poetry*, Sidney explicates his distinction between the brazen world of nature and the golden worlds of poetry by arguing:

> Neither let this be jestingly conceived, because the works of the one be essential, the other in imitation or fiction; for any understanding knoweth the skill of the artificer standeth in that Idea or fore-conceit of the work, and not in the work itself. And that the poet hath that Idea is manifest, by delivering them forth in such excellency as he hath imagined them. Which delivering forth also is not wholly imaginative, as we are wont to say by them that build castles in the air; but so far substantially it worketh, not only to make a Cyrus, which had been but a particular excellency as nature might have done, but to bestow a Cyrus upon the world to make many Cyruses, if they will learn aright why and how that maker made him.[3]

Much heated discussion has been occasioned by these sentences, and especially by the three central terms, Idea, fore-conceit, and work (or literary text). It is perhaps not unfair to say that the whole course of Sidney's treatise, as well as its applicability to Renaissance literature in general, depends upon how we conceive the relationships between his words. As I have argued in detail elsewhere, Sidney's terms show us how Renaissance poets thought about the metaphoric nature of both their own and their readers' work.[4]

An Idea is an abstract universal, implanted in the human mind by God (infused, as Sidney implies, "with the force of a divine breath"). The poet neither teaches nor constructs Ideas; rather, he reminds the reader of Ideas present, although perhaps "forgotten" through misuse or lack of use, in the latter's mind. The conceit[5] is an abstract relational concept, a hypothetical option or a latent potential. It is a first metaphoric imitation of the abstract Idea and hence the initial mimetic step in fashioning that Idea into an action, in putting the Idea to work. The verbal poem, or work, is the second metaphoric imitation of the Idea, its concrete materialization or manifestation. As

Sidney later describes this final stage of the mimetic process, the Idea is delivered, figured, or bodied forth in the narrative images and speaking pictures of the text.

Elsewhere in the *Apology*, Sidney clarifies these three terms by drawing out the mimetic and metaphoric relations between them. "Poesy," he argues, "is an art of imitation" (p. 79). Although such "imitation" glances occasionally at conventional descriptions of poetry's relation to an exterior world, Sidney is more interested in how mimesis orders and controls the internal process of poetic making. Xenophon, to cite his own example, "imitates" in his poem an Idea within his mind. He makes the Idea manifest, that is, by creating two metaphors of it—a conceptual conceit and a verbal text. If we think of this process in linguistic terms, we might say that Xenophon begins with an abstract noun, "Rule" or "Right Rule." His first mimetic and metaphorizing act is to conceive an infinitive by which that Idea can be activated—"to rule." Finally, he fashions a particular character who acts according to that infinitive and who can therefore serve as a verbal metaphor of actual "ruling."

Sidney himself hints at such a linguistic paradigm when he addresses, significantly, the problem of poetic misreading. Arguing against *mysomousoi*, or poet-haters, Sidney notes that these railers frequently misinterpret and thus falsely imitate the most excellent of literary texts. When Agrippa ironically condemns science and Erasmus ironically commends folly, the poet-haters misconstrue their witty jests as a license to carp at all learning. "But for Erasmus and Agrippa," Sidney writes, "they had another foundation, than the superficial part would promise." Their intentions and meanings, that is, were concealed behind the ostensibly literal words of their texts. In failing to recognize that fact, the poet-haters have read like all ignorant "faultfinders, who will correct the *verb* before they understand the *noun*, and confute others' knowledge before they confirm their own" (p. 100; my italics).

Sidney's example is susceptible to two different interpretations, but both illustrate the mimetic and metaphorizing process he envisions. His noun clearly represents the Ideas Erasmus and Agrippa had in mind. The verb may represent the Erasmian or Agrippan text, the verbalization of the Idea which has been fashioned by, or taken its formal shape from, the infinitive fore-conceit. In this case, the poet-haters have failed to understand the metaphor that is the text, as well as the true subject (the Idea) to which the metaphor points. Sidney may, however, be suggesting a broader linguistic model. The verb of his statement may refer to the *railing* of the poet-haters and thus to the ethical actions which the poetic texts incite. The texts themselves offer illustrations of the conceptual options *to rail* and therefore represent limited manifestations of the poets' Ideas. The poet-haters, failing to understand the metaphoric relation between Idea and conceit, imitate the wrong part of speech. In this interpretation the entire poetic act is embraced by Sidney's three terms: the noun is the poet's Idea; the fore-conceit is the infinitive poem; and the verb is the reader's subsequent ethical work. Obviously, such a model is here used to explore problems of wrong reading, but we may glimpse in the process a hint of the way such reading conditions further making: the poet-haters, who initially "misconstrue" the poets' words, end by "misconstructing" their own ethical activities. To misread is a metaphorical adumbration of a miswriting, and he who is a "faultfinder" becomes, in Sidney's eyes, a subsequent "wrong-speaker."

Later in the *Apology*, Sidney fashions a debate between a philosopher and an historian. The debate begins in earnest when the historian argues that he teaches an active virtue whereas the philosopher teaches only a disputative virtue, or, as Sidney rephrases it, the philosopher "giveth the precept, and the other the example" (p. 84). Both disciplines, he then argues, are incomplete educationally because each provides but half the necessary truth. The poet, however, who "coupleth the general notion with the particular example," participates in and completes both studies.

Again Sidney implies a linguistic model. The Idea, as an abstract universal, is the special province, the object and the subject, of philosophy. Particular texts or works, as instances of experiential contingencies, are the province of history. Poetry serves as the mimetic and metaphoric relation between the two (it "coupleth" them). It demonstrates how the noun-Ideas of philosophy are bodied forth in the gerund-texts of history by providing the formal and activating principle of mimesis, the infinitive fore-conceit.

The linguistic model proposed in the *Apology* is a succinct summation of common Renaissance assumptions about how poetry is made and used. It is clear, however, that these notions are not ours. We hardly conceive of Xenophon's Cyrus inspiring other Cyruses, and the whole concept of mimesis makes us uncomfortable. Yet unless we understand how Sidney's poetic process unites both poet and reader in the same act of metaphoric imitation, we may fail to see why reading and writing are equally problematic for a poet like Spenser.

Let us clarify Sidney's scheme by means of a Spenser poem. Behind the *Epithalamion* lies the originating abstract Idea, *Love*. Spenser's first mimetic act was to fashion that Idea into a fore-conceit capable of giving both direction and form to his subsequent verbal narrative. In this case, we can propose the infinitive *to love* as Spenser's conceit. Each element of the narrative then imitates this conceit by bodying it forth in particular verbal acts of *loving*. In theory, this is true not only of the characters in Spenser's poem—lover, beloved, priest, nymphs, merchants' daughters, all demonstrate activities or ways of loving—but also of its images, its structures, and, of course, its themes. For example, the process by which the single torch in stanza 2 grows steadily to "a thousand torches flaming bright" in stanza 23, and that by which the solitary voice of the lover singing to himself becomes an ever-expanding choir of earthly and heavenly anthems are verbal metaphors of the way love flows outward from the blessed pair to embrace and be embraced by all of creation. They are speaking pictures of particularized *loving* and again imitate various ways in which *to love*. Or, more exactly, we see that the conceit *to love* is the principle which fashions all the discrete verbal acts of *loving* into a metaphoric unity. If we take the additional step of asking what universal is metaphorically revealed in the multiple options *to love*, we arrive at the originating Idea, *Love*.

What, then, does the *Epithalamion* teach us? Not individual acts of loving, but why and how to love. It teaches us why we must and how we can re-fashion our own loving to the Idea that Love is. Thus we can say that each stage of Spenser's making involves the formation of a metaphor. The conceit metaphorically speaks the Idea, just as the text metaphorically speaks the conceit. And Sidney, therefore, can conclude that poetry is a "representing, counterfeiting, or figuring forth to speak metaphorically."[6] Metaphorically here refers primarily to the internal stages of mimetic making; yet the poet's Idea is an analogue to that innate in the mind of the reader, just as both are metaphors of the true Idea of Love-as-Marriage existing in the mind of God. Mimesis and metaphor thus imply and implicate each other.

Although we have been emphasizing the poet's stages of writing, we have also hinted at the reader's obligation when confronted by a text like the *Epithalamion*: he must reverse the mimetic process of the poet. Whereas the poet transfers an Idea into a text, the reader must transfer the text into an Idea. He must disembody the textual particulars back into the conceit and the Idea out of which they were originally bodied forth. He can accomplish this task only by understanding why and how the text is metaphoric. Recognizing that, he will be led to the abstract principles the text imitates. Sidney suggests the following scheme: the reader's senses receive the poem's images and speaking pictures; his imagination perceives its structure or groundplot; his reason discursively understands the fore-conceit; his intellect meditates on the Idea; and his will promotes the subsequent imitative action.

The final step is the most difficult since it transfers the reader from a literary to an ethical action and since it depends upon several prior achievements. First, the reader must recognize the fore-conceit as a metaphoric imitation; second, he must understand that as an infinitive, the conceit provides the model by which any Idea becomes an action; and third, he must realize that the conceit can direct his ethical imitation just as it directs the poet's verbal imitation. Once the reader of the *Epithalamion* has learned why and how Spenser has made that text, he will have re-cognized the Idea of Love-as-Marriage and the model by which to love. He can then imitate the poet's "art of imitation": he can body forth in his own actions the Idea in his own mind which the poem has now illuminated. It is important to be clear on this analogy: both poet and reader imitate an Idea by bodying it forth in particular and concrete work, verbal in the first instance, moral in the second. The conceit, the mimetic model by which such figuring forth is accomplished, thus draws poet and reader into the same activity of making.[7] Such an analogy has widespread implications for all Renaissance poetry. It will allow Spenser, for example, to argue consistently that writing poetry is a moral activity and that moral activity is poetic making. If the reader is envisioned, therefore, as a potential maker, the poet can be seen as a preceding reader. "Rightly to devise" and "to read aright" may ultimately be collapsed into a single metaphoric activity.

We can support this conception of the reading process by looking briefly at another Renaissance theorist, Marsilio Ficino. Discussing an architectural Idea, Ficino argues:

> In the beginning, an architect conceives an idea of the building, like an Idea in the soul. Then he builds, as nearly as possible, the kind of house he has thought out. Who will deny that the house is a body, and that it is very much like the incorporeal idea of the builder in likeness to which it was made? Furthermore, it is to be judged like the idea more because of a certain incorporeal plan than because of its matter. Therefore, subtract its matter, if you can. You can indeed subtract it in thought, but leave the plan; nothing material or corporeal will remain to you. On the contrary, these two will be exactly the same internally, both the plan which comes forth from the builder and the plan which remains [unmaterialized in the mind of] the builder.[8]

Ficino's "plan," because it is defined generically ("the kind of house he has thought out"), is a fore-conceit, a first metaphoric imitation of the Platonic Idea of House. It is clear that a reader following Ficino's instructions would de-materialize the text-house in order to perceive the form which that text imitates. By that means, he learns as well the mimetic process and the precise metaphoric stages by which the Idea of a building can be bodied forth into a particular house.

With the *Epithalamion*, then, we could say that the reader must *read through* the textual images, structures, and characters to the form, the conceit, which the text imitates. Having done so, he learns why and how the maker made that text. He learns, in short, the infinitive model by which all human actions body forth human absolutes—virtues, vices, or what else. It is for this reason that both Sidney and Spenser consistently use the term "conceit" rather than "Idea" to refer to the unique lesson of poetry. The Ideas are in the human mind; what man must learn, and what poetry teaches him, is the model by which such Ideas can be made manifest in the actions of his will.

As we know, Sidney and Spenser conceive of poetry as playing a far larger role than simply teaching ethical action. For Spenser, poetry becomes instrumental in societal and religious reform. Again and again, his poems take us beyond the problems of isolated and individual characters to political and social issues. The private speaker who begins the *Epithalamion* has, by its close, been brought into public relation not only with his beloved but also with his neighbors, his country, his church, and even with all the blessed harmony of saved Christian souls both past and future. Spenser clearly thinks of the song that is the *Epithalamion* as itself an instrument whereby such societal and cosmic concords are effected, or at least as a means by which we, as poets and readers, can actively participate in such a wedding, refashioning ourselves according to the model of heavenly love. Sidney also conceives of poetry in these terms, whether he is thinking about England's participation, through its literature, in the European Protestant League, or whether he is thinking more specifically about poetry's role in reforming individual man:

> This purifying of wit—this enriching of memory, enabling of judgement, and enlarging of conceit—which commonly we call learning, under what name soever it come forth, or to what immediate end soever it be directed, the final end is to lead and draw us to as high a perfection as our degenerate souls, made worse by their clayey lodgings, can be capable of. . . . to know, and by knowledge to lift up the mind from the dungeon of the body to the enjoying his own divine essence. [p. 82]

To Sidney, the "ending end" of poetry is nothing less than the highest of Christian callings—the reformation of man.

Obviously, both Sidney and Spenser inherit much of this urge towards renovation and reformation from the humanist tradition. But to concede this point is not also to admit that the reformation of man is a naive ideal arbitrarily grafted onto their poetic theories. Rather, it is a careful and logical extension of those theories. In fact, it is precisely that extension that underlies and gives point to Sidney's analogy between the poet-maker and the heavenly Maker. The poet, like all men, is a narrative character in God's Poem, the Book of Creation. By learning God's "art of imitation," he learns why and how he himself has been bodied or figured forth and, in turn, how to fashion or refashion himself according to the Idea by which he was originally made. The poet, in short, is the true metaphor of God: he teaches us how to imitate the image or Idea of divinity which has been implanted in our souls, as well as how to imitate the process of imitation by which that Idea has been bodied forth to speak metaphorically, to call us to metaphor and to the mimetic activity of making metaphors. It is ultimately this task that both legitimizes and directs the poet's vocation as Sidney and Spenser understand it. And it is this task both authors have in mind when they consider the responsibilities of the Right Poet.

Neither Spenser nor Sidney, of course, is the first Renaissance thinker to pursue art to such elevated or consecrated heights, and once more we might look to Ficino for an analogous statement. As Cassirer reminds us, Ficino thought not only about the relation between divine creation and artistic re-creation but also about the place of art in the reformation of man:

> According to Ficino, the whole point of religious and philosophical *knowledge* is nothing other than the eradication from the world of everything that seems deformed; and the recognition that even things that seem formless participate in form. But such knowledge cannot content itself with mere concept; it must be transformed into action, and prove itself through action. Here begins the contribution of the artist. He can fulfill the requirement that speculation can only state. Man can only be certain that the sense world *has* form and shape if he continually *gives* it form. . . . Seen in this light, however, art no longer lies outside the province of religion but becomes a moment of the religious process itself. If redemption is conceived of as a renovation of the *form* of man and of the world, i.e., as a true *reformatio*, then the focal point of the intellectual life must lie in the place where the "idea" is embodied, i.e., where the non-sensible form present in the mind of the artist breaks forth into the world of the visible and becomes realized in it.[9]

Poetry teaches man the art of re-forming, the skillful process by which a mental Idea can make itself manifest in particular experiential activities. To use the terms of another Renaissance figure, art can teach us the mimetic processes by which man was "well formed in his creation, deformed in his corruption, and reformed in Grace."[10] By such grace, and with the grace of poetic instruction, man can refashion or re-form himself according to the *imago Dei* by which he was originally formed and which remains implanted but forgotten in the human mind.

Once the conception of poetry and its role in human existence has been extended to these concerns, the responsibilities that accrue to right speaking and right reading are measurably heightened. One sign of the new status accorded both activities is the kind of metaphor to which they are subjected. The poet now discovers his ideal mimetic model in the creative act of God: as a maker, the poet participates in and furthers the unfolding in human time of the Maker's Word. The reader, of course, finds his ideal model in the Son who hears, echoes, and bears living witness to that Word by making it manifest in human action. Yet such metaphors measure only poetic successes. To understand the ways in which writing and reading become problematic for the Renaissance poet, we must be alert to the metaphors which define or articulate not the success but the abuse of the Word: the parodic false maker, like Satan or Archimago or Despair, whose misconstructions threaten uncreation rather than recreation; the fault-finding misreader, like Redcross, like Adam, like the *mysomousoi*, who refuses the reformation offered him and who therefore slides continuously toward ultimate deformation. Between such positive and negative metaphoric models, both the Renaissance poet and his reader must locate their literal places.

Poetry is an art of imitation that figures forth in order to speak metaphorically. This assertion is both definition and warning. The defensive postures we find being adopted by Renaissance poets like Sidney and Spenser are concessions to that warning, an open acknowledgment that the imitation poetry calls us to can be abused and misused. The most common manifestation of this awareness is the routine distinction both authors make between those poets and readers who remain faithful to the fact that poetry speaks metaphorically and those who would reduce poetry to literality. For Sidney, this orientation is demanded by the very nature of his task—to answer those who have slandered the good name of poetry by calling its literal effects into question, and to remind such literary antagonists (both "wrong-speakers" and "faultfinders") what poetry is and does. For Spenser, the rhetoric of defense would seem to be a freer choice: he is not answering particular charges against poetry, and he has no apparent antagonists. Yet the frequency with which Spenser places either his own voice or his poems on the defensive suggests that the freedom of this choice is not as great as we might expect. Indeed, it could be argued that it is precisely Spenser's acceptance of the Sidneyan theory that poetry speaks metaphorically that commits him as well to Sidney's rhetoric of defense. For Sidney's theory does more than define the metaphoric nature of the poetic act: it also identifies the literalizing abuses to which that act is susceptible. These abuses range from internal errors of the poet's own pen (copying the ancients literally rather than using them as metaphoric groundplots for profitable inventions, indecorously mixing disparate generic models without accommodating them to a broader metaphoric conceit), to epistemological errors regarding the poet's language (literal-minded dichotomies of fact or fiction, truth or lie, precept or example, which are avoided only by understanding how poetry speaks metaphorically), to external threats posed by a variety of either poor or perverse readers (presuming that the sign of Thebes on a stage door identifies a literal place, or simply refusing, like Alexander of Pherae, to see any metaphoric relation between the literal text and literal human experience).

Spenser was particularly alert to this aspect of Sidney's work. As a consequence, his desire to announce himself as a Sidneyan Right Poet was, in his own mind, dependent upon his ability to marshall an adequate defense against the abuses Sidney identifies. He had, that is, to prove his own claims of right speaking and to guard his texts against the threat of wrong readings by making the metaphoric nature of the poems a constant and central focus. The defensive strategies he adopts in order to accomplish these goals occasion much of the drama of his poetry. It is possible to argue that Spenser's typical poem is shaped largely by an internal dialogue with itself, one voice continually opening the textual words, figures, and genres to greater metaphoric extension and the other continually striving to fix and enclose them in literal reductions. The first voice is usually characterized as either a true poet or a right reader; the second is a fictional antagonist, either false poet or false reader, against which the first voice must constantly defend itself. Part of the purpose of this study is to attempt a fuller understanding of such internal dialogues and to show why Spenser feels so compelled to create fictional antagonists in order to defend himself and his texts.

The larger purpose of the study is to explore Spenser's conception of and use of metaphor. The Sidneyan model of how poetry speaks metaphorically will greatly assist this task, but it will not take us far enough. For ultimately, Sidney does not confront the poet's darkest doubts about how any metaphor can be misconstrued or misconstructed. Spenser, however, constantly doubts his own language, his own abilities "rightly to define" in that language, and his reader's ability "rightly to read" that language. It is therefore not enough to see metaphor as an answer to the problems of poetic abuse, for metaphor itself can be misused. Our task, then, is to understand the conditions under which even metaphor becomes susceptible to either right use or misuse.

Some years ago, Rosemond Tuve tried to correct what she took to be a false impression of Renaissance allegory by arguing that it is not a closed system of fixed narrative and extra-narrative equivalences, but a rhetorical strategy of pointing toward what never can be verbally or even conceptually fixed and limited. Allegory, in short, was a mode of adumbrating significant relations, not a mode of predetermined analogies.[11] Current views of poetic metaphor tend to fall into similar conceptual perspectives. "To speak metaphorically" thus ranges from drawing particular and limited analogies to suggesting a multiplicity of relations. What we need to see is that Spenser himself is conscious of these two ways of conceiving metaphor. A metaphoric equivalence can be used to supply an answer, close a text, or bring its speaking to an end. Yet metaphor can also be a groundplot for further invention, an opening of a text to increased conversation, an incentive to re-creation. When we examine the particular ways in which Spenser's poetry speaks metaphorically, we thus situate ourselves at the center of a linguistic controversy. We become not only observers but also participants in the drama of a text which must itself face the conflicting urges to close and to open, to declare and to suggest, to prescribe and to offer. To follow the course of the Spenserian metaphor is to track the poet's doubts about and his faith in both the language and the beings to which he has bound himself. Finally, it is to watch the fascinating project of a man trying to articulate the ways in which language speaks to us about the ways we speak the language.

Part I. The Minor Poems

Chapter 1. *The Shepheardes Calender*

The Sidneyan terms we have been using to sketch Spenser's poetic tasks and problems were not available, in 1579, to the aspiring author of *The Shepheardes Calender*. Spenser had yet to meet his younger colleague, and Sidney had yet to set out his poetic theories. Nonetheless, the assumption that poetry speaks metaphorically was at the heart of the literary tradition both men inherited. And while Spenser could not have understood the implications of metaphoric speaking as Sidney was to articulate them, it is easy enough to see that his early conceptions about metaphor accord with the scheme we have just proposed.

To disclose the metaphoric nature of the *Calender*, it is best to focus on its most conventional elements—the various literary kinds by which Spenser shapes both the individual eclogues and the work as a whole. By watching Spenser manipulate the generic terms of the poem, we can recover his basic presumptions about how poetry speaks metaphorically and some of the dangers such speaking occasions.

In her studies of Renaissance genre theory, Rosalie Colie suggests that the conceptual form of any literary genre be thought of as a way of perceiving, a "mental set" or "fix" upon the broader, experiential reality.[1] Implicit in her argument is the notion that genre, because it represents but one way of looking at reality, also mimetically limits that reality by reducing and particularizing it. Although Colie does not make use of Sidney's *Apology*, her view of genre finds considerable support in his verbal paradigm; in turn, that paradigm helps to define the precise nature of the generic decisions a poet must make and to place those decisions within the stages of poetic imitation.

Knowledge, or perception, is a literary as well as a philosophical Idea. Sidney calls it *architectonike*, an abstract ideal composed of self-knowledge, ethical and political wisdom, and the skill to put that wisdom into practice. Regardless of its exact term, perception is the educative Idea of any literary work. Individual poetic genres provide conceptual possibilities for achieving that Idea; they propose infinitive models by which to know or to perceive. Genre, therefore, can be taken as the formal fore-conceit of literary perception, a transitional form mediating between wisdom in the abstract and concrete verbal knowledge. Particular texts written in or according to a given genre illustrate acts of perceiving.[2] Within the literary system, then, the relationships between poetry, pastoral, and "Ye goat-herd gods," for example, are the same mimetic and metaphoric ones Sidney draws between Idea, fore-conceit, and text. Pastoral figures forth poetry as "Ye goat-herd gods" figures forth pastoral. In theory, it follows that pastoral, as a literary fore-conceit, is also a perceptual distortion, because a limitation, of the infinite possibilities of poetry as a whole, the Idea of poetry. Analogously, "Ye goat-herd gods," regardless of its stature as a poem, is a perceptual distortion of the numerous possibilities of the pastoral genre.[3] Every time a poet commits himself to a formal genre, he limits what he can see. By actually writing in that genre, he precludes additional points of view.

Yet it is wrong to think of genres as merely distorting texts of perceiving or distorted fore-conceits by which to perceive. As an infinitive model, genre must be kept conceptually neutral. For while genre may disclose and direct the particularizing movement from comprehensive perception to specific acts of perceiving, it also reveals the imitative method by which individual points of view can be abstracted to universal perception. This interplay between materializing and abstracting, particularizing and generalizing, individualizing and universalizing, literalizing and metaphorizing governs all generic systems and all texts written according to such systems.[4]

One slight adjustment can complicate this interplay. Suppose someone were to misunderstand either the neutrality of the genre or its place in the mimetic stages. Suppose, for instance, he were to read the textual railing of Erasmus's Moria as wisdom, as perception abstracted and universalized rather than perceiving individualized. We, like Sidney, would say he has misread the Encomium; he has not understood the ironic relationship between the verbal text and Erasmus's noun-Idea. He has, in effect, short-circuited the Sidneyan paradigm by failing to see the generic fore-conceit which both determines and reveals the paradoxical nature of Moria's oration. As we have seen, Sidney scoffs at such misreaders, calling them "faultfinders" and "wrong-speakers," but he does not explain how to correct their misreadings or how to guard one's text against their literary abuses.

Even before being exposed to Sidney's terms, Spenser was concerned with the misuse of literary forms. He populates The Shepheardes Calender with a variety of "wrong-speakers" and "faultfinders," shepherds whose narrative actions are judged as if they were literary imitations. In making these judgments, Spenser repeatedly implies a conception of genre much like the one just outlined. Those shepherds who use generic models only to limit or narrowly enclose their perceptions are guilty of literalizing and distorting poetic fore-conceits; they are consequently viewed as either misreaders or false poets. Those who abstract from the generic models a broader, more universal view of reality both read and write correctly. Spenser seems to derive these distinctions between right and wrong readers from their ability to recognize why and how poetry speaks metaphorically.

By judging his characters, furthermore, Spenser also suggests that the artistic processes of disembodying generic models into higher Ideas or figuring them forth into particular texts are ethical activities. Generic conceits, that is, provide not only poetic but also moral choices, and the art which bodies them forth in one sphere or medium is a metaphor for that which puts them to work in the other. Any misunderstanding of the metaphoric nature of the literary genre is thus analogous to the ethical error of severing a particular act from the larger system of moral options which gives value and meaning to all individual choices.

Reading the *Calender* in these terms may seem unduly moralistic, especially for those eclogues that E. K. designates as simply plaintive or recreative. Yet we need to remember how carefully we are excluded from the shepherds' limited pastoral world. E. K.'s introductory letter to Harvey, his classifying "Argument," and his textual glosses all compel a particularly literary perspective. Not simply ornaments to render the poem an instantaneous "classic," these appendages help to define our relationship to the shepherds as, above all, a literate audience reading about men in the process of becoming literate. We are reading our own origins—how literature comes to and can shape our literate lives. It is precisely this connection with the shepherds that guarantees our interest in their actions and identifies the metaphoric meaning of those actions to our own lives. The morality of our judgments, therefore, is not to be registered so much in censure of the shepherds as simply in the recognition that their narrative actions are conditioned in tangible ways by their use of sophisticated literary vehicles they do not fully understand. For Spenser, as for us, the theme of correct application of literature to ethics is a fundamental background to the otherwise entertaining pastoral drama.

To see how Spenser establishes this literary background and the place of genre in that background, we can begin by focusing on the most directly apprehendable of the poetic imitations, the dramatic oppositions of the text itself. The fullest account of these oppositions is given by Patrick Cullen, who argues that Spenser structures the *Calender* by placing a pagan, Arcadian viewpoint in confrontation with a Christian, Mantuan one.[5] Within the individual eclogues, this dramatic conflict shapes the thematic debates: youth versus age, spring versus winter, active life versus contemplative life, and so on. Rendered in schematic fashion, Cullen's argument unfolds the central Arcadian-Mantuan opposition into a Sidneyan groundplot. The Arcadian perspective metaphorically signifies spring, youth, the high estate, passion, confidence and participation in the world, ambition, and celebration; its speakers are Cuddie, Willie, Palinode, Morrell, and Hobbinoll. The Mantuan perspective metaphorically signifies winter, old age, the low estate, reason, *contemptus mundi*, withdrawal, and elegy; its speakers are Thenot, Thomalin, Piers, Colin, and Diggon Davie.

Although we could follow Cullen in using this groundplot to display and dispose the several thematic strands of the poem, it is more immediately relevant in pointing to one way the text speaks metaphorically. The focus on spring, for example, is a narrative element of the Arcadian "mental set," defining a perspective and determining certain actions. As such, it functions continuously as a metaphor of all the other Arcadian elements and consequently of the textual genre itself. This fact is not surprising, since Colie's studies have shown us that the formulae associated with particular genres tend to become metaphors of those genres and thus employable as any other rhetorical figure. What is somewhat surprising is that a given element, like spring, from the Arcadian string also serves as a metaphor of its antithetical Mantuan "set": spring-winter, youth-old age, and so on. No single element occurs as a literal or discrete textual fact; it is internally metaphoric from the start.

This double play of the narrative metaphors is in part a consequence of Spenser's decision to begin his year with January, a decision sufficiently dramatic and novel to call forth a lengthy explanation by the ever-alert E. K. Indeed, E. K.'s terms invoke the Christian-pagan, Mantuan-Arcadian sets even before the poem itself begins. The Janus face of January thus occasions the double-talk, as it were, of all the subsequent metaphoric elements.[6]

The metaphoric nature of Spenser's genres becomes even clearer when we consider the relation between pastoral itself and the Arcadian-Mantuan forms it engenders. The Renaissance pastoral, as Spenser inherited it, was already a kind of Arcadian-Mantuan double-talk, because "pastoral provided a mode for the juxtaposition of contending values and perspectives."[7] Pastoral, then, can be seen as a metaphoric fore-conceit of conflicting possibilities; it is that metaphor which accommodates the textual disparities and dichotomies into which the poet has bodied it forth. Conversely, the literal oppositions of the verbal narrative—the Mantuan-Arcadian groundplot—are to be resolved by the reader back into the metaphoric conceit that shapes the narrative. A closer look at some typical eclogues will reveal this metaphorizing process.

The April eclogue on Elisa and the November one on Dido are dramatic and thematic centers of the work as a whole; both represent moments in which the linear progression of time through the year is transcended. In April, Spenser moves backwards in time to recreate Elisa as the mythic spring goddess of fertility and regeneration. As the Fourth Grace of text and woodcut, Elisa stands as a permanent center, unchanged and unmoved, within the yearly cycle. Dido, recreated as a heavenly spirit, is similarly unchanging and unmoving. Both figures achieve eternity through a form of investiture: Elisa in the garb of nature, Dido in that of the spirit. But what is the relationship between them? If Elisa represents a natural, seasonal immortality and Dido a Christian one, are we to interpret the figures as dialectical opposites, as imitative metaphors of one another, or as complementary aspects of the same continuum? To answer these questions, we must shift our gaze away from the textual details to the informing generic models controlling and determining those details.

In April, Colin constructs a pastoral blazon, festive and optimistic, celebratory in tone; in November, he makes a formal dirge or threnody, elegiac and lamenting. Spenser exploits the two textual genres for their dictional and rhetorical oppositions of compliment and complaint, praise and blame. On the level of the generic fore-conceit, however, the dichotomy of compliment and complaint is resolved in the epideictic infinitive to laud.[8] The textual structures of the pagan blazon (Arcadian) and the Christian dirge (Mantuan) both originate in the broader genre of the literary hymn (Pastoral). They represent limited narrative options of bodying forth the generic infinitive, and the reader's attempt to resolve their conflicting surface figures leads him to interpret those figures metaphorically. The disparities of the textual genres, then, direct us to disembody narrative images and actions back into the abstract generic fore-conceits which they imitate. The textual terms, the groundplot that Spenser invents, become the groundplot for our own profitable invention in turn, an invention now reversing the poet's mimetic process.

In the February eclogue, Spenser fashions a similar textual opposition. As Cuddie and Thenot argue about the cycle of seasons and the respective virtues of spring and winter, their dialogue takes the form of a conventional youth versus age débat. At the end of the eclogue, Thenot tells a fable about an oak and a briar to support his own perspective. As Cullen's thematic analysis suggests, Spenser does not present the fable as a simple parallel to the debate, for the oak and the briar serve as perverse and tragic extensions of the two shepherds. By setting the textual débat and the textual fable against one another, Spenser forces both to speak metaphorically of the mixed genre which subsumes the two arguments in a broader vision and which offers the reader an opportunity to accommodate the narratively disparate perspectives. The reader, in short, conceives the metaphoric infinitive which shapes both textual genres into the poetic whole of this particular eclogue. In this case, to scorn might be invented as the fore-conceit of the whole, although it is not necessary to agree on a specific infinitive or its generic set in order to understand the strategy by which the text is made to speak metaphorically.

As a third example, we can look briefly at the August eclogue. In the first half of the poem, Perigot and Willye argue the "mischaunce" of love; in the second half, Cuddie sings of Colin's similar misadventure. But again Spenser sets the two versions of "complaining" in dialectical opposition by heightening the rhetoric of their respective textual genres: the comic parody of the song-contest versus the "dooleful" seriousness of the *planctus*. As in "February," Spenser's mixing of the two textual genres within the same eclogue leads the reader to a subsuming, accommodating frame (the complaint genre) and a broader, shaping fore-conceit (to complain).

What we have been describing in these three eclogues is the mimetic process by which genre itself speaks metaphorically.[9] No one would deny, of course, that the eclogues are metaphoric, but their metaphoric nature is usually defined by supplying external referents for the textual figures. These need not be specific topical allusions—Elisa as Queen Elizabeth, the oak as Leicester, Cuddie as Edward Dyer—but may be moral virtues, a sort of thematic metaphorizing of the figures in the poem. The point is, however, that the figures would be metaphoric without any historical or thematic referents; or, more exactly, before they can be extended to historical or thematic significance, they should be understood as already metaphoric elements of the extended groundplot which expresses the Arcadian-Mantuan oppositions. The textual genres speak metaphorically the various fore-conceits they body forth. It does not matter on this level whether we dispose the text along an Arcadian-Mantuan plot at all, for these perspectives are always carefully controlled by conventional literary kinds: *planctus*, débat, fable, mock-epic, blazon, beast epic, encomium, song-contest, dirge, lament, and so forth. It is not an external referent that commands our attention but the nature and use of these internal literary metaphors.

Once we begin to address the question of how the textual kinds are to be used, we bring the poetic model into metaphoric relation with the ethical model and begin to discriminate between readers of the narrative and readers within the narrative. The September eclogue is a convenient example. Diggon Davie, having left the idyllic realm of innocence to wander "about the world rounde," falls, as it were, into experience. He learns the corruption of the city, the vanity of earthly ambition, the folly and presumption of false shepherds. As a consequence, he interprets all existence as dark and threatening, and he takes the terms of his generic perspective—here pastoral satire—as literal and accurate reflections of reality. In the terms of Cullen's groundplot, he has so literally bound himself to the Mantuan view that he fails to perceive any good in life. Hobbinoll, on the other hand, having remained in the safety of his idyllic realm, has not experienced the Fall. Yet he too interprets all existence in the literalizing terms of a generic perspective—the golden age idyll. As Diggon's eyes are blind to the presence of good, Hobbinoll's are blind to the presence of evil: there are no wolves, he argues, in Christendom. Both characters erroneously presume that the generic terms are literal rather than metaphoric and thus constitutive of disparity (experience versus innocence, evil versus good, despair versus euphoria) rather than unity or completeness. Each fails, in short, to see that his own perspective metaphorically implies and can metaphorically be accommodated to the other's.

In the July eclogue, Spenser again dramatizes the effects of misreading. Thomalin, interpreting all existence in the literal terms of his Mantuan genre,

praises only the low estate and patient humility; Morrell, equally given to literalizing the terms of his Arcadian genre, "reads" only the high estate and
aspiration. Neither sees that the hills over which they argue offer a continuum of ethical possibilities and thus void the dichotomies into which they
have trapped themselves. In each eclogue, the activities of the shepherds—
their choices of setting, their occupations, their capacities for seeing, and especially the argumentative stances they take in attacking one another—are
literal actings out of their one-dimensional and literal-minded perspectives.
Improper reading of their textual genres has thus led the shepherds into ethical error, into foolish faultfinding and wrong speaking. The shepherds use
their generic models only to limit or dichotomize ethical action; they rarely
open those models to metaphoric synthesis. For Spenser, however, and for
the readers of the narrative, the generic models are always *genera mixta*.[10]
They do not necessitate either/or alternatives but offer ethical challenges and
opportunities. The poetic activity of locating a conceit capable of avoiding
arbitrary dichotomy is thus a metaphoric lesson in and a metaphoric model
of the ethical activity of preventing arbitrary and prematurely disjunctive
choices.

Against his wrong-reading and faultfinding shepherds, Spenser sets two
ideal poets, one historical, the other mythic. The first is Chaucer, called
Tityrus after and frequently aligned with Virgil; the second is Orpheus.
Spenser defines both poets in the same terms. In "February," Thenot describes the songs of Tityrus as follows:

> Many meete tales of youth did he make,
> And some of loue, and some of cheualrie.   [ll. 98–99]

In "June," Colin laments:

> The God of shepheards *Tityrus* is dead,
> Who taught me homely, as I can, to make.
> He, whilst he liued, was the soueraigne head
> Of shepheards all, that bene with loue ytake:
> Well couth he wayle hys Woes, and lightly slake
> The flames, which loue within his heart had bredd,
> And tell vs mery tales, to keepe vs wake,
> The while our sheepe about vs safely fedde.   [ll. 81–88]

In "October," the "Romish" Tityrus is described as one who

> left his Oaten reede,
> Whereon he earst had taught his flocks to feede,
> And laboured lands to yield the timely eare,
> And eft did sing of warres and deadly drede,
> So as the Heauens did quake his verse to here.   [ll. 56–60]

And finally, in "December," Spenser refers in passing to the songs (the plural is significant) Colin has learned from Tityrus.

The result of these descriptions is that Tityrus, as the arch-poet, represents a figurative merging of poetic choices and generic perspectives. He sings merry tales and lamentations, simple love songs and martial epics. E. K. directs us to this generic emphasis by glossing the lines from "October" cited above:

> in these three verses are the three seuerall workes of Virgile intended. For in teaching his flocks to feed, is meant his Æglogues. In labouring of lands, is hys Georgiques. In singing of wars and deadly dreade, is his diuine Æneis figured.

It is precisely his ability to alter and combine generic perspectives that assures Tityrus's fame and influence as a poet. He stands, therefore, as a counterpoint to Colin, who now sings only one lamenting song, and he symbolizes the poetic combination of perspectives that Colin is unable to achieve. Colin's January and December songs are identical *mono*logues: they are the only eclogues in the *Calender* that do not combine disparate viewpoints but choose a single option. By that choice, Colin seals his death, both ethically and poetically. The true or Right Poet, Spenser implies, is he who is able to transcend the limited sets of the individual textual genres by imagining metaphoric conceits or by constructing mixed forms which actualize differing perceptual options. The poet who cannot do this, who commits himself totally to but one narrative genre, limits himself to but one act of perceiving. All he can do is repeat that act over and over, as December repeats the somber and wintery conclusions of January. Right Poets progress through the calendric options; false or inadequate poets remain where they begin.[11]

Orpheus is mentioned only once in the *Calender* proper, but the allusion occurs in the crucial poetic debate of "October":

> Soone as thou gynst to sette thy notes in frame,
> O how the rurall routes to thee doe cleaue:
> Seemeth thou dost their soule of sence bereaue,
> All as the shepheard, that did fetch his dame
> From *Plutoes* balefull bowre withouten leaue:
> His musicks might the hellish hound did tame.   [ll. 25–30]

The significance of this reference lies in the notion of the opening lines, that of Cuddie's framing individual and discrete notes into harmonious song. We recall E. K.'s epistle to the *Calender*, in which he commends the poet for

> his dewe obseruing of Decorum euerye where, in personages, in seasons, in matter, in speach, and generally in al seemely simplycitie of handeling his matter, and framing his words.   [p. 7]

In a later passage, E. K. continues this praise:

> For what in most English wryters vseth to be loose, and as it were vngyrt, in this Authour is well grounded, finely framed, and strongly trussed vp together. [p. 9]

The idea of framing is repeatedly mentioned in the *Calender* (see also "June," ll. 57, 78; "August," l. 3, among others), but the most important instance occurs in E. K.'s gloss on the lines immediately preceding the Orpheus passage in "October." Explaining the Orphic origins of poetry, E. K. argues:

> some learned man being more hable then the rest, for speciall gyftes of wytte and Musicke, would take vpon him to sing fine verses to the people, in prayse eyther of vertue or of victory or of immortality or such like. At whose wonderful gyft al men being astonied and as it were rauished, with delight, thinking (as it was indeed) that he was inspired from aboue, called him vatem: which kinde of men afterwarde framing their verses to lighter musick (as of musick be many kinds, some sadder, some lighter, some martiall, some heroical: and so diuersely eke affect the mynds of men) found out lighter matter of Poesie also, some playing wyth loue, some scorning at mens fashions, some powred out in pleasures: and so were called Poetes or makers. [p. 100]

Framing, to E. K., is a mimetic and metaphoric challenge to match an invented structure to ethical reality.[12] In all three of his glosses, E. K. seems to define the artistic skill of such framing as tuning[13] the generic decorum to various human emotions, attitudes, and experiences. E. K., in short, is identifying the origins of poetry with the same metaphoric relationships between literary and ethical models that Spenser and Sidney take to be the ends of poetry. And it is precisely his focus on activities of framing that leads E. K., in the "Generall Argument," to use the poem as a groundplot of his own invention: he "frames" the tale into "three formes or ranckes" according to which "every thing herein [may] be reasonably" divided. More interesting than the plaintive, recreative, and moral divisions themselves is simply E. K.'s urge to frame the poem into a conceptual scheme. If we are correct in assuming that Spenser directs our attention to shaping infinitives rather than textual structures, then E. K. proves a capable reader of the poem. He understands that the acts of framing dramatized in the individual eclogues must themselves be abstracted, disembodied into the fore-conceits which they imitate.

In the epilogue, Spenser directs us beyond E. K.'s tripartite groundplot—for ultimately that is what E. K. fashions—to the originating Idea of the poem as a whole:

> Loe I have made a Calender for euery yeare,
> That steele in strength, and time in durance shall outweare:

> And if I marked well the starres reuolution,
>> It shall continewe till the worlds dissolution.   [ll. 1-4]

The frame of the "Calender" in these lines is neither a textual structure of twelve months nor a groundplot of rhetorical divisions. Neither is it, in the terms of S. K. Heninger, a microcosm metaphorically revealing the harmonizing principles of the macrocosm;[14] nor, in the terms of the present discussion, a new generic form metaphorically revealing the mimetic principles of the poetic Idea. It is certainly all of these things and more, but every attempt to verbalize the final frame is bound to be inadequate. What we need to see is that Spenser here forces us beyond the conceits we have formulated in order to frame his textual narratives (which are themselves activities of framing); we must now abstract from the conceits themselves a larger formal frame from which both they and the individual eclogues have been mimetically and metaphorically bodied forth.

The difficulty of perceiving the formal Idea of the poem is acknowledged by the poet himself, for even as he affirms such a frame, Spenser is forced to qualify his poem's expression of it. The "if" of line 3 of the epilogue clearly implies that the urge to embrace and articulate the universal is no more successful in the poem as a whole than the mimetic models of the textual genres have been for the shepherds within the poem. No matter how complex the final poetic form is, no matter how universalized or abstracted from the particular textual elements, the frame of the "Calender" is still metaphoric.

One reason this is so, of course, is because the poetic Idea is itself a metaphor for the reader's ethical Idea, just as the poetic text is a metaphor of the reader's ethical action. The self-defensive qualification, therefore, occasions the final shift in the focus of the epilogue away from the accomplishments of the poet to the mimetic challenge to the reader. Significantly, Spenser prepares for that shift by punning on a word that brings his own and his reader's activities into metaphoric relation. "If" he has accurately "marked" (i.e., written) his own metaphors and if the reader has correctly "marked" (i.e., read) them in turn, then the poem may prove "a free passeporte" to the "profitable invention" of both. And if the reader has thus learned his metaphoric relation to the poet, Spenser can, in effect, turn the poem over to him. He can "aske no more" because no more can be said; the metaphoric speaking and the rewards of the poet must give way to the substantial and intelligent response of the discerning reader. *Merce non mercede*!

In early and relatively uncomplicated terms, *The Shepheardes Calender* identifies the major components of Spenser's poetic: a dramatic confrontation of textual elements to force metaphoric abstraction and accommodation, the use of wrong speakers and wrong readers within the narrative to instruct and defend the right speaker and right readers of the narrative, and an insistence that the models of mimetic making serve equally for literary and for ethical works. Each of these strategies reveals a distinct aspect of why and how poetry speaks metaphorically. In the remainder of this study, we will trace Spenser's explorations of these aspects of metaphor and his growing awareness of what metaphoric speaking implies and demands.

Chapter 2. "The Ruins of Time"

Sidney is the first theoretician to offer Elizabethan poets a comprehensive definition of why poetry speaks metaphorically and a verbal model of how it speaks metaphorically. He is also the first to emphasize the two major problems that can render that model ineffective, namely, improper writing and improper reading. And while he does not himself offer any specific safeguards against false writing or false reading, he does force the poets who follow him to confront both problems openly and directly. It is imperative, therefore, to understand exactly how Sidney raises these questions and how his humanist followers tried to answer them.

In the course of defending poetry against foolish "faultfinders" and "wrong-speakers," Sidney makes two important concessions. Although he insists that poetry moves men to virtue more effectively than any other art, he also acknowledges that some men are either too ignorant (like the *mysomousoi*) or too stubborn (like Alexander Pheraeus) to be moved at all. No matter how excellent the literary text, there will be those who cannot or will not read it correctly. Similarly, despite his assertion that man's erected wit can create reformative poetry, Sidney is quick to admit that man is just as capable of abusing poetry. Such abuses range from technical errors—copying the ancients slavishly, composing "cold" sonnets, or indecorously mixing the comic with the tragic—to moral perversions—teaching wrong notions about God or "infect[ing]" the fancy with unworthy objects. Obviously, these two concessions, which encompass the entire poetic act, demand careful and cautious attention. Yet Sidney, by focusing on a conceptual art rather than specific artificers or artifacts, is able to avoid addressing either problem directly.

Indirectly, however, the *Apology* does propose an argument on the literary conditions which result in either false reading or false writing. When the *mysomousoi* do not recognize the noun behind the Erasmian text, or when Alexander does not perceive the relationship between Euripides's textual image and his own situation, these readers have failed primarily in understanding the metaphoric nature of the literary work. They read the textual metaphors as though they were literal, forgetting that poetry intends "to speak metaphorically." Thus, while the forms of their misreadings are clearly distinct— the *mysomousoi* represent a misunderstanding of the internal metaphoric principles of poetry, whereas Alexander represents a misunderstanding of the external metaphoric functions of poetry—the same condition allows and determines their interpretive errors. Sidney's conceptions of wrong writing are equally grounded in the metaphoric nature of the text. The writer, like the reader, must remember that poetry speaks metaphorically. To forget that essential truth leads to literalized notions of imitation, like classical emulation, or to positing metaphoric images as if they were ontological truths. Again Sidney appears to divide miswriting into internal and external errors, both conditioned by the failure to understand how poetry speaks metaphorically. In short, both poet and reader face two analogous obligations: to perceive the metaphoric stages of the verbal model, and to understand the metaphoric relationship between the "golden world" of a poem and the natural world outside the poem.

If such problems are only implicit in the *Apology*, they could hardly remain so for the humanist poets who came after Sidney. Engaged in a practical literary exercise which depended upon both their own and their readers' poetic skills, they had to confront openly the questions Sidney had raised. Spenser, in particular, is alert to these questions from his earliest poems. The need to establish an authority and a validity for his own speaking voice involves him from the start of his career in an ongoing exploration of the differences between wrong speaking and right speaking, between false poets and true ones. His recognition of the problem Sidney poses thus forces him into constant self-defense. Spenser's strategy for solving the problem is equally consistent: in poem after poem he fashions wrong speakers who serve as negative examples for validating the words of his own right-speaking voice. Both voices, moreover, are judged by two Sidneyan premises: first, that the principal distinction between true and false speaking can be measured by the speaker's awareness of the metaphoric status of his speech; and second, that such speech is, according to the Sidneyan model, an ethical action and thus subject to moral evaluation. False speaking is a metaphoric example of wrong acting just as wrong acting is a metaphoric instance of false speaking.

The same strategy can be seen in Spenser's treatment of right and wrong readers. In order to ensure a correct reading of his poem, he habitually includes within the narrative internal readers who illustrate both proper and improper responses to poetry. Again Sidney's assumptions provide the evaluative measure: false reading fails to recognize metaphors as metaphors and itself represents a metaphoric instance of immoral action.

"The Ruins of Time," the opening poem in Spenser's 1591 volume of *Complaints*, is a particularly clear example of these strategies, as well as a convenient illustration of Spenser's familiarity with and ability to exploit the Sidneyan verbal paradigm. Early Spenser criticism dismissed "The Ruins" as nothing more than a commissioned elegy on Sidney hurriedly combined with a clumsy redaction of Du Bellay's *Antiquitez de Rome*. It was quick to point out the triteness of the themes, the fragmentary state of the text, and the unimaginative treatment of the Dudley line.[1] Recent criticism has been more sympathetic: Nelson shows how the numerical stanzaic scheme synthesizes the poem's disparate parts; Maclure urges an occasional and thematic unity to the work; and Bayley argues that Spenser succeeds in the very immortalization he posits as the function of poetry.[2]

"The Ruins" is indeed unified by Spenser's focus on the function of poetry,[3] but we severely narrow that focus by thinking immortalization is the poet's sole task. Rather, we need to see that Spenser presents poetry and the immortality it confers in a carefully defined Sidneyan context. Immortalization, as the poem shows, is a process of passing the fore-conceits of ethical action from one generation to the next. Poetry both preserves those fore-conceits and teaches the mimetic process by which they figure forth abstract Ideas of the past in contemporary moral action. By enriching the memories of its readers, enlarging their conceits, poetry serves as an effective instrument of both private and public reform. "The Ruins of Time" thus pays the dead Sidney the highest of literary compliments by demonstrating in practice the principal theorems of the *Apology*.[4]

At the same time, the poem is seriously flawed, in part by its frequently prosaic style, but more importantly by Spenser's inability to maintain a consistent speaking voice. The ostensible narrator, Verlame, is at times a misanthropic voice of golden-age nostalgia; at others, an authorially sanctioned voice of dutiful eulogy and moral exhortation. Nor is this the only confusion. Colin Clout, Spenser's surrogate in the poem, seems clearly to usurp the narrating role from Verlame at two crucial moments; and the anonymous "it" that presents the twelve "notable images" or "speaking pictures" at the end of the poem represents a third narrator. Initially, it appears that Spenser had some intention of aligning these distinct narrators with his three objects of address—the public realm of England, the Dudley-Sidney family, and the obligations of the private poet. By using a different narrator for each subject, Spenser might have been trying to explore more fully the various demands of his own multiple poetic roles and responsibilities. Unfortunately, even this scheme is not consistently developed or maintained, and Spenser seems unaware that his characterizations work against rather than with each other. This is especially true of Verlame, who treats public, family, and private matters, but who is reliable only in her eulogy on the Dudleys. She vacillates, in other words, between a false reader and a right poet, as Spenser seems unable to decide whether he wants her to represent a "sad ensample" or a positive image of notable virtue.

"The Ruins" opens conventionally with a dedication to Mary, Countess of Pembroke, in which Spenser announces his poetic purpose: to memorialize Sidney's name and race in order to satisfy those who have chided him for his silence. The first section of the poem proper (ll. 1–175) is a dream-vision in which the poet-observer encounters Verlame and listens to her lament the destruction of her city. The section ends with the lady complaining that no poet has recorded her loss except Camden, "the nourice of antiquitie, / And lanterne vnto late succeeding age" (ll. 169–170). Verlame next laments the history of the Dudley family (ll. 176–343), from Robert Dudley through Ambrose and Mary Dudley, to Philip and Mary Sidney. Two motifs recur throughout this section: that each family member bequeaths a pattern of virtue to succeeding members, and that no poet has mourned the individual deaths. Verlame calls upon Colin Clout to sing a plaintive song, and the second section ends with Colin accepting the charge:

> Yet whilest the fates affoord me vitall breath,
> I will it spend in speaking of thy praise,
> And sing to thee [i.e., Sidney].[5]   [ll. 309–311]

The third section of the poem (ll. 344–455) opens a more general lament by asking how many lie unsung because they did not patronize poets or poetry. Only the Orphic poet can keep the memory alive or teach the truth of the universal ruins of time. Returning to the frame of the dream-vision, Verlame once more universalizes her lament and offers herself as an "ensample" of "such vaine illusion" as the world is wont to trust (ll. 456–490). The dreamer, "inlie grieuing" over what he has heard, remains silent and dumb. At length, for "demonstration," he is given a pageant of twelve icons (ll. 491–672) and the poem ends with Spenser's envoy.

Although it avoids the problem of the different speaking voices, this overview of the poem uncovers three primary themes. First, Spenser forces us to accept an analogous and metaphoric relationship between man and society by making Verlame's lament that no poets have praised her identical to her lament that no one has eulogized the Dudleys. The analogy suggests in each instance the poet's obligation to create out of the past "notable images" of both public and private virtues. Only by this means, the poem argues, can present societies or individuals understand the patterns by which they should fashion, or refashion, themselves. Second, because the poet's recreated vision of the past provides a model for present action, it offers an answer to the seemingly universal ruins of time. Again Spenser exploits the analogy between public society and private family: Verulame proves its societal virtues by imitating and keeping alive the "notable image" of Rome; in the same way, the descendents of the Dudley family ensure the excellence of their individual lives by imitating and keeping alive the exemplary virtues of their ancestors. Third, the poet's obligation to a literary tradition is itself analogous to and a metaphoric example of the relationships between past and present cities or between past and present family members. That is, Spenser teaches London to imitate and emulate Verulame, and the Countess to imitate her brother, by himself imitating Sidney and the poetic principles Sidney espouses.

It is clear that this formulation of themes implies a continual opening of individual topics to metaphoric relationships. Sidney, the announced subject of the poem, is serially portrayed by his relation to a poetic tradition, a private family, and a public society. Indeed, we might argue that it is precisely these multiple relations that define the conceit "Sidney."[6] Yet Sidney himself, or even Sidney as a "notable image," is not the sole subject of the poem. Of more concern to us and to Spenser are those who have survived Sidney's death—London, the Countess, and Spenser himself. Each of these figures participates in the same metaphoric relationships to a poetic tradition, a private family, and a public society. Moreover, the relationships of any one of these figures is a complex metaphor for the relationships of the others. "The Ruins" may be described, then, as Spenser's attempt to define an Idea of excellence by developing the spheres of metaphoric correspondence such an Idea would have to embrace. The Idea of the poem could not be verbalized in any more precise way: it is the aggregate of relationships the poem displays. What can be articulated is the principle by which the various spheres are related, the principle by which they are revealed to be and by which they make themselves metaphors of each other.

We could rephrase the poetic problem in simpler terms. Ethical action, as portrayed in "The Ruins," consists of a simultaneous commitment to poetic, familial, and societal obligations. The task of each individual is, first, to discover which potential actions will fulfill all three obligations at the same time; and, second, to learn how to put those potential actions to specific work. The poet's own process of imitation is a metaphoric and artistic example of these ethical tasks, for he too must discover a conceit capable of expressing the poetic, familial, and national features that make up the characters he praises as ethical. And he must fashion those characters in such a way that all three traditional obligations are textually fulfilled. The poet's own task, therefore, duplicates the individual's he would move: his fore-conceit teaches the first ethical lesson; his text, as an action itself, teaches the second. And now, of course, we observe a Sidneyan twist to the paradigm, for the poet's metaphoric imitation of an Idea of metaphoric relationships is itself a metaphor of the reader's ethical imitation. Hence, the chief point of interest for a reader of "The Ruins" is not how Sidney or the Countess or Verlame act in relation to their poetic, familial, or societal duties, but how the poet metaphorically imitates those actions in the textual act of his poem. As Sidney's *Apology* leads us to expect, the poet's "art of imitation" teaches the mimetic method by which any abstract virtue is bodied forth in specific, material form.

In the dedication to "The Ruins," Spenser makes two important points: that Sidney was the patron of his young muse, whose death has cut off "anie further fruit"; and that the poet intends the poem as a dutiful remembrance and "renowning" of "that noble race" from which Sidney and the Countess have sprung. His completion of the poem is thus envisioned as proof of Sidney's effective patronage and tutelage. "The Ruins of Time" is itself the "further fruit," the reformative ethical action, of one "reader" who has been moved by the dead poet's words. This seemingly innocuous assumption reveals again Spenser's refusal to countenance literal-minded discriminations. Like Sidney, he collapses the distinctions between poet and reader and between poem and action. The Right Poet is initially a right reader, and his poem is an ethical action vindicating that reading. Such conflations are crucial to Spenser's designs for moving his reader. Since all poets are right readers, all right readers ought also to be creative right poets. Whether they "create" poems or ethical acts, they demonstrate the "fruit" of proper teaching. Significantly, Sidney's own definition of the end of poetic instruction uses the same image:

> For who will be taught, if he be not moved with desire to be taught? and what so much good doth that teaching bring forth . . . as that it moveth one to do that which it doth teach. For, as Aristotle saith, it is not *gnosis* but *praxis* must be the fruit.   [*Apology*, p. 112]

By returning his first-fruits[7] to Sidney, Spenser affirms the ethical value of his poem, approves his perception as a right reader of Sidney's work, and accepts the moral responsibility of his literary ancestry. His proper reading of Sidney moves him to enroll in the legion of Right Poets that Sidney traces and eulogizes in the *Apology* and to which he calls all would-be English artists.

Spenser further argues that he will eternalize Sidney's own "noble race," referring here not only to the line of reforming poets given in the *Apology*—and to which Spenser now assigns Sidney himself—but also to Sidney's family lineage and to the English nation as a whole. By insisting that "race" be interpreted in all of these senses, Spenser takes his first step toward ensuring that each particular lineage be seen as a metaphor for the other two. Consequently, both the public history of England and the private history of the poet must be interpreted as participating directly in praise of the Sidney family. More significant, perhaps, praise of England and praise of the Dudleys must also effect a metaphoric encomium of Spenser himself. Like all of his poems, "The Ruins" announces and praises the New English Poet by illustrating his ability "to speak metaphorically."

As stated earlier, the opening frame of "The Ruins" consists of Verlame's lament over the loss of her city and her accusation that no poet has eulogized that city. The female genius of Verlame is here set in analogous relationship to Mary Sidney: both have suffered a loss which poets have failed to mourn. Verlame begins her lament with a conventional *ubi sunt* catalogue and then focuses, in turn, on Rome (to which she is related as daughter to mother, "Princesse" to "Empresse"), Troynovant (her "elder sister"), Verulame itself, and finally, by implication, London. Throughout this tracing of the "family" line, Verlame's chief complaint is:

> But me no man bewaileth, but in game,
> Ne sheddeth teares from lamentable eie:
> Nor anie liues that mentioneth my name
> To be remembred of posteritie,
> Saue One that maugre fortunes iniurie,
> And times decay, and enuies cruell tort,
> Hath writ my record in true-seeming sort.   [ll. 162–168]

Only Camden, whose lantern allows succeeding ages "to see the light of simple veritie" and who constructs an eternal mnemonic monument of her, ensures Verlame's continued existence through time. This narrative pattern—a temporal loss finally redeemed by a poetic monument—governs each of the subjects broached in the remainder of the poem.

It will be noted, however, that Verlame's continued existence is not in fact ensured by Camden's monument, nor is her loss redeemed by his mnemonic text. Camden's history presents only an image of Verulame's virtues, a literary imitation of the conceit of civic virtue which Verlame herself represents.[8] Only when that conceit is reembodied in the actual society of contemporary London will the loss of Verulame be fully redeemed and its virtues live again. Like Sidney, Spenser insists that it is not the literary text but ethical action that is the "ending end" of literature. The importance of Camden's history is not diminished by this interpretation, for that work provides the means by which Verulame's past excellences are transferred to the present London. By singling out Camden, moreover, Spenser identifies the kind of potentially reforming text he would like to write and the kind of ethical action he wants to inspire by means of that text.

Although Spenser's intentions in this section seem clear, his characterization of Verlame needlessly complicates his statement, for she actually performs a dual role. As a voice urging public reform, Verlame speaks with authority and truth; as a voice of private lament, Verlame is highly suspect. She is foolishly proud of the material splendor of her city and considerably less than honest in her account of Bunduca's raid. Her attitude is so consistently materialistic that it contaminates even the conceit of Rome. Is the Rome imitated by Verulame one of individual and civic achievement or one of superficial pomp and moral decadence? Is it, that is, the Rome of Renaissance humanists or the Rome of Protestant propagandists? As the editors of the Variorum and, more recently, James Nohrnberg, have pointed out, the frequent echoes of biblical Lamentations in the speech of Verlame suggest that she is more like a tragic figure of earthly vanity than a heavenly genius of Christian consolation.[9] Even her central complaint is ambiguous: are poets legitimately attacked for their failures, or are they made the scapegoats for Verlame's own failures?

Probably Spenser did not recognize the difficulties he has created here. He needed a public voice that could serve as a metaphoric extension of the Countess and a literal excuse for broadening the poem's subject. Without Verlame, the poet's function, and the Idea of the poem, would be restricted to private and family matters; with her, both the poet's task and the poetic Idea enlarge to include public and communal reform. But while Spenser needs Verlame, the kind of lament he gives her undercuts the very reason for employing her. Rather than a spokesman for positive public reform, she illustrates a sinful private perspective. Less interested in teaching contemporary London than in bemoaning the vanished glories of her own past, she becomes both a "wrong-speaker" and a pompous "faultfinder."

Verlame represents an early version of the Spenserian strategy defined in the opening pages. As both false poet and false reader of her own "sad ensample," Verlame clarifies the responsibilities of Spenser's right speaking and cautions his audience about their responsibilities of right reading. Yet the precise nature of Verlame's failures needs to be seen clearly. The rhetoric with which Verlame mourns her vanished glory is not, in itself, wrong; nor is her lament that poets have not praised her. What is wrong is Verlame's apparent literalizing of her terms. She never seems to understand that the *ubi sunt* catalogue is a metaphoric warning against materialistic and literalistic values or that poetic praise is a metaphoric challenge to public reform. And if these errors define her wrong speaking, then one can see that the same failure defines her wrong reading, for Verlame never recognizes the metaphoric relationships that her own lament discloses. Her loss and the Dudley losses are literal and discrete; they do not, in her view, form any complex metaphor.

Verlame's failures, and the literalizing misinterpretation which occasions them, are clarified in the remainder of the poem. The response of the Countess to the poet's song, for example, will reveal the selfish limitations of Verlame's vision. Similarly, the public lineage the poem ultimately displays—a metaphoric line much like Britomart's conception of Troy-Rome-Troynovant—corrects Verlame's notion that her city is simply and literally destroyed. In each case, the poem posits metaphoric correspondences that Verlame is unable to see, and it thereby instructs us that the Idea toward which the poet is directing us must be broader than any one of his subjects. Her failures of perception thus serve to dramatize what Spenser successfully sees and what we are invited to see.

In the second section of the poem, Verlame laments the deaths of several Dudleys. Here, of course, Spenser could not have Verlame's authority—as either poet or reader—questioned, for that would cast suspicion on the very praise he sets out to record. Yet we should observe a consequence of this shift in Verlame's status: Spenser has, in effect, conceded that it is easier to "read" another's situation than one's own. By itself this is hardly a profound thought, but in the context of Sidney's discussion of the difficulties of right reading it comes close to implying that all readers are like Alexander Pheraeus. And if poetry therefore offers the reader an opportunity to see in the literary metaphor what he can't see in himself, it does so only to the extent that the poet teaches him that the poetic image is indeed metaphoric. It would be unwise to suggest that Spenser is fully conscious of these thoughts in "The Ruins of Time," but even here we can see him broaching a view of right speaking which makes the poet himself responsible for a reader's right reading. As his alertness to this responsibility grows, so too will the narrative energies he is forced to commit to fulfilling it.

Verlame begins her serial eulogy of the second section with Robert Dudley, the first Earl of Leicester, Sidney's uncle, and Spenser's own early patron. With his death, Verlame argues, only defamers and "faultfinders" thrive[10] because no one has fashioned Dudley's due fame:

> He now is dead, and all his glorie gone,
> And all his greatnes vapoured to nought,
> That as a glasse vpon the water shone,
> Which vanisht quite, so soone as it was sought:
> His name is worne alreadie out of thought,
> Ne anie Poet seekes him to reuiue;
> Yet manie Poets honourd him aliue.   [ll. 218–224]

As a glass of virtue, Dudley presented his contemporaries with a living "notable image"; since no poet has revived that image, no model of virtue now remains. Hence Verlame criticizes Colin Clout, accusing him of "guiltie blame" for not having praised Leicester in song. Since Leicester is Spenser's first patron, the accusation strikes with particular force and reminds us of the charges brought against the poet in the dedication. That is, it brings Spenser's past obligations to the dead Leicester to bear metaphorically on his present obligations to the dead Sidney.

To clarify Colin's failure, Verlame turns abruptly to Ambrose Dudley, also deceased, but who continues to live in his widow, Anne:

> So whilst that thou, faire flower of chastitie,
> Dost liue, by thee thy Lord shall neuer die.   [ll. 251–252]

As this lesson teaches the Countess of Pembroke her responsibility to the dead Sidney, it also teaches Spenser his own poetic obligations and he immediately, through Colin, accepts the charge:

> Thy Lord shall neuer die, the whiles this verse
> Shall liue, and surely it shall liue for euer:

For euer it shall liue, and shall rehearse
His worthie praise, and vertues dying neuer.   [ll. 253–256]

The intricate rhetorical structures here—from a simple pun to the incremental *conduplicatio*—and the careful merging of poetic voices as the fictive
Verlame becomes indistinguishable from the dedicating Spenser,[11] force a
metaphoric identification between the poet's recreated image and the widow's
recreated life. Both imitate, by bodying it forth, a conceit of Dudleyan virtue.
The family process of succeeding generations imitating their ancestors' virtues is now extended through Mary Dudley,[12] Francis Dudley, Edward Dudley, thence to Sidney, Mary's son, who also kept alive and clarified the image
of excellence begun by the "Grandsire." Again merging the speaking voices,
Spenser finally accepts Verlame's challenge and dedicates himself to singing
the praises of Sidney and of Sidney's sister, in whom Sir Philip now presumably "lives":

So there thou liuest, singing euermore,
And here thou liuest, being euer song
of vs . . .   [ll. 337–339]

So thou both here and there immortall art.   [l. 343]

The importance of this section of the poem cannot be overemphasized. It
serves first to demonstrate that despite the deaths of individual family members, each succeeding member keeps alive, by imitation, the pattern of virtue, the conceit of excellence, which defines the family line. The poet himself
becomes a member of this line by joining Sidney in song, by imitating
Sidney's singing, and by his new relationship with the Countess, his own succeeding patron. This last act signifies that the imitative and metaphoric lesson
has been learned, for the Countess now imitates both Leicester and her
brother by becoming the patron of the present poet.[13] Family line becomes
poetic line, just as national line becomes family line, and the notable image of
virtue each line praises and imitates is the same—Sir Philip himself.
    We see here one positive effect of Spenser's decision to use Verlame as the
poetic narrator. By allowing her to voice the complaint, Spenser avoids the
difficulty of having the Countess lament her own family losses. Verlame thus
suffers the moral censure which accrues to any complaint, while the Countess's very silence affirms her proper moral action. Similarly, Spenser is able to
affirm the Countess as a right reader of his own text by dramatizing Verlame's
failure. Verlame, "reading" her own "sad ensample," cannot see either the
positive imitative values or the metaphoric equivalences it implies. The
Countess, reading of her sad example, not only understands those values and
those metaphors, but subsequently bodies them forth in her own ethical
action.
    It is in this context that section 3 turns to the issue of patronage:

> But such as neither of themselues can sing,
> Nor yet are sung of others for reward,
> Die in obscure obliuion, as the thing
> Which neuer was . . . .   [ll. 344–347]

Only by cherishing poets and poetry can the family descendants learn how to imitate the virtues of their ancestors. To say that Spenser is here making a bold-faced plea for patronage is to mistake the issue. The Countess is already his patron, if not in fact then certainly within the fiction of the poem. Spenser is therefore universalizing, abstracting the conceit of virtue which the Countess has already set to ethical work. His poetic text stops to instruct us in the reading process by performing the very "disembodiment" it requires. The poet, now a reader, moves from a literal "text" of one private patron to the public principle of literary patronage. Through a series of mythic examples, Spenser praises the power of poetry to effect the immortality of virtuous deeds and families. Those who "will with vertuous deeds assay / To mount to heauen, on *Pegasus* must ride, / And with sweete Poets verse be glorifide" (ll. 425–427). So bold an assertion, usually dismissed as blatant self-serving, is the logical conclusion of one line of Spenser's praise of the Countess. It is also, of course, a larger argument: that only the poetic image of a notable virtue can provide an instructive and moving pattern for subsequent praise-worthy ethical action. As the first section of the poem teaches the poet his public responsibility, the second teaches him a more private responsibility. Whether he portrays national or familial images of virtue, the poet instructs the present in how to imitate the excellences of the past.

Spenser concludes this section of the poem by copying the final words of the *Apology*. Sidney mockingly curses anyone who has so "earth-creeping a mind that it cannot lift itself up to look to the sky of Poetry":

> Yet thus much curse I must send you, in behalf of all poets, that while you live, you live in love, and never get favour for lacking the skill of a sonnet, and, when you die, your memory die from the earth for want of an epitaph.
> [*Apology*, p. 142]

Spenser, without Sidney's wit, still mirrors his thought:

> O let the man, of whom the Muse is scorned,
> Nor aliue, nor dead be of the Muse adorned.   [ll. 454–455]

Once more the literal poetic imitation validates and affirms the broader notion of imitation the poet is trying to demonstrate.

Spenser's return to the dream-vision frame at the end of the poem is initially somewhat puzzling. As Verlame concludes her lament, the observer mourns in silence, having "no words to say" and laboring to wrest meaning from "her doubtful speech." The speaker here must be distinguished from the voice of Spenser himself in such lines as the paean to Sidney (ll. 309–343). This narrator is temporally prior to the poem: he has listened to Verlame but cannot yet sing himself. The narrator's puzzlement may be the logical result of Verlame's own ambiguity. Not sure that she is a reliable authòrity and perhaps, like her, unable to perceive the metaphoric equivalences between the three spheres she has addressed, the narrator does not yet understand his own poetic role. His problem is clarified by what he now sees:

> At length by demonstration me to teach,
> Before mine eies strange sights presented were,
> Like tragicke Pageants seeming to appeare.   [ll. 488–490]

The six images which he now watches figure forth Verlame's own condition.[14] Presented by an anonymous and characterless figure, the "tragicke Pageants" serve as visual emblems, speaking pictures, of the ruins of time. They reveal, in their objectivity, the inadequacy of Verlame's lament over the loss of her city. But significantly, sight of them leaves the observer still "distraught twixt feare and pitie": fear, we presume, because he has unwisely accepted Verlame's cynical view that all is lost, and pity because he has yet to understand the full metaphoric truth of the visions. He needs six additional emblems, all related specifically to the historical Sidney and metaphorically to the Orphic power of poetry to immortalize "for endless memorie." The emblems of Sidney correct those of Verlame; pity and fear are purged by consolation and hope. Or rather, the narrator discovers his own voice and his own moral stance precisely between the dual series. By mediating between fearful images of societal ruin and hopeful images of individual transcendence, he locates and defines the metaphoric correspondences of his own poem. Again the Right Poet is initially a right reader. Having read the "teach[ing]" correctly, he can turn, in the Envoy, to summarize his own lesson, drawing attention first to the conceit of excellence now identified with the dead Sidney, then to the three metaphoric spheres in which that conceit is to be, and has been, bodied forth—the Countess's own life, the contemporary society, and his literary text. Public, family, and private realms are all exhorted to imitate the pattern of Sidney's "immortall spirite," which has now, through the poem, "enriched" their memories and "enlarged" their conceits.

The twelve "notable images" with which the poem ends offer additional interpretive opportunity, for they obviously bear the same relation to the poetic narrator as the poem bears to us. Consequently, as they reveal to him the fore-conceit of the poem proper, so they should reveal metaphorically to us a conceit capable of making the poem a "groundplot" of our own "profitable invention." As the poem urges, poetry is responsible for providing such images for individuals and societies to "read." But it is also responsible for articulating the virtues those images re-present. If, that is, poetry is an art of verbalizing abstract nouns, it is also an occasion for nominalizing concrete verbs. In "The Ruins," the noun-Idea which is finally, if unspecifically, nominalized is Imitation itself. The Idea of metaphoric imitation, narratively exposed and partially defined by the poet's meditation on the deaths of Verulame and Sidney, is bodied forth first in Spenser's decision to shape three distinct and metaphoric actions by means of the conceptual infinitive *to imitate*. The public realm defines its creative excellence by attempting to imitate Rome, Verulame, and Troynovant; the Countess transforms her life by trying to imitate the Dudleys and the Sidneys; Spenser himself sets out to imitate the principles of the *Apology*. The public, family, and poetic actions narrated in the poem, then, body forth in their own respective terms the literal effects of such *imitating*. The poetic process thus names, praises, and demonstrates in mimetic action the virtue it seeks to evoke in the reader who understands how the poem was made.

We must take care, however, not to overemphasize the verbal nature of this paradigm. It is easy enough to see that the narrative actions of any of the poem's characters consist of imitating antecedents. But if we seek the imitative principle, then it is not sufficient merely to draw out the figures of the past which such actions seek to imitate, for the simple reason that this method could not reveal the ways in which the imitating actions are also metaphors of each other. In order to learn the poetic fore-conceit, we must perceive the implicit relationships between the discrete narrative elements. It is not the poet, but the reader, who verbalizes that relationship as a specific infinitive. The Idea of the poem, however, is not recoverable in verbal terms. We could call it Imitation in the abstract, and argue that it embodies, simultaneously, a notion of poetic, familial, and societal progress, a standard by which such progress is measured and evaluated, and a set of relationships which must obtain among all spheres that so progress. But this is probably as far as we could go in articulating the poetic Idea. And even this articulation would be inappropriate without a clear consciousness of how inexact and distorting our words for the Idea are. Still, if the poet has made that Idea manifest "in such excellency as he hath imagined" it, then it should be possible for us to imagine it in turn.

Chapter 3. *Daphnaida* and *Colin Clout*

In "The Ruins of Time" and *The Shepheardes Calender*, Spenser tries to expose the errors of "foolish faultfinders" or wrong readers. In both poems, such readers fail repeatedly to understand the metaphoric nature of the literary vehicles they use and they therefore commit themselves to narrowly conceived and literal-minded ethical options. In the *Calender*, Spenser identifies these options as either/or dichotomies: either one is young or old; either active or contemplative; either comic or tragic. For the mind that thinks literally, all observation resolves into such disjunctive terms. The mind that perceives metaphorically, however, both avoids and voids the false dichotomies to which literal readings are inevitably committed.

In *Daphnaida* and *Colin Clout*, Spenser pursues these same problems, although here he dramatizes the errors of "wrong-speakers" or false poets. Again the pastoral genre, conceived as a metaphoric fore-conceit of perceptual possibilities, furnishes the context for the drama; and again the touchstone of proper use of the literary form is the ability to understand that it speaks metaphorically. We may expect, then, that the false poet, like the false reader, literalizes his generic options into textual dichotomies that falsify the metaphoric conceits; the Right Poet, like the right reader, creates a metaphoric text that is faithful to the nature of his conceit. Instead of describing the particular verbal paradigms in these two poems, we will focus here on the dramatic strategy itself: why Spenser adopts it, what additional literary problems he uncovers by using it, and what poetic lessons he draws from it.

We should also recall that in *The Calender*, Spenser practices a kind of literary exorcism. By making the literalizing errors of a series of misreaders the center of his narrative, he tries to cleanse his own reader of such mistakes. In the present poems, he inverts the defensive strategy. By exposing the errors of false speaking, he tries to ensure the success of his own right speaking.[1] This defensive maneuver offers him, moreover, a narrative opportunity to explore, through surrogate poet-figures, the responsibilities of any poet who presumes to speak correctly. In effect, then, the defense is also a definition, as Spenser tries once more to present himself as a Sidneyan Right Poet.

It may seem odd to propose a link between *Daphnaida* and *Colin Clout*, for the poems seem to have little in common. The *Daphnaida* is a clever redaction of Chaucer's *Book of the Duchess*,[2] a conventionally elegiac and public poem eulogizing Lady Douglas Howard, deceased wife of Sir Arthur Gorges. *Colin Clout*, in contrast, is an original and subjective account of Spenser's self-promoted failure to gain Elizabeth's favor or support, a pastoral satire on the corruption of the court, and a private lament at having to return to Ireland.³ Yet when viewed in conjunction, the two poems show striking similarities. That Spenser invites such comparison is clear, not only by his passing reference in *Colin Clout* to Alcyon's grief over Daphne's death, but also by having Colin gratuitously remind his shepherd audience of Mansilia, "she to whom *Daphnaida* / Vpon her neeces death I did complain" (ll. 510–511).

Both the *Daphnaida* and *Colin Clout* concern shepherd-poets who fail, in a general sense, to come to terms with reality. In the *Daphnaida*, the poet's reality is death: like Orpheus, he has lost his beloved, journeys through a kind of hell, turns his imaginative powers to invective and misanthropy, and ends a rather pathetic victim of his own despair. He becomes, in other words, a type of failed Orpheus, whose songs shift dramatically from creative reformation to willful deformation. In *Colin Clout*, the poet's problem is that both courtly and country realities fail to accord with his literary visions of them. He too "loses" his beloved, either because she judges him as unworthy or because his poetic role in her court is usurped by false poets. And he too retreats from his poetic responsibilities, turns to invective and despair, and ends by withdrawing from life altogether. Like the black pilgrim of the *Daphnaida*, Colin Clout is cast as a failed Orpheus figure who abandons the proper Sidneyan obligations of moral and societal reform.

Of particular interest in both poems is the way each shepherd-poet overturns his pastoral realm. Although the specific terms of their inversions are different, the questioning of the pastoral genre as a viable literary model is a clear effect of both poets' actions. In *Daphnaida*, the pastoral elegy, whose function is always to place the austere fact of death in a broader, more natural, and hence less terrifying perspective, becomes, for the black pilgrim, a myopic antipastoral which sees death as the only reality and which is blind to all universal order and justice. The usual pastoral consolations are here twisted into a perverse poetic uncreation, as willful an act of deforming and defaming pastoral assumptions about the unity and goodness of human existence as Lear's raging calls upon Nature to disnature herself into elemental chaos. In *Colin Clout*, the entire basis of political and satiric pastoral is turned on its head: the court, the acknowledged subject and audience of such pastoral, is presumed incapable of correctly perceiving its value; and Colin's retreat to a simpler life among the shepherds isolates country from city in a way that denies the pastoral any social or civilizing function.⁴ Even the country does not escape Colin's invectives as the idyllic landscape turns into a wasteland of wretchedness and exile.

In both poems Spenser deploys a common paradox: the traditional pastoral spokesman, the shepherd-poet, is effective as a reforming, civilizing voice precisely because his vision transcends his pastoral place. Even though he is a pastoral figure, he understands that the generic *topoi* and *loci* are by definition metaphoric. In the present poems, however, the two poet-figures are resolutely literal-minded. Their pastoral locales do not provide them with broader—because simpler and clearer—perspectives; instead, their pastoral places yield myopic and distorted views which arbitrarily close them off to more encompassing visions. Alcyon constantly perceives and speaks in terms of false dichotomies: black versus white, death versus life, spring versus winter, praise versus blame. Colin Clout thinks and speaks in the same disjunctive terms: country versus city, love versus lust, presence versus absence, here versus there. By revealing the errors of such literalizing, Spenser explores the tragic consequences of the refusal or the inability to speak metaphorically. He shows us, in short, the literal effect of trying, as Sidney says, "to correct the verb before . . . [we] understand the noun."

i

Spenser wastes little time in complicating the pastoral world of the *Daphnaida*. His poem, the opening stanzas explain, is not intended to assuage anyone's sorrow or to cure him "whose heauie mynd / With griefe of mournefull great mishap [is] opprest" (ll. 1–2). The poem begins, in other words, by ironically disclaiming its own generic purposes. It is a tale of the "wofulst man aliue," and the reader who expects the standard elegiac consolation is warned to look elsewhere:

> But who so else in pleasure findeth sense,
> Or in this wretched life dooth take delight,
> Let him be banisht farre away from hence:
> Ne let the sacred Sisters here be hight,
> Though they of sorrowe heauilie can sing;
> For euen their heauie song would breede delight:
> But here no tunes, saue sobs and grones shall ring.   [ll. 8–14]

Obviously, Spenser is playing several literary games in this stanza. He denies all aesthetic control while manipulating the intricate rhyme royal, and he manages to invoke the muses even in the process of banishing them. Such discrepancy between what the poet says he is doing and the skill actually shaping the poem forces the reader from the start to adopt a metaphoric perspective.[5] He must interpret the speaker's denial of art as both a metaphor for his "troublous" emotions, and a metaphoric insistence on the reality—the literalness—of his grief. The conventional metaphor of artlessness, of what Ivor Winters calls the "fallacy of affective form,"[6] seeks to deny that the speaker's grief is either metaphoric or conventional. Thus the poem complicates its status as elegy by compounding its controlling voices. At this point, the reader's perspective seems closer to the poet's than to the narrator's: he

sees the artistic order of the poem as a metaphor of external and creative control of which the speaker is unaware. He might expect, then, that Spenser
will use his own presence in the poem to instruct the narrator in the justness
of Providence by means of a Sidneyan analogy: as the poet stands behind and
orders the poem, so God stands behind and orders human existence.

Yet this comforting aesthetic and metaphoric irony does not mask the fact
that the traditional pastoral consolation, as well as the reader's familiarity
with the convention, are immediately challenged. Spenser's subtle variation
of the classical admonition, "Hence, hence profane," issues a direct threat to
the reader's facile presumptions. "Profanity," in this case, is assuming either
"sense" or "delight" in life or poetry. The reader who continues to read the
poem is cautioned that he enters at his own peril and only by giving up his
view of human existence as divinely ordered and beneficently controlled.
Lasciate ogni speranza voi ch'entrate! To escape being censured by the poet as a
fool, the reader must adopt the potentially distorted singleness of vision soon
to be personified in the black pilgrim.[7] The importance of Spenser's strategy
is again clarified by the usual generic intentions: if the pastoral elegy functions to "remind the pastoral mind that nature is not only a provider, but also
a destroyer: that it generates from its womb not only life, but also death,"[8]
then Spenser has inverted the poetic form. It is not death that the genre has
forgotten, but life, "sense" and "delight." And insofar as the reader willingly
enters this pastoral world, he may be seeking not a consolation in terms of
Christian syntheses of life and death, gain and loss, joy and grief, but an expression of his darker intimations that there is no such equilibrium, that
death and despair rule all and everywhere. The man in black may thus be
considerably more seductive than he initially appears, for despite his extreme
point of view he still articulates a recognizably human perspective.

As the narrator accosts the man in black for the first time, we learn that he
is not merely a "sory wight," "like to some pilgrim," but a poet:

> *Alcyon* he, the iollie Shepheard swaine,
> That wont full merrilie to pipe and daunce,
> And fill with pleasaunce euery wood and plaine.   [ll. 54–56]

Alcyon, in other words, is, or was, the very person originally banished from
the poem—he who finds both "sense" and "delight" in life. It is important to
stress this point, for only when we see the relationship between Alcyon's
present unkempt condition and his earlier status as a poet can we understand
the human and literary danger his failure in the poem represents. Spenser's
initial exploration of that failure comes with Alcyon's fanciful tale about his
"faire young Lionesse."

Spenser's critics have been as bewildered as his narrator at this curious allegory, but its function in the poem is clear enough if we are alert to the literary

questions Spenser is raising. The lioness is "White as the natiue Rose before the chaunge, / Which *Venus* blood did in her leaues impresse" (ll. 108–109). The black poet's perception of his youthful love is an idealizing fiction of innocence preceding experience, and he makes use of the standard pastoral *topoi* of the earthly paradise:

> . . . shee became so meeke and milde of cheare,
> As the least lamb in all my flock that went.   [ll. 125–126]

> Safe then and safest were my sillie sheepe,
> Ne fear'd the Wolfe, ne fear'd the wildest beast:
> All were I drown'd in carelesse quiet deepe:
> My louely Lionesse without beheast
> So careful was for them, and for my good.   [ll. 134–138]

Alcyon's fable is a poetic wish-fulfillment: the savageness of life becomes not only tame but actively protective. Of course, such fictional innocence cannot survive the test of experience and the shepherd's lioness is killed by a "cruel Satyre." Even this act of destruction is a poetic re-creation, not a factual report.[9] The entire fable is a conventional pastoral trope whose purpose, generically, is to introduce and exorcise the fear of death. But the shepherd-poet misuses his own tale. To him it provides merely an evasion of the reality of Daphne's death, and, as we later learn, it also falsifies the process of her dying by making it wantonly destructive and tragic (Daphne accepts her dying as God's final blessing). Like his later embracing of the antipastoral invective, Alcyon here uses the poetic form as simple escape. His artistic rendering of death fails to teach him the broader human perspective; it leads him only "afresh to waile and weepe" (l. 169).

What, the reader is forced to ask, has gone wrong here? Why doesn't the pastoral form of the shepherd's tale instruct and console him? Why do both Alcyon and the narrator fail to understand the fable?

> Yet doth not my dull wit well vnderstand
> The riddle of thy loued Lionesse.   [ll. 176–177]

This is not the naive obtuseness of Chaucer's comic narrator: Spenser's narrator is totally cut off from Alcyon's meaning because he is given only a metaphoric vehicle; he does not, and cannot, know its tenor. He is led to assume, therefore, that the lioness is not metaphoric at all. The further irony here is that Alcyon too has forgotten that his fable speaks metaphorically. Like Marvell's complaining nymph, he so loses himself in the poetic recreation of his lost innocence that he fails to learn any appropriate response to the human reality behind that loss. And having failed to find consolation in the pastoral terms, he turns in the remainder of the poem to antipastoral rage against all creation.

In effect, Spenser returns here to the narrative strategy of *The Calender*; but rather than creating different figures to body forth the textually conflicting options, he here collapses those figures into one. The pastoral foreconceit, as in *The Calender*, allows both fable and invective, both praise and blame. Alcyon embraces each option in turn, unaware that each metaphorically points to the other or that both are capable of being abstracted into a metaphoric conceit. His literal speaking thus prevents him from learning any metaphoric lesson. He does not see, in other words, that the pastoral terms of his initial fable provide, because of their status as metaphors, a warning of the loss that is to come. In the same way, he will not see that the metaphoric terms of his invective offer hope that life will continue. As a consequence of such literal speaking, Alcyon will turn against his first pastoral form when it fails to accommodate his experience, literally inverting it in the false hope that that will provide a satisfactory answer. Of course, it does not: the invective merely ensures Alcyon's commitment to yet another set of literalized pastoral terms.

We might observe here a further difference between Chaucer's elegy and Spenser's. The poet-figure in Chaucer's poem is the narrator himself. Unable to sleep because he has "so many an ydel thought" and "fantasies" in his head, the Chaucerian narrator decides to read a book, the rhymed romance of Seys and Alcyone. After failing to understand this tale, he falls asleep over the book and dreams of the black knight. At the end of the poem, he awakens and decides to put his own dream-vision into rhyme. Chaucer wants us to understand that the narrator's ability to put his experience into poetry is a sign of his having finally learned the metaphoric lesson which the romance first opened to him.[10] The movement of the poem is thus to present a poetic *consolatio*, to test that metaphoric vision by having it encounter and accommodate a specific experience, and then to reaffirm its validity by re-creating it poetically at the conclusion of the tale. The poetic ordering of experience is, therefore, a positive value in Chaucer's text.

To Spenser, such optimism is naive, for it presumes that the narrator-poet recognizes the metaphoric nature of his terms. To demonstrate that this need not be so, Spenser shifts the poetic focus from the narrator to Alcyon and thereby ultimately questions the very thing Chaucer affirms—the "auctoritee" of literature or the usefulness of poetry in directing ethical action. In more specific terms, Chaucer assumes that the translations of literature to life and life to literature are simple and direct. The romance of Seys and Alcyone teaches the narrator how to deal with the experience of the black knight and that experience teaches him how to write *The Book of the Duchess*. For Spenser, both translations are problematical. Alcyon's experience with Daphne results in a falsely literal text, and that text in turn occasions Alcyon's perverse ethical actions. In each case, he fails to recognize the metaphoric nature of the literary terms. As a consequence, he cannot satisfactorily accommodate either death to life or literature to experience. The literary form does not provide an appropriate directive to ethical action. In fact, Spenser implies that it may even distort or deform human action when it is abused as Alcyon abuses it.

Alcyon's misuse of his poetic materials is seen most clearly in the difference between his fable of Daphne's death and the actual experience the fable represents. As he later admits to the narrator,

> Yet fell she not, as one enforst to dye,
> Ne dyde with dread and grudging discontent,
> But as one toyld with trauell downe doth lye,
> So lay she downe, as if to sleepe she went,
> And closde her eyes with carelesse quietnesse;
> The whiles soft death away her spirit hent,
> And soule assoyld from sinfull fleshlinesse.   [ll. 253–259]

Daphne's death is hardly the wanton and tragic murder depicted in the fable, but a natural and inevitable end to her earthly pilgrimage. She dies neither complaining nor sorrowing, and she tries to console Alcyon for his apparent loss by teaching him how to accept and view it:

> *Alcyon*, ah my first and latest loue,
> Ah why does my *Alcyon* weepe and mourne,
> And grieue my ghost, that ill mote him behoue,
> As if to me had chaunst some euill tourne?
>
> I, since the messenger is come for mee,
> That summons soules vnto the bridale feast
> Of his great Lord, must needs depart from thee,
> And straight obay his soueraine beheast:
> Why should *Alcyon* then so sore lament,
> That I from miserie shall be releast,
> And freed from wretched long imprisonment?   [ll. 263–273]

The sudden intrusion of the Christian bridal feast into the pastoral framework demands a radical adjustment be made both to Daphne's death and to her view of life's wretchedness.[11] Alcyon, like the reader, must see that both death and life are reinterpreted by Daphne in terms that, while not at odds with the poem's earlier pastoralism, certainly qualify and redefine it. Death is not a loss of innocence, but the regaining of innocence; not a severing of the marriage ties, but a true binding of them; not an evil chance, but divine fulfillment. Similarly, the "wretched long imprisonment" is not, as Daphne's next lines affirm, a definitive judgment on the horror of life, but a

Christian *contemptus mundi* which metaphorically warns Alcyon against putting total faith in, or even venting total rage against, a fleeting existence:

> Our daies are full of dolour and disease,
> Our life afflicted with incessant paine,
> That nought on earth may lessen or appease.
> Why then should I desire here to remaine?
> Or why should he that loues me, sorrie bee
> For my deliuerance, or at all complaine
> My good to heare, and toward ioyes to see?   [ll. 274–280]

Yet Daphne's description of the *contemptus mundi* has precisely the wrong effect on Alcyon. In forcing him to readjust his earlier account of the world of innocence, her language ironically provides him with a new account of the world of experience. And Alcyon, who reads both metaphors literally, merely substitutes one pastoral paradigm for another, failing to see the metaphoric relationship between them. He fails, in other words, by assuming that the literal terms of each pastoral option exclude those of the other; he cannot see the conceit which joins them and which defines them both as "pastoral."

The description of Daphne's death continues to emphasize her ascent, not to a literal Elysium, but to a pastorally accommodated heaven of "Saints and Angels in celestiall thrones." Yet rather than leave either his hero or his reader with the false assumption that ethical action is now over or assured, Spenser pushes the lesson of metaphoric accommodation one step further by having Daphne charge Alcyon with a specific task:

> Yet ere I goe, a pledge I leaue with thee
> Of the late loue, the which betwixt vs past,
> My young *Ambrosia*, in lieu of mee
> Loue her: so shall our loue for euer last.   [ll. 288–291]

Although it has elicited little interest or commentary, the presence of the child in the poem is a minor Spenserian achievement. We might notice first that neither Alcyon's fable nor his subsequent rage once mentions the child. In his wrathful "pilgrimage," Alcyon has obviously failed to accept the one responsibility Daphne placed upon him. His solipsistic and narcissistic grief is therefore also human irresponsibility—he abandons his sole daughter, the pledge of the seemingly glorious love he so grievously laments, and he consigns that love to a frozen death because he cannot renew it by loving his daughter. Even more striking is the fact that Ambrosia is not a fictional name like Alcyon or Daphne, but the actual name of Sir Arthur and Lady Howard's real daughter. By keeping the historical name, Spenser ingeniously demonstrates the ability of the literary form to accommodate literal human experience and to direct particular ethical action. Alcyon, however, does not acknowledge that accommodation or the metaphoric option it provides. He sees and speaks only the literalized terms of universal death and destruction.

Alcyon's complaint involves the same dissociation of form and content that we have noted in the opening of the poem. Through seven sections of seven seven-line stanzas, Alcyon curses the absence of order and meaning in life. That his bitter invective is itself a perfect formal sign of universal order is clear; what is not so clear, perhaps, is that Spenser calls into question the value of the poetic ability to order experience in this fashion.[12] That capacity, he suggests, is at best a dubious value if the very figure who conceives it is unable to understand its metaphoric significance or to transfer its lessons so as to order his own life. Alcyon remains unaware, therefore, that the literary form of his measured threnody conflicts dramatically with the chaos of his emotions and his thoughts. He is unable and unwilling, in Sidneyan terms, to translate fictional action into ethical action.

Even the content of Alcyon's lament enforces this point. In calling for a universal deformation, Alcyon still cannot escape his literalized literary world:

> Let birds be silent on the naked spray,
> And shady woods resound with dreadfull yells:
> Let streaming floods their hastie courses stay,
> And parching drouth drie vp the christall wells;
> Let th'earth be barren and bring foorth no flowres,
> And th'ayre be fild with noyse of dolefull knells,
> And wandring spirits walke vntimely howres.   [ll. 330–336]

"Spenser expected his audience to recognize that what Alcyon demands here is yearly and naturally accomplished: the silence of the birds on winter's bare branch; the uncontrollable spring floods; the summer drought; and finally winter's flowerless sterility."[13] Alcyon has taken the stock metaphors of the pastoral pathetic formula and perversely extended them to literal finality. Certainly Alcyon fails to see that the yearly cycle continues, and we can judge his grief as willful self-pity; but his greater error is in literalizing the pastoral metaphors in the first place. Alcyon is simply a bad reader and writer of pastorals, for he never recognizes that the generic metaphors are metaphoric. In both of his songs—the fable and the threnody—he makes the same mistake of assuming that the poetic conventions are literal records of his own emotional condition and his own experiential situation. For Spenser, as for Sidney before him, such an error renders poetry not only useless in terms of human experience, but even dangerous.[14]

Like "The Ruins of Time" and *The Shepheardes Calender*, the *Daphnaida* is a poetic defense. The dramatization of how poetry can be abused is, at least in part, an attempt to ensure that this poem is used correctly. Against the false-speaking Alcyon, therefore, is the Right Poet Spenser. As evidence of his own success, Spenser puts forth the *Daphnaida* itself. The poem consists of three distinct versions of pastoral: the dream-vision in which a narrator encounters a bereaving shepherd (the largest frame); a pastoral fable of an innocent existence at one with nature; and a pastoral complaint on the experience of alienation from nature. For Spenser, the poetic task is to demonstrate how the pastoral conceit allows and accommodates these perspectives, how each functions as a metaphor of the others. In the process of fulfilling that task, he has taught a much larger lesson, applicable to any literary form: that unless poetry is allowed to speak metaphorically, both its *gnosis* and its *praxis* will be abused.

ii

If Spenser began *Colin Clout* as a self-promoting fiction of his failure to gain favor or patronage at the English court, he soon realized that more significant issues were at stake in the poem. Where and to whom does the New Poet sing? Can a poet outside the court legitimately participate in Sidney's line of national Right Poets, or must he present himself as a banished country voice speaking in appropriately diminished tones? Certainly these are questions which Spenser, home again in Kilcolman, must have asked himself. In part, *Colin Clout* is his attempt to answer them.

Coming home is an action so charged with value that it requires some effort to see it as a potentially negative or culpable retreat. For a poet writing in the early 1590s, with the fabled progression of Virgil before him, it would take a similar effort to see the literary dangers of the pastoral: it too was deeply embedded in unquestioned merit, and yet it too could become a self-consoling retreat. It is a sign of Spenser's critical self-honesty that he is well aware of the hazards in both choices. His decision, therefore, to write a pastoral about coming home ought to be understood as a conscious effort to vindicate and to validate his own poetic motives and intentions.

The drama of this effort consists in Spenser's analysis of the ethical ambiguities involved in each choice—to come home and to write pastorals—as well as in his ability to show how these choices are metaphorically related. That is, Colin's homecoming offers Spenser a dramatic opportunity to examine the strengths and limitations of his own generic decision and to test the correctness of his own understanding of the poet's place and function. More specifically, Colin's failure measures Spenser's success.[15] When he comes home again, Colin forsakes his public responsibilities as a poet and abandons the court of Elizabeth-Cynthia to false speakers and false doers. He fails, in Spenser's judgment, to sing in his proper place, and he thus commits himself, like the black pilgrim in the *Daphnaida*, to futile invective and solipsistic exile. By making that judgment, Spenser assures us (and himself) that his own choices are not so narrowly conceived, and that he has not really left the court at all. He still speaks for and to that court, regardless of where he now is. The differences between poet and persona, therefore, are focused on the issue of place, on where each perceives himself to be or where "home" actually is.

Colin Clout opens with Hobbinol's description of how the "shepheards nation" suffered during Colin's absence and revived when he returned:

> Whilest thou wast hence, all dead in dole did lie:
> The woods were heard to waile full many a sythe,
> And all their birds with silence to complaine:
> The fields with faded flowers did seem to mourne,
> And all their flocks from feeding to refraine:
> The running waters wept for thy returne,
> And all their fish with languour did lament:
> But now both woods and fields, and floods reviue,
> Sith thou art come, their cause of meriment,
> That vs late dead, hast made againe aliue.   [ll. 22–31]

Hobbinol's words suggest a simple, but crucial, equation: absence equals deformation and death; presence equals reformation and life. The significance of these terms can be seen by comparing them to a conventional Elizabethan description of the effects of Orphic poetry. In a 1595 epyllion entitled *Orpheus His Journey to Hell*, Orpheus tells us how his songs have affected the pastoral realm:

> The whilom desart plaines where nothing grew,
>   now fertill by the meanes my musicke made:
> Gin now againe for sorrowe to renew
>   their olde accustomable wearie trade.[16]

Now that Orpheus is absent, lamenting for and seeking the lost Euridice, the lands he once reformed begin to transform themselves back into formless desert. The point here is that Orpheus, as the poetic instrument of a civilizing and reformative power, is morally obligated to exercise that power. When he fails to do so, the forces of destruction ascend. Hobbinol's equation, then, suggests that Colin shares in Orpheus's poetic power to reform, and implies that Colin also shares the Orphic responsibility that accompanies that power. If he fails to exercise that power correctly, or in the proper place, he is responsible for the deformation which inevitably occurs.

Hobbinol speaks in these opening lines about the pastoral realm, but if his equation is valid, it also applies to the court. We must understand, therefore, that in addition to defining the importance of the concept of place to the poem and arguing that the nation's health is dependent upon Colin's presence, Hobbinol's terms impose an ethical choice on Colin. Since his presence in one realm would seem to require his absence from the other, Colin's problem is not what but where to sing.

The issue of place is further elaborated when Cuddy asks about the "other" land to which Colin has journeyed with the Shepheard of the Ocean. Colin's answer is rhetorically structured by syntactic oppositions of place: there versus here, that country versus this one:

> Both heauen and heauenly graces do much more
> (Quoth he) abound in *that* same *land*, then *this*.
> For *there* all happie peace and plenteous store
> Conspire in one to make contented blisse:
> No wayling *there* nor wretchednesse is heard,
> No bloodie issues nor no leprosies,
> No griesly famine, nor no raging sweard,
> No nightly bodrags, nor no hue and cries;
> The shepheards *there* abroad may safely lie,
> On hills and downes, withouten dread or daunger:
> No rauenous wolues the good mans hope destroy,
> Nor outlawes fell affray the forest raunger.
> *There* learned arts do florish in great honor,
> And Poets wits are had in peerlesse price:
> Religion hath lay powre to rest vpon her,
> Aduancing vertue and suppressing vice.
> For end, all good, all grace *there* freely growes,
> Had people grace it gratefully to vse:
> For God his gifts *there* plenteously bestowes.
>
> [ll. 308–326, my italics; see also ll. 292–307]

The most obvious effect of these oppositions is an inversion of the usual pastoral *loci*. The city becomes the privileged happy place to which the poet accords all the stock pastoral blessings: plenty, contentment, peace, security, and grace. The country becomes the inhospitable wasteland of wretchedness, famine, hues and cries, outlaws, and discord. More than an attack upon Ireland, the description places Colin in an extremely ironic position, for the wasteland that he implicitly attacks is the very one to which he has come home. That choice is immediately called into question.

Not so obvious, perhaps, is the fact that Colin's disjunctive oppositions of this country versus that, of here versus there, lead him to both a false view of the poem's places and a false choice between them. He presumes, in other words, that the pastoral country is literally habitable, a viable option to living at court. For Spenser, of course, the pastoral place is strictly metaphoric: it is a private and poetic vision in which questions of public responsibility can be posed in simplified form. If it entertains contraries such as city versus country or public versus private, it does so only to enforce an accommodation of things which frequently, in other contexts and other places, seem irreconcilable. Therefore, while much of *Colin Clout* is structured upon the dual poles of court and country, the poem ultimately shows that duality to be false. There is no "country" in the literal sense of a separate place. In fact, we can see this voiding of oppositions at the very start of the poem. Hobbinol argues, as we have seen, that Colin's obligations are to "the shepheards nation." Yet the term "nation" defines the pastoral country as a metaphor, as a function of Cynthia's realm and her court, not as a literal rural place. "Here" and "there" are, from the opening lines, collapsed into one "nation," and the poet's function is defined as serving and reforming that nation.[17]

Once we see the issue of place in these terms, then it is clear that Colin's task is not to choose between ostensibly opposing places but to recognize how such spatial dichotomies function metaphorically to define the one place. That is, the textual oppositions of here and there, this country and that, serve to broaden the understanding of "nation." Both court and country are, from this perspective, metaphoric imitations of the larger, accommodating term. As metaphors which are bodied forth in a narrative text, they are allowed to develop their own unique contributions to that subsuming whole. To conceive the nation as a court reveals certain things about it; to conceive it as a rural country reveals others. The conceit "nation" not only encompasses both but also reveals the relationship between them. Insofar as Colin's decision to come home fails to recognize that relationship, it can testify only to his failure to understand how pastoral speaks metaphorically.

In order to clarify Colin's misunderstanding, Spenser introduces the Shepheard of the Ocean. The Shepheard, whose journey in the poem exactly reverses Colin's, is the Right Poet at "home" both here and there, in both this and that country. Spenser makes this point by again focusing on the matter of place. When we first hear the Shepheard, he is lamenting how Cynthia "from her presence faultlesse him debard" (1. 167). Though absent from his lady, however, the Shepheard does not cease to serve her nor does he really presume her presence is limited to a literal court. As he explains to Colin while they are sailing on the sea—a place Colin perceives only as a wilderness of horrid beasts and ghastly dread—

> These be the hills (quoth he) the surges hie,
> On which faire *Cynthia* her heards doth feed:
> Her heards be thousand fishes with their frie,
> Which in the bosome of the billowes breed.   [ll. 240–243]

> Those be the shepheards which my *Cynthia* serue,
> At sea, beside a thousand moe at land:
> For land and sea my *Cynthia* doth deserue
> To haue in her commandement at hand.   [ll. 260–263]

> And I among the rest of many least,
> Haue in the Ocean charge to me assignd:
> Where I will liue or die at her beheast,
> And serue and honour her with faithfull mind.   [ll. 252–255]

From the Shepheard's point of view, Colin's distinctions between here and there, as well as Hobbinol's dichotomy of presence and absence, do not obtain. Cynthia rules everywhere, and that fact makes all places legitimate arenas of service to her. The Shepheard defines, therefore, not only the full spatial dimensions of Cynthia's "nation," but also the metaphoric sense in which here and there, presence and absence must be taken. To the "faithfull mind," such oppositions falsify the service and honor all shepherds owe by suggesting that one can literally be absent from Cynthia's nation and thus not responsible for duty to that nation.[18]

As the two poets finish singing, the Shepheard again raises the question of Colin's proper place:

> He gan to cast great lyking to my lore,
> And great dislyking to my lucklesse lot:
> That banisht had my selfe, like wight forlore,
> Into that waste, where I was quite forgot.
> The which to leaue, thenceforth he counseld mee,
> Vnmeet for man, in whom was ought regardfull,
> And wend with him, his *Cynthia* to see:
> Whose grace was great, and bounty most rewardfull.   [ll. 180–187]

Since Colin has been quoting the Shepheard directly, we might ask why Spenser here has him merely paraphrase his companion's words. The answer might well be that Spenser wants to indicate that Colin misunderstands the issue of place from the beginning. Even in these lines recording his decision to leave home, Colin thinks in dichotomies. This land is luckless, banishment, wasteful; the court is grace-ful, bounteous, and "rewardfull." If the Shepheard uses these terms, he clearly means them metaphorically. Colin's place is an "vnmeet" wasteland because Colin perceives it as literal and as literally distinct from Cynthia's nation. Colin does not know the relationship between this land and that, and thus cannot know the duty he owes. What the Shepheard offers, therefore, is not a literal change of place but a growth in metaphoric perception, an enlarging of Colin's view of his "lucklesse lot" to a recognition of his societal responsibilities.

The songs of Colin and the Shepheard relate this question of place to the analogous question of genre by demonstrating that pastoral has a legitimate service to perform for the court. As Colin and he take turns piping and singing, Colin tells the lay of Mole, Mulla, and Bregog, and the Shepheard responds with a complaint about Cynthia's unjust treatment of him. It is clear that Spenser intends the two songs to complement one another: the "auncient truth confirmed with credence old" is immediately reaffirmed and given particular application by the Shepheard's lament. The function of the fable is thus to provide the Shepheard with a pastoral metaphor of his own situation. And the lesson the fable teaches is a metaphoric equivalent of the Shepheard's own ethical values of honoring and serving with a "faithfull mind": "For Loue will not be drawne, but must be ledde" (l. 129).[19] Since the Shepheard follows by reaffirming his love for and duty to the queen, he apparently learns the metaphoric lesson.

The remainder of the poem charts Colin's journey to Cynthia's court by a succession of three portraits. The first (ll. 194–328), which treats Colin's ocean voyage, is the broadest in scope and the most abstract. Presented largely by the Shepheard of the Ocean, the portrait defines in appropriately pastoral terms the regions and the legions attendant upon the queen. The pastoral metaphors are designed to teach Colin what Cynthia's "nation" means by figuring forth its virtues in a language he can understand. But when Colin tries to apply the Shepheard's terms, he does so by subjecting them to the very dichotomies they seek to invalidate. Hence, he splits the Shepheard's unified nation into this land and that, here and there; and he interprets the Shepheard's idealizing metaphors as a literal attack upon his own wretched wasteland. Besides showing Colin as a foolish "faultfinder," these lines imply an even greater error. By literalizing the Shepheard's metaphors, Colin wrongly anticipates an ideal court. And here Spenser reveals, for the first time perhaps, a surprising distrust even of speaking metaphorically. For if the pastoral metaphors lead men to develop false expectations about human society, they may also lead men to reject that society when it fails, as it must, to live up to the metaphoric ideals. As we will see, this is precisely what happens to Colin. Unable to recognize the relationship between the "reality" of Cynthia's court and the ideal the Shepheard draws, he becomes increasingly disillusioned with reality.

In the second portrait (ll. 330–648), Spenser recasts the pastoral metaphors that explain Cynthia's "nation" into a metaphoric description of her court. The shepherd-legions that husband the queen's various lands are here replaced by the shepherd-courtiers and court ladies that define her "presence." Such metaphoric adjustment affirms the ethical value of the pastoral terms, for the pastoral is shown to be capable not only of accommodating but also of explicating the court's activity. That is, the love and service defined by the pastoral metaphors of the first portrait are now brought to bear upon the courtesy of the second. Courtesy itself is thus presented as a poetic and ethical action which figures forth the dual obligations to love and to serve the queen.

The role of poetry in Cynthia's court is to provide a metaphoric demonstration of how such obligations can be fulfilled. Poetic courtesy, then, consists of singing the glory of the queen's name ("to blow / Their pipes aloud, her name to glorifie") or praising those who make up her "presence." This much Colin seems to learn: his praise of the court poets and ladies surrounding the queen participates in the courtesy by which her glory is attested; and his praise of Cynthia herself teaches his shepherd-peers "her name . . . in knowen terms to frame." In short, Colin seems to come into his full poetic maturity in this section. His songs of court instruct the country; his songs of the country presumably teach the court. Even Cynthia herself affirms the value of his verses:

> The shepheard of the Ocean (quoth he)
> Vnto that Goddesse grace me first enhanced,
> And to mine oaten pipe enclin'd her eare,
> That she thenceforth therein gan take delight,
> And it desir'd at timely houres to heare,
> All were my notes but rude and roughly dight.
> For not by measure of her owne great mynd,
> And wondrous worth she mott my simple song,
> But ioyd that country shepheard ought could fynd
> Worth harkening to, emongst the learned throng.   [ll. 358–367]

With such success, it is no wonder Thestylis asks, "Why didst thou euer leaue that happie place?" (l. 654).[20]

We have come again to the crucial term, for despite Colin's apparent success, he has still not understood the metaphoric nature of place. We get a hint of this even as he describes the shepherd-poets attendant on the queen: "There is good *Harpalus*"; "there is *Corydon*"; "there is sad *Alcyon*"; "there eke is *Paladin*"; "there is pleasing *Alcon*"; "there is old *Palemon*"; "there is *Alabaster*"; "and there that Shepheard of the Ocean is." Colin still perceives a literal distinction between here and there that his own songs deny. And because he is now here, not there, Colin assumes that his poetry no longer participates directly in the queen's service. This is especially clear in the way he suddenly cuts off his praise of the court ladies:

> But if I all should praise as they deserue,
> This sun would faile me ere I halfe had ended.
> Therefore in closure of a thankfull mynd,

I deeme it best to hold eternally,
Their bounteous deeds and noble fauours shrynd,
Then by discourse them to indignifie.   [ll. 578–583]

Unlike the Shepheard of the Ocean, whose "faithfull mind" refuses to admit such dichotomies as presence versus absence, and who continues to serve and honor Cynthia wherever he is, Colin allows a literalized conception of opposing places to stop his song. The praise which he is bound by duty to record remains locked and enshrined in the "closure" of his mind; he will not even submit it to the spatial extension of discourse.

As a consequence, Colin's final portrait of the court is based upon those disjunctive contraries that obtain only in a mind closed to metaphoric relationships. The mind that is unfaithful to the metaphoric identification of here and there also perceives literal oppositions between happy states and annoyed states, between public good and private self-regard, between love and lust, praise and blame, speaking the truth and dissembling. And to the mind that perceives in these terms, there is little reason to believe that a "silly" country poet has any role or function in the city court.

This conclusion is implicit in the way Colin answers Thetylis's question about why he has left the presence of the queen he "so feelingly" deifies:

Happie indeed (said *Colin*) I him hold,
That may that blessed presence still enioy,
Of fortune and of enuy vncomptrold,
Which still are wont most happie states t'annoy:
But I by that which little while I prooued:
Some part of those enormities did see,
The which in Court continually hooued,
And followd those which happie seemd to bee.
Therefore I silly man, whose former dayes
Had in rude fields bene altogether spent,
Durst not aduenture such vnknowen wayes,
Nor trust the guile of fortunes blandishment,
But rather chose back to my sheep to tourne,
Whose vtmost hardnesse I before had tryde,
Then hauing learnd repentance late, to mourne
Emongst those wretches which I there descryde.   [ll. 660–675]

In a sense, Colin simply refuses the challenge of life at court, refuses to risk falling into misfortune or disfavor. Yet he records that refusal in terms that return us to the standard opposition of the poem's opening—country contentment versus city discontent. When we recall that Colin has actually reversed the earlier dichotomy, we may again suspect that he is abusing the literary formulae. "Here" is a land of pastoral innocence; "there" is one of "annoyed" experience.

The fact that the poem shows such dichotomies to be false is not here as important as understanding why Colin comes back to them. He does so because the pastoral metaphors have betrayed him. The idealizing terms of the first two portraits have led Colin into presuming that the court is literally a "blessed presence" of blameless felicity. When he discovers that it is something more—"fortune," "enormities," "guile," and so on—he concludes that the fault lies with the court itself rather than with his terms. A mind so closed to experience that it is unable or unwilling to accommodate its own imaginings to the reality it discovers beyond itself is also unable to perceive the function of the literary metaphors. Colin values the pastoral metaphors not for what they reveal about human experience, but because he sees them as a literal option to such experience.[21]

In part, the final section of Spenser's poem is designed to correct Colin's error. By demonstrating how the pastoral is capable both of revealing false service to and false love of the queen, and of teaching right love and service, Spenser insists that, unlike Colin, he directs his own pastoral to the court. He may, like Colin, have come home again, but his poetic choices are not made with a closed mind. Like the Shepheard of the Ocean, he still faithfully honors and serves his queen.

As we have already said, Colin's final speeches in the poem embrace the disparities to which a literalizing mind is subject. In his first attack, he accuses the court of discourtesy, of perverting the obligation to serve the queen:

> For sooth to say, it is no sort of life,
> For shepheard fit to lead in that same place,
> Where each one seeks with malice and with strife,
> To thrust downe other into foule disgrace,
> Himself to raise: and he doth soonest rise
> That best can handle his deceitfull wit,
> In subtil shifts, and finest sleights deuise,
> Either by slaundring his well deemed name,
> Through leasings lewd, and fained forgerie:
> Or else by breeding him some blot of blame,
> By creeping close into his secrecie;
> To which him needs, a guilefull hollow hart,
> Masked with faire dissembling curtesie,
> A filed toung furnisht with tearmes of art,
> No art of schoole, but Courtiers schoolery.   [ll. 688–702]

The ideal of courtesy, which Colin describes in his second portrait of Cynthia's presence, has here been inverted. The skill by which men fashion all their actions to honor the queen is turned, by a cunning twist of "poetic" wit, from the art of *conceit* to the art of *deceit*.[22] To Colin, such dissemblings are purely literal. To Spenser, however, they speak metaphorically to reveal a poetic abuse even worse than Colin's: the abilities to feign, to devise sleights and "subtil shifts," to mask, and to appear eloquent (and hence, by humanist logic, wise), are all "arts" that false courtiers have learned from the poet. But if poetry is responsible in some sense for such perversions, it is also responsible for disclosing them. Only by demonstrating the metaphoric relationship between grace and disgrace, between conceits and deceits, can poetry remain faithful to the real world it seeks to reform.

Colin continues his attack upon the court by focusing on the "vaine votaries of laesie loue." Love, he argues, is "all their talke and studie,"

> But they of loue and of his sacred lere,
> (As it should be) all otherwise deuise,
> Then we poore shepheards are accustomd here,
> And him do sue and serue all otherwise.
> For with lewd speeches and licentious deeds,
> His mightie mysteries they do prophane,
> And vse his ydle name to other needs,
> But as a complement for courting vaine.   [ll. 783–790]

Again Colin is content merely to identify the court's perversion, and once he has named such love as lust he dismisses the court entirely:

> But who so else doth otherwise esteeme,
> Are outlawes, and his [Love's] lore do disobay.
> For their desire is base, and doth not merit,
> The name of loue, but of disloyall lust:
> Ne mongst true louers they shall place inherit,
> But as Exuls out of his court be thrust.   [ll. 889–894]

The irony of these lines is that the court itself is "exiled" from the closure of Colin's mind. Since it does not live up to the ideals Colin has so literally accepted, he banishes both the place and the actions which he perceives as antithetical to those ideals.

For Spenser, of course, Colin has again misunderstood his own place and function. Cuddy calls Colin the priest of love—

> Well may it seeme by this thy deep insight,
> That of that God the Priest thou shouldest bee—   [ll. 831–832]

and Colin himself agrees that the ideal of love needs a fit spokesman:

> Of loues perfection perfectly to speake,
> Or of his nature rightly to define,

> Indeed (said *Colin*) passeth reasons reach,
> And needs his priest t'expresse his powre diuine.   [ll. 835–838]

What he does not see is that "perfectly to speak" of love does not mean speaking only of "loues perfection." Colin's false dichotomies once more condemn him to false choices. The poet's task is to correct improper actions of love by teaching right loving. This is, in fact, precisely what Colin had done earlier in the poem when his metaphoric fable taught the Shepheard how to act in the face of the queen's displeasure. Such successful poetic lessons cannot arise, however, where the poet seeks to deny that wrong loving exists or to dismiss it from his vision by calling it another name.

It is no accident that Spenser has Colin, at the conclusion of the poem, enclosed in a world of private lament. His error is not quite the same as those who falsely interpret love's lore, but perhaps it is just as dangerous. At least the courtiers, however falsely, are attempting to put poetic lessons into public practice; Colin merely withdraws into the closure of his own mind. His private mode represents a failure to accept the poet's public role and hence a failure to achieve, even to attempt, any ethical reform. Life is not an idyllic pastoral, and the attempt to literalize the metaphors of the pastoral fiction is "world denying" (l. 950), a living death of exile in a "wasteful" place.

In this context, it is instructive to reexamine Colin's description of one of the courtly shepherd-poets, Alcyon:

> And there is sad *Alcyon* bent to mourne,
> Though fit to frame an euerlasting dittie,
> Whose gentle spright for *Daphnes* death doth tourn
> Sweet layes of loue to pensiue plaints of pittie.
> Ah pensiue boy pursue that braue conceipt,
> In thy sweet Eglantine of *Meriflure*,
> Lift vp thy notes vnto their wonted height,
> That may thy *Muse* and mates to mirth allure.   [ll. 384–391]

The failed poets of both our poems meet here in the same terms. Alcyon, like Colin, has turned away from the world and from life. Death has driven him, as corruption drives Colin, into self-regarding and self-pitying complaint. And he, like Colin, must learn that his poetic gifts carry with them public responsibilities which cannot be denied or dismissed. Significantly, Alcyon, as Colin must be, is urged to sing again his "sweet layes of loue" in order to lift up and cheer his fellow man. And he is urged to do this by reexamining "that braue conceipt" which may "lift vp" both his own song and his courtly peers to "as high a perfection" as they are capable of.

iii

Both Alcyon and Colin, however they are distinguished, share an intention "rightly to define" love's nature. But in the process of attempting "t'expresse his powre diuine," both fail to discover an appropriate way to speak of the wholeness of love and thus fall into false dichotomies. At issue, it seems, are the terms of definition that rightly define. Spenser himself implies that such terms "passeth reasons reach," and that they can be learned only by a mind that is "faithfull" to the conditions of metaphor. We may see in such discriminations a poet who is worried about the closures of his own expression. Indeed, Spenser seems to perceive closure, literalizing, as a constant danger of all expression. The urge to define, to subject experience to rational statement, to find a literal truth among metaphoric possibilities—such intentions too frequently result in distortion and misperception. To speak—or to read—rightly, is to defy such urges, to remain conscious of the metaphor as metaphor, and to be faithful to the Idea that surpasses both reason's and expression's reach.

If Spenser thought about this issue in the Sidneyan terms we employed in the Introduction, then his fears about even right speaking are neither groundless nor surprising. The excellence of the poem resides in the Idea, yet the Idea can be known—expressed or interpreted—only by insisting upon the distortions inherent even in a metaphoric conceit. The poet, like the reader, must understand and accept these conditions of articulated speech. Having done so, he will also understand that he cannot "rightly . . . define" the metaphor for which no metaphor is itself wholly adequate. He can point the way, but he cannot finally "place" us at the site where all dichotomies are resolved.

Chapter 4. *The Amoretti*

In the *Amoretti*, Spenser again tries "rightly to define" the nature and the power of love. We might expect, therefore, that the ways of misperceiving and falsely expressing love that have engaged the poet in the *Calender*, the *Daphnaida*, and *Colin Clout* will once more serve as dramatic foils to his own right speaking. As those poems have taught us, the obligation to express correctly predicts a double commitment—to remain faithful to the fact that poetry speaks metaphorically, and to defend the poetic metaphors against those intelligences that would reduce them to literality.

The descriptive title Spenser accords his collection of sonnets is evidence of the poet's consciousness of these obligations. Love, or *Amor*, is the Idea lying behind and shaping the sequence. The eighty-nine sonnets, or *amoretti*, that comprise the sequence are literary acts of loving, textual metaphors of the abstract Idea. The task of the poet is to reveal the fore-conceit by which these *amoretti* are metaphorically figured forth. By conceiving the whole in these Sidneyan terms, we can redirect the critical energies usually spent in charting the narrative progression of the sequence or in describing the individualized personalities of its lover and his beloved.[1] For regardless of how these elements are defined, narrative progress is nothing more than a Sidneyan groundplot, and the lover and his lady are but "notable images." Both must be unfigured along the linguistic stages of mimetic making in order to learn how they speak metaphorically.

Much has been written about the groundplot of the *Amoretti*, and some of it is relevant to our concerns. The most obvious thing to say is that Spenser habitually repeats whole poems, parts of poems, or specific image patterns in different contexts throughout the sequence. In fact, these repetitions—actually transformations—are so consistent that almost all of the individual sonnets could be arranged in identifiable mini-sequences within the sequence as a whole.[2] It is also clear that such minor sequences are themselves subjected to three large structural and thematic divisions. Generally speaking, the first twenty-two sonnets are controlled by a broadly sketched Petrarchan context, and sonnets of several distinct groups (calendric sonnets, sonnets on the "cruel fayre," pride sonnets, eye sonnets) are all focused through the Petrarchan perspective. In the middle forty-five sonnets, Spenser seems intent upon complicating the terms by which love is defined. The singleness of the Petrarchan view gives way to a context in which Petrarchan, neo-Platonic, Ovidian, and Christian perspectives all compete with and clash against one another. In the final twenty-two sonnets, the multiplicity of viewpoints seems again to resolve into one as Spenser tries to articulate a Christian synthesis.[3]

All of this is obvious enough, but the precise nature of the divisions—whether they are thematic, calendric, liturgical—is not as important as the necessity which gives rise to them. Rather than thinking of the divisions as a narrative fact, we should ask whether they answer to a particular poetic problem. In "The Ruins of Time," Spenser defines the notable image of Sidney by situating it in three distinct contexts: a national line, a family line, and a poetic line. Such contexts, as we have seen, are narrative places, rhetorical *loci*. The definition Spenser intends in the poem cannot itself be located in any one place; it is a composition which the poet makes by relations to and among all three places. In *The Shepheardes Calender*, each eclogue is again a rhetorical *locus*, and the terms of its dialogue are unfolded according to the decorum of such a place. But the meaning of the whole poem is something Spenser creates out of relations between the twelve individualized sites. In *Colin Clout*, the same strategy obtains. Love, as the poem defines it, embraces diverse places and correlates the diverse kinds of loving discovered in or occasioned by such places. In the *Amoretti*, place is again central and complex. Each sonnet, each individual text of loving, is a site in which love's meaning is expressed. But that site is also party to other and larger places: the mini-sequences connecting similar poems or the structural divisions connecting dissimilar ones. As in his earlier poems, what the poet makes is precisely the metaphoric lines by which these places are related.

In all four poems, Spenser conceives of place as continually opening out to other places. At the same time, places can become enclosures, as they do for Verlame, Colin, and the shepherds of the *Calender*; such closing of place, or closing off of place, Spenser associates with misspeaking and misreading. Place is thus metaphoric, and Spenser is dealing in these instances with discriminations between semantic spaces. Spaces that remain open are guaranteed to be metaphorical; those that are closed are reduced to the literal. The various divisions of the *Amoretti*, then, are rhetorical safeguards by which Spenser keeps his semantic sites open to metaphoric extension. Our task, therefore, is not to name a given place, or even to name the kind of loving that is set to work in that place, but to learn the relations the poet makes between places. "Rightly to define" is to demonstrate how the text is made to speak metaphorically of a site that is beyond it.

We can begin this work by looking yet once more at the obviously calendric sonnets. The first of these is Sonnet 4, a New Year's poem, set in January, but looking forward to the awakening of spring and Cupid, and calling upon the beloved to "prepare [her] selfe new loue to entertaine." Although Spenser has some original fun with the diction and the puns, the sonnet itself is perfectly conventional and heavily dependent upon the classical *carpe diem* motif. Despite the fact that it is still winter, the promise of spring is seemingly fulfilled within the poem as the flowers quite literally take over the final eight lines. Fifteen sonnets later, Sonnet 19, spring formally arrives. Like Ronsard before and Herrick after him, Spenser affirms the sanctity of seasonal love by directing a "quyre of Byrds" to sing "anthemes" and "lays" in its honor, and by having "all the woods" reecho those hymns. Again the *carpe diem* urge lies behind the poem, even though the major focus is on the lady's rebellion from Love's law, her willful disobeying of the natural "precepts."

In Sonnet 62, after "one year is spent," New Year's comes round again. As in Sonnet 4, the temporal change leads the lover to envision a more hopeful season of clear weather, fresh joys, and reciprocated love. Yet the tone of this poem is very different from that of Sonnet 4. The eagerness, the confident word-play, even the rather bold, brash challenge of the final "prepare your selfe," have given way in Sonnet 62 to a more somber pleading and a greater awareness that some of winter's gloom is likely to linger on:

> The weary yeare his race now hauing run,
>   the new begins his compast course anew:
>   with shew of morning mylde he hath begun,
>   betokening peace and plenty to ensew.
> So let vs, which this chaunge of weather vew,
>   chaunge eeke our mynds and former liues amend,
>   the old yeares sinnes forepast let vs eschew,
>   and fly the faults with which we did offend.
> Then shall the new yeares ioy forth freshly send,
>   into the glooming world his gladsome ray:
>   and all these stormes which now his beauty blend,
>   shall turne to caulmes and tymely cleare away.
> So likewise loue cheare you your heauy spright,
>   and chaunge old yeares annoy to new delight.

How inappropriate the *carpe diem* injunction of Sonnet 4 would be to this poem. Fresh youth and wanton love are not addressed at all. Instead of awakening a lusty hour, these more exprienced lovers are both enjoined to amend their lives, eschew old faults, and cheer their heavy and possibly sinful spirits.

Sonnet 70 repeats the spring song of Sonnet 19, and although the *carpe diem* urge reappears in one of its strongest forms, its meaning is fundamentally altered again by the changed tone:

> Fresh spring the herald of loues mighty king,
>   in whose cote armour richly are displayd

all sorts of flowers the which on earth do spring
in goodly colours gloriously arrayd:
Goe to my loue, where she is careless layd,
    yet in her winters bowre not well awake:
    tell her the ioyous time wil not be staid
    vnlesse she doe him by the forelock take.
Bid her therefore her selfe soone ready make,
    to wayt on loue amongst his louely crew:
    where euery one that misseth then her make,
    shall be by him amearst with penance dew.
Make hast therefore sweet loue, whilest it is prime,
    for none can call againe the passed time.

As in Sonnet 19, the lady is threatened with a penalty if she does not "wayt on loue." But here the call to love, to seize the day, is chastened by the speaker's own wry smile at the conventional injunction and by the strong biblical overtones of lines 5–6. Sonnet 70 is one of a small group of climactic sonnets drawing on the Song of Songs[4] and on the coming of spring that blesses the lovers in the biblical text (2 : 10–12):

> My welbeloued spake & said vnto me, Arise, my loue, my faire one, & come thy way. For beholde, winter is past: the raine is changed, and is gone away. The flowers appear in ye earth: the time of the singing of birdes is come, & the voice of the turtle is heard in our land.[5]

The *carpe diem* exhortation, therefore, is focused through the perspective of the symbolic marriage celebrated in the Song. The beloved in this sonnet is not asked, as she was in Sonnet 19, to wait upon Cupid's crew, but to love as she ought, as "the Lord vs taught."

How are we to articulate the relationships between these four sonnets? If we suppose a sequential progress through the "sequence," then the obvious calendric pairing (Sonnets 4 and 62; Sonnets 19 and 70) is a secondary structure abstracted from a prior pairing within contextual sites (Sonnets 4 and 19; Sonnets 62 and 70). The kind of loving expressed in Sonnet 4, for example, is determined by a sequence of semantic situations: first, by the Petrarchan context in which the poem is initially perceived; second, by calendric analogy to the second poem in that context (19); and third, by a calendric analogy to a third poem situated in a different context (62). Each poem in the sequence alters the perspective and the placement of the initial calendric sonnet. And in this way, Spenser ensures that the terms of that initial sonnet remain open to metaphoric extension. Sonnet 4 "speaks metaphorically" Sonnets 19, 62, and 70.

We could draw the same conclusion by observing how the poet-lover perceives his own terms. In Sonnets 4 and 19, King Cupid and the *carpe diem* injunction pronounced in his name are both interpreted literally by the poet-lover. His sense of the poetic and ethical dimensions of his words is limited by the equally literal seasons in which the poems are situated. Sonnets 62 and 70 transform both the literal seasons and their literal terms into metaphors. The threshold of New Year's Day becomes a metaphor for personal reformation and renewed commitments of all kinds, and the promise of spring becomes a metaphor for the spiritual uniting of all existence. The repetition of the seasonal site thus discloses the error of the poet-lover's initial perceptions, for we now see that even Sonnets 4 and 19 are metaphoric adumbrations of the broader perspectives in 62 and 70. The "mighty king" of Sonnet 70 is not only itself metaphoric, but also redefines the "King" of Sonnet 19 as a metaphor; and the metaphoric confession-contrition-amendment of Sonnet 64 rewrites the *carpe diem* of Sonnet 4 as a metaphoric prefiguration of itself. The speaker has learned, in the later poems, to open his earlier terms and places to new and larger accommodations which are themselves metaphoric extensions of those earlier terms. He has learned, in short, to speak metaphorically.

Sonnets 22 and 68 form another calendric pairing and provide another opportunity for metaphoric transformation. But in this instance Spenser complicates the interpretive problems of both his speaker and his reader by revealing that even metaphoric speech is susceptible to falsifying closure. At first glance, the relationship between these two sonnets seems to duplicate those we have already drawn. The enclosed and literal place of worship in Sonnet 22 is radically opened to metaphoric extension in 68: the "holy day" of interiorized devotion in the early poem becomes, in the later one, "this day" which reaches back to "death and sin" and forward to eternal life "in felicity." Similarly, the temple within the mind in Sonnet 22 is opened in 68 to admit not only worship of the lady, but also man's devotion to God as well as God's love for man.

But if we ask how the lover of Sonnet 22 goes wrong, it is clear that his error does not result from the kind of literalizing we have seen in Sonnets 4 and 19. He is perfectly conscious of the fact that both his "seruice" and his "sacrifice" are metaphors fashioned by imitating the devotions of "this holy season." In effect, what the speaker here has forgotten is the heart of his own metaphors. By failing to see how such metaphors point beyond themselves, he has again settled for an incomplete definition.

Sonnet 68 presents the action from which all of love's metaphors derive: Christ's sacrifice is not a fictional metaphor but a literal fact. As a result of that sacrifice, all other loving is metaphorically situated. Man's love of God metaphorically imitates Christ's love of man: "thy loue we weighing worthily, / may likewise loue thee for the same againe." Man's love of man metaphorically imitates God's love of man: "and for thy sake that all lyke deare

didst buy, / with loue may one another entertayne." The speaker's love of
his mistress must find its metaphoric site among these loving relationships.
The "gentle deare" whose "owne goodwill" allows the lover to capture her in
Sonnet 67 not only reenacts Christ's sacrificial act, but also is allowed to do so
because Christ has defined her as one of "all lyke deare." Similarly, the "entertainment" to which the lady is called in the first calendric sonnet is here
redefined not as the closed metaphoric devotion of Sonnet 22 but as the radically metaphoric entertainment by which loving "one another" participates in
loving God and being loved by God.[6] Even the structure of Sonnet 68 enforces this opening of the metaphoric places. The mistress is addressed only
through and in proper subordination to the prayer of the first eight lines. Unlike Sonnet 22, which replaces heavenly love with a narrowly conceived, even
if metaphoric, earthly love, Sonnet 68 insists that the metaphoric relations
between all forms of loving inform the activity of any one of them.

The profundity of Sonnet 68 does not lie simply in its Christian dogma, but
in its radical transformation of all the metaphors of loving that appear in the
Amoretti. It defines the literal act by which all such metaphors arise and to
which all such metaphors must be referred. All acts of loving are metaphoric
imitations, and it is precisely Spenser's continual reformulation of those
metaphoric acts, his constant opening of them to ever larger metaphoric relation, that reveals the mimetic principle.[7] We hardly need add, perhaps, that
this poetic activity is itself metaphoric of appropriate ethical action.

We have dealt thus far with only the most obvious of the metaphoric recre-
ations in the *Amoretti*, but if our conclusions are valid, we should find a similar strategy at work in other mini-sequences. Sonnet 7 begins a series of sonnets treating the mistress's eyes:

> Fayre eyes, the myrrour of my mazed hart,
>   what wondrous vertue is contaynd in you
>   the which both lyfe and death forth from you dart
>   into the obiect of your mighty view?   [ll. 1–4]

As we might expect, the contextual placement of the poem within the sequence predicates a semantic commonplace. The poet-lover merely elabo-
rates the Petrarchan contrariety: when the lady smiles, he is "inspired";
when she frowns, he is "fyred." Apparently unable to conceive the eyes in
any other terms, he can only keep repeating the simplistic life-death dichotomy the commonplace gives rise to. Spenser's own wry judgment on such
reductive literalizing implies not that the Petrarchan trope is wrong, but that
to the speaker it has become a semantic trap.

That the speaker's perspective is arbitrarily limited is revealed in the very
next poem:

More then most faire, full of the liuing fire,
    kindled aboue vnto the maker neere:
    no eies but ioyes, in which al powers conspire,
    that to the world naught else be counted deare.
Thrugh your bright beams doth not the blinded guest
    shoot out his darts to base affections wound;
    but Angels come to lead fraile mindes to rest
    in chast desires on heauenly beauty bound.
You frame my thoughts and fashion me within,
    you stop my toung, and teach my hart to speake,
    you calme the storme that passion did begin,
    strong thrugh your cause, but by your vertue weak.
Dark is the world, where your light shined neuer;
    well is he borne, that may behold you euer.

Here the lady's eyes serve only reforming functions—framing, fashioning, teaching, and calming—and the poet-lover seems to have corrected the Petrarchan excesses of Sonnet 7 by invoking a new semantic convention, here loosely neo-Platonic. He seems also to understand in this sonnet that "rightly to define" the lady's eyes means finding a suitable metaphor. Hence the eyes are not eyes, but "ioyes"; and the lover gazing into them sees not affections' dart, but "heauenly beauty." It is clear, however, that this positive reading of the eyes arises not by metaphorically accommodating the contraries of the preceding sonnet, but by excluding half of its terms.

Sonnet 9 takes the speaker a step further:

Long-while I sought to what I might compare
    those powrefull eies, which lighten my dark spright,
    yet find I nought on earth to which I dare
    resemble th'ymage of their goodly light.
Not to the Sun: for they doo shine by night;
    nor to the Moone: for they are changed neuer;
    nor to the Starres: for they haue purer sight;
    nor to the fire: for they consume not euer;
Nor to the lightning: for they still perseuer;
    nor to the Diamond: for they are more tender;
    nor vnto Christall: for nought may them seuer;
    nor vnto glasse: such basenesse mought offend her;
Then to the Maker selfe they likest be,
    whose light doth lighten all that here we see.

What was implicit in Sonnet 8 here becomes explicit as Spenser parodies his speaker's quest for an adequate metaphor by mocking the intelligence that seeks such a metaphor in literal-minded equivalences. Throughout the first section of the sequence, and well into the second, the speaker tries out the various literary conventions by which he might express the lady's eyes. Most of these are broadly Petrarchan, as Sonnets 7, 10, 12, and 16; some are loosely neo-Platonic, as 8 and 21; and some potentially Christian, as 9 and 24. But in every case, the speaker pursues the conventions only to reductive ends. Even when he recognizes that the contextual tropes are metaphoric, he does not see that they are metaphors for the other contextual tropes as well. In a sense, we could say that the conventional models provide the poet-lover with literal situations in which he can act out differing ways of loving. But like the shepherds in the *Calender*, or Alcyon, or Colin, he merely substitutes one semantic site for another and thus fails to conceive the relationship between them.

For Spenser, however, the interplay between discrete texts of loving discloses a broader metaphor from which all textual figures have been "figured forth." And this metaphor, rather than excluding specific contextual options, seeks to accommodate them all. By reading the conceit *to love* or the Idea *Love* behind the different texts of *loving*, we learn that those texts speak metaphorically. As we get on in the sequence, the speaker too learns to read in this way. In fact, it is exactly his growing ability to perceive metaphorically that charts his progress within the sequence. By the end of the middle section, he has learned to appropriate and approximate the voice of the poet by using conventional tropes to explore what remains constant in the varieties of loving rather than abusing them by assuming that one kind of loving precludes another. Like the Shepheard of the Ocean, he becomes "faithfull" to the metaphoric nature of his discrete sites of loving and begins to avoid the kind of dichotomizing his earlier literal-mindedness gave rise to.

The rhetorical interplay between metaphors that close by literal reduction and those that open by metaphoric extension shapes another mini-sequence on capture and captivity. The series begins with the very first sonnet:

> Happy ye leaues when as those lilly hands,
>> which hold my life in their dead doing might
>> shall handle you and hold in loues soft bands,
>> lyke captiues trembling at the victors sight.   [ll. 1–4]

Captivity is clearly metaphoric in these lines, a sign of the mistress's acceptance and prophetic of the speaker's future love and happiness. Sonnet 10 repeats the metaphor but situates it within a literalized Petrarchan context. The literal implications of tyranny, massacre, and vengeance control the next several appearances of the trope and thus occasion the speaker's growing complaint. In Sonnets 11, 12, 14, 29, and 37, the metaphoric captivity the speaker initially desired has become a literal place from which he wishes to escape. Sonnet 37 presents the altered perspective in its clearest terms:

> Fondness it were for any being free,
>   to couet fetters, though they golden be.   [ll. 13–14]

The initial trope has again become a semantic trap and the speaker's escape is made to depend upon his recovery of the metaphoric sense of his term.

His reformed image of captivity comes dramatically in Sonnet 65, but Spenser prepares very carefully for this new image by once again making the contextual site an opportunity for speaking metaphorically rather than a condition of semantic reduction. In Sonnet 62, as we have seen, the speaker prays that both he and his mistress will "chaunge old yeares annoy to new delight," and in Sonnet 63 he sights "the happy shore" which promises "the ioyous safety of so sweet a rest." As Sonnet 64 shows, this shore is the mistress herself, now perceived as "a gardin of sweet flowres." Because this biblical metaphor is so crucial to understanding the metaphoric speech of Sonnet 65, it is worth a slight digression.

The central metaphor of the Song of Songs is, of course, the enclosed garden, the *hortus conclusus*: "My sister my spouse is as a garden inclosed, as a spring shut vp, and a fountaine sealed vp" (4:12, Geneva Bible). Enclosure, shutting up, is not a negative or life-denying act here, for it is precisely because the garden is enclosed that it flourishes; because it is sealed, the lover is unafraid to enter it, to taste "the ioyous safety of so sweete a rest."

> My welbeloued is gone downe into his garden to the beds of spices, to fede in the gardens, and to gather lilies.   [Song 6:1]

The Great Bible combines the description of the sealed garden and the lover's entry into it in its translation of the fourth chapter:

> A garden well locked is my sister, my spouse, a garden well locked, and a sealed well. The fruits y are planted in thee are lyke a very Paradyse of pomgranates with swete frutes . . . a well of gardens, a wel of lyuinge waters, which renne down fro Libanus. . . . yee y my beloued maye come into my garden and eate of the swete fruites that growe thereon.

In an annotation on the word "locked" in this passage, Henry Ainsworth writes: "*Barred*: that is, close shut . . . which is for safetie and defense, that no evill should come thereon, no enemies should enter."[8] Captivity, therefore, is neither destructive nor delimiting; it is instead a guarantee of safety and productivity if correctly viewed. The Song of Songs thus gives the lover the means of transforming his previously literal understanding of captivity. As we shall see, this enables the lover not only to "offer" captivity to his mistress, but also to explain to her exactly what such captivity means.

But there may be even more behind Spenser's use of the Song of Songs at this dramatic point in the sequence. The repeated incident of the maid's taking hold of her love and bringing him into her house not only furthers the notion that captivity is productive, but foreshadows both the climactic Sonnet 67, in which the deer-love returns willingly to be caught and led in by the reformed lover, and the *Epithalamion*, where the lover first takes his bride by the hand and later leads her into the bridal chamber to consummate their union. In the third chapter of the Song, the maid says:

> I founde him whome my soule loued: I toke holde on him and left him not, til I had broght him vnto my mothers house into the chamber of her that conceiued me.   [3:4]

John Dove explains this passage: the maid does not grab her lover as Potiphar's wife grabbed Joseph, for he was able to slip away from her. The maid holds the lover as the Christian must hold Christ, "as Iacob did, which held not the Angels garment, but the Angell himself; not the shadow but the substance."[9] Although the lover loses his freedom to captivity, the result is nourishment:

> I wil lead thee & bring thee into my mothers house: there thou shalt teache me: & I wil cause thee to drinke spiced wine, & newe wine of the pomegranate.   [8:2]

Captivity is thus doubly sustaining: as in Sonnets 76 and 77, the lover is fed with the "sweet fruit of pleasure"; the lady, as in Sonnets 65 and 68, is taught the sweet fruit of Christian doctrine.

Sonnet 65, then, demonstrates not only that the lover's literalizing and reductive perception of captivity has been strikingly altered, but also that he has now adopted the role of the instructor sanctioned by the biblical text:

> The doubt which ye misdeeme, fayre loue, is vaine,
>> that fondly feare to loose your liberty,
>> when loosing one, two liberties ye gayne,
>> and make him bond that bondage earst dyd fly.
> Sweet be the bands, the which true loue doth tye,
>> without constraynt or dread of any ill:
>> the gentle birde feeles no captiuity
>> within her cage, but singes and feeds her fill.
> There pride dare not approach, nor discord spill
>> the league twixt them, that loyal loue hath bound:
>> but simple truth and mutuall good will,
>> seekes with sweet peace to salue each others wound:
> There fayth doth fearlesse dwell in brasen towre,
>> and spotlesse pleasure builds her sacred bowre.

The lover admits, in lines 3–4, that he had formerly misconstrued bondage as a literal captivity, loss of freedom as dreaded constraint. But now, understanding the metaphor of the "true loue knot," the sweet bands of love, he argues that only in such captivity is the soul completely free. "The gentle birde feeles no captiuity / within her cage, but singes and feeds her fill." Singing and feeding are metaphorically related again to the two roles the lover now assumes: the teacher of the mistress and partaker of her sweet fruits. As in the enclosed garden of the Song of Songs, there is multiple nourishment within the captivity of love in the *Amoretti*.

In Sonnet 67 the mistress, apparently having learned the lesson given her by the lover in Sonnet 65, allows herself to be "gotten hold of" as the bridegroom in the Song. Both lover and lady have learned to interpret captivity metaphorically. No longer reducing it to falsifying dichotomies, they open the term to accommodating paradox. The validity of their new perspective is immediately affirmed in Sonnet 68: Christ, triumphing over sin and death, "didst bring away / captiuity thence captiue vs to win." Man's captivity to sin is rewritten by his full acceptance of his greater captivity to Christ, a captivity both educating and nourishing:

> being with thy deare blood clene washt from sin,
> may liue for euer in felicity.

Even Christ here proves a mimetic lover: adopting the literal role of man's captivity, Christ captures captivity itself, rendering it only metaphoric. The lovers' love, insofar as it reflects, imitates, Christ's own act, reflects as well Christ's freeing love.

Two final sonnets measure the lovers' success. In Sonnet 71 the lover tells the lady that just as her needlework "is wouen all aboue / With woodbynd flowres and fragrant Eglantine," so shall what seemed a prison in which love has trapped her be "with many deare delights bedecked." The reference to the spider in line 3 of this poem recalls the description of the spider in Sonnet 23. There the lover compared his labor to win the lady to a spider whose web was merely "fruitlesse worke . . . broken with least wynd." Now, however, the spider and the bee live in peace and safety in the enclosure of the garden, aware of the necessity for captivity. And the web is full of fruit for both of them.

In Sonnet 73, the lover plays true and false views of captivity against one another. Captive within his own prison of the self, the lover breaks free to give himself over to the "seruile bands" of the "fayre tresses" of the lady's "golden hayre." Spenser once again doubles back upon his own poems, here on the literal interpretation given in Sonnet 37 of the net of hair as entangling and entrapping. Then, expanding the image he had already used in Sonnet

65, Spenser has the lover fly as a bird "to feed his fill" on the lady's eyes. Those eyes, seen throughout the early stages of the sequence as literal sources of destruction, now are metaphoric nourishment. Finally, the lover prays to be encaged as a bird in the mistress's bosom, where, as he said in Sonnet 65, captivity is not captivity at all but the freedom to learn, to feed, and to sing:

> perhaps he there may learn with rare delight,
>   to sing your name and praises ouer all
> That it hereafter may you not repent,
>   him lodging in your bosome to haue lent.   [ll. 11–14]

The strategy by which Spenser opens his textual metaphors to other and more encompassing accommodations is remarkably similar to the kind of *entrelacement* Rosemond Tuve describes in the continued metaphor of *The Faerie Queene*. As specific images or motifs are repeatedly placed in distinct contextual situations and shown to fulfill the semantic requirements of each place, their metaphoric nature is both ensured and illustrated. The textual transformations, in other words, guarantee the openness of all semantic places. Such freeing of place and of the literal vocabularies that places give rise to is itself a poetic imitation of Christ's redemptive act. For the Christ who frees love opens the space in which love is imprisoned in literal dichotomies, transforms that place into a metaphor that voids all dichotomy. Christ's freeing of love thus frees as well all ways of expressing love. "In Christ," Erasmus tells us, "everything is created anew, and vocabulary is wholly transformed." [10] The conventional vocabularies of Petrarchan or neo-Platonic love need not, therefore, be denied or even satirized, only opened to metaphoric status. The languages of traditional loving speak metaphorically of the divine injunction "to love," and the poet's task is to reveal the mimetic process by which such speaking has been "created anew." Such poetic reformation proposes a model, moreover, for ethical action. Lovers within and without the poetic narrative must learn that the various forms of loving available to them are legitimate only insofar as they are metaphorically accommodated to the lesson which "the Lord vs taught"—"to love" one another as we love Him and as He loves us.

It is precisely in these terms that Spenser opens even the site of Christ's loving to further metaphoric extension. Christ enters the textual sequence in order to force all literal narrative places into accommodating Him; but His action is itself metaphoric of the Idea of Love which He too imitates. The reformation which Christ accomplishes is thus a model rather than an end, and the poet's new task at the conclusion of the sequence is to reveal how such a model resolves all places into one, or frees all desire to love to aspire to the divine Idea of Love.

The typical Elizabethan sonnet sequence ends in a separation. In the terms of the present discussion, separation would necessarily involve a return to reductive dichotomies: lover and beloved, presence and absence, this place and that. At first glance, Spenser seems to confirm this sense of separation by placing his lover in the conventional condition:

> Lackying my loue I go from place to place,
>   lyke a young fawne that late hath lost the hynd:
>   and seeke each where, where last I sawe her face,
>   whose ymage yet I carry fresh in mynd.
> I seeke the fields with her late footing synd,
>   I seeke her bowre with her late presence deckt,
>   yet nor in field nor bowre I her can fynd:
>   yet field and bowre are full of her aspect.   [Sonnet 78, 1−8]

In the normal sequence, such spatial separation would imply the lady's final rejection of the persistently physical lover.[11] Here, however, the spatial terms are again opened to the metaphoric condition of the beloved in the Song of Songs: separation is not rejection, and those who seek will find. This separation does not question but affirms the success of the narrative lovers.

The final separation is very different from this traditional pattern. The lovers are still in love, but are driven apart by lies and slanders. In other words, once the lovers try to broaden their private, internal dialogue of love to include an external, public community, mistrust and misunderstanding result. Spenser sketches this outward movement clearly and precisely. Sonnet 85[12] laments that "the world . . . cannot deeme of worthy things"; nonetheless, says the poet-lover, he will continue to trumpet abroad his lady's praise and the world can choose whether "to enuy or to wonder." As the next sonnet, the first of the separation group, demonstrates, the world chooses to envy:

> Venemous toung tipt with vile adders sting,
>   Of that selfe kynd with which the Furies fell
>   theyr snaky heads doe combe, from which a spring
>   of poysoned words and spitefull speeches well.
> Let all the plagues and horrid paines of hell,
>   vpon thee fall for thine accursed hyre:
>   that with false forged lyes, which thou didst tel,
>   in my true loue did stirre vp coles of yre.[13]

Six sonnets after Spenser tells us he has completed Book VI of *The Faerie Queene*, the Blatant Beast, having already escaped from Calidore's iron chains and threatened the poet himself, enters the sonnet sequence and forces the lovers apart by interpreting their reformed love as a lie. In the face of that public slander, the lover fails to be consoled even by contemplating "the Idaea playne," and he ends the sequence mourning his absent beloved.

Although it may not be possible to understand the full import of the "venemous toung" to Spenser without examining Books V and VI of *The Faerie Queene*, some tentative suggestions may be offered.[14] The Beast represents the public world, the community, within which the lovers must find their ultimate success. What the lovers have thus far achieved is not denied, but it is seriously qualified.[15] One measure of that qualification is the surprise by which we suddenly realize how closed a space the lovers have inhabited to this point. Once their private place is opened, however, we see that their loving must now be figured forth in an act of marriage affirmed and sanctified by the human community called upon to witness that sacrament. Without that public sanctification by what the Prayer Book calls "his congregation," the activity of Christian loving and the reformation it should occasion would literally be displaced. The deformative slanders of the Beast, therefore, separate not only the lovers from each other, but also the entire community from the unfolding and regenerating love of God.

It is ultimately the metaphoric place of human loving within divine Love that leads Spenser to both the Christ of Sonnet 68 and the Song of Songs throughout the concluding section of the *Amoretti*. The redemption which Christ offers and the spiritual union of which the Song speaks establish the obligations that right loving must fulfill. Like the Song itself, the state of matrimony, as the Prayer Book defines it, is a metaphoric participation in "the spiritual marriage and unity betwixt Christ and his Church."[16] By breaking off his sequence prior to this moment of private, public, and divine unity, Spenser seems to imply that the success of each place depends upon the others. The lovers' final achievement, therefore, is measured not only by their metaphoric relation to Christ's act of redeeming love, but also by our metaphoric relation to their reforming love. The Idea of Love accommodates all three places and all three metaphoric imitations. And unless we imitate the lovers' imitation we, like the "venemous toung," deprive them of their due place in the figuring forth of divine Love. We also, of course, deprive ourselves of a place in the redemption love offers. We are the community that must sanctify the lovers' love, and we can do so only by now metaphorically transferring their poetic re-formation into our own ethical reformation.

At this point, we may begin to measure one aspect of Spenser's achievement in the *Epithalamion* to follow. Just as he there calls upon all the muses, nymphs, young maids and virgins, fresh boys, minstrels, merchants' daughters, and even the high heavens to come and celebrate the public moment of the wedding, so he calls upon the community of the poem's readers to stand with the couple before the holy priest and bless their matrimonial union. We become, in effect, the participating congregation, praising the happy pair and sanctifying through the poetic ritual the public success of their "tymely ioyes." [17] Our engagement in this poetic sacrament is precisely the ethical activity for which the lesson of the *Amoretti* prepares us, and to which it incites us. Only our active participation in the rite of this loving can assure the lovers and ourselves that the poem is "for short time an endlesse moniment."

Chapter 5. *The Fowre Hymnes*

The Fowre Hymnes is the final panel in the extended portrait of loving that Spenser begins in the *Amoretti* and centers in the *Epithalamion*. Of the many strategies by which this portrait is drawn, Spenser's shifting narrative modes are perhaps the most intriguing. The *Amoretti*, as we have seen, is essentially a dramatic poem in which an initially literal-minded lover learns to speak metaphorically. The *Epithalamion* is a ceremonial poem in which the private poet learns the public place of the wedding sacrament. And *The Fowre Hymnes* is a meditation on the divine cosmic principles which that sacrament metaphorically imitates. In a sense, Spenser's progress through the three poems is measured by the extent to which their speakers are able to open the terms of love to increasingly larger metaphoric accommodation. Paradoxically, such metaphoric extension is brought about by a turning inward, by the gradual effacement of a dramatic and objectified speaker into the poet's own internalized meditation. The narrative shifts, in other words, attest to the poet's growing confidence in his ability "rightly to define" the nature and power of love. By the final panel, he feels no need to defend his speech against the closures of a literalizing intelligence—he even parodies that need at the opening of the third hymn. Even more surprising is the fact that the poet's movement within, rather than excluding the reader from a progressively private text, increasingly draws that reader into the metaphoric activity of making such a text. How Spenser accomplishes this feat is the burden of the present chapter.

All readers of *The Fowre Hymnes* would probably agree with William Nelson's observation that Spenser's "method is a complex system of parallels and contrasts." [1] But they might not understand that Nelson's formulation unconsciously reiterates Sidney's description of the poetic act. System, as an abstract form or scheme, is a Sidneyan Idea; parallels and / or contrasts are particular verbal structures and thus constitute a text; method is a poetic process or fore-conceit. Most criticism on *The Fowre Hymnes* has focused narrowly on only one of these poetic elements. The majority of studies has addressed the systems or Ideas behind the work—neo-Platonic ladders of love, medieval schemes of mystical ascent, and conventional Renaissance debates of passion versus reason or earthly love versus spiritual love. [2] Occasionally, studies have demonstrated the textual patterns of Spenser's adumbrating imagery—metaphors of light, myths of creation, Cupid-figures, or spatial metaphors of ascent and descent. [3] In Sidneyan terms, both approaches fail to locate the principle of imitation by which the two are related. The textual images have not been shown to be metaphoric embodiments of the proposed systems, and the systems have never been defended specifically as abstracted metaphors of the text. But if the Sidneyan poetic is indeed at work in Spenser's poem, then it is precisely these imitative relationships that we must uncover. By analyzing a sequence of major images in the poem,[4] we ought to be able to disclose the fore-conceit, which, in turn, should reveal Spenser's formal Idea.

Obviously, there are several image clusters which run throughout *The Fowre Hymnes*; so it is difficult to draw definitive conclusions from the study of any one. That caveat made, it is still possible to argue that the cluster involving various images of light and fire is central to Spenser's poem. The poet begins the work "t'asswage the force of this new flame" that Cupid has kindled in him, and he concludes by urging the reader to "look at last vp to that soueraigne light" of Christ. He tells us, moreover, that the contemplation of various forms of light is actually circular, for he discovers in the fourth hymn that the source of the flame which initially urged him on in the first was not Cupid, but Christ, that purer flame which "kindleth loue in euery godly spright." We might expect, therefore, that the cluster of light images in the poem proceeds in an orderly and traceable line, or circle. Yet the sheer number of such images conceals that order, for major images of light appear at least ninety-two times in the poem, in multiple variations and with frequently conflicting meanings.[5] The words "light" and "fire" occur some sixty-five times. In order to disclose a groundplot to Spenser's development, therefore, it is necessary to locate the metaphoric source of both fire and light. Fortunately, that source is readily available in the more encompassing image of the lamp, which appears only eight times in the poem but which clearly enlightens the poem's metaphoric process.

As both receiver and producer of light, the lamp serves as an appropriate image of the poet's own task and function, as a suitable vehicle for his intellectual quest in the poem, and as a conventional metaphor for the object of that quest, Christ. The mimetic relationship between Lamp-Christ and lamp-poet, furthermore, duplicates the Maker / maker analogy described in the Introduction; and this metaphoric imitation opens, in turn, a relationship between God's Poem and the poet's: "Thy word is a lamp unto my feete: and a light unto my path" (Psalm 119:105).

The lamp, then, guides Spenser's journey up and down the levels of creation, and his narrative progress through the four hymns can be envisioned as a sequence of discovering various lamps, each kindled by another lamp, until he arrives at the ultimate nonkindled and self-kindling Lamp of divine light. And if this sense of the progress of the *Hymnes* is correct, we can focus it more sharply by suggesting that the journey is structured by the intention "to enlighten."[6] As lower lamps are "enlightened" by higher ones, they are led to "en-lighten" themselves of earthly dross so as to rise to ultimate "enlighten-ment." This process, moreover, enlightens the poet in such a way that he is able to enlighten his readers in turn. Initially, then, we can conceive of the lamp as a complex poetic metaphor of the poet's Sidneyan purpose: it an-nounces his end as nothing less than exalting the reader to full Christian enlightenment.

The first appearance of the lamp occurs in "An Hymne in Honovr of Love." Frail earthly lovers, inflamed by sparks from Cupid's "empoisned darts," devote themselves to "piteous" adulation of their earthly ladies:

> The daies they waste, the nights they grieue and grone,
> Their liues they loath, and heauens light disdaine;
> No light but that, whose lampe doth yet remaine
> Fresh burning in the image of their eye,
> They deigne to see, and seeing it still dye.   [HL, ll. 129–133]

This lamp is the "glorious beame" of the physical beauty of the lady ("the image of their eye"), a lamp which actually blinds rather than enlightens be-cause it encourages the lover to accept it as sole and final source. But Spenser has prepared carefully for this lamp, and thus cleansed our perception of it, by distinguishing between the fire which inspires animals to multiply in order to "quench the flame" of desire (HL, l. 102), and that "heauenly fyre" which leads man to aspire beyond procreation to "th'immortall flame / Of heauenly light," which is "Beauties glorious beame" (HL, ll. 107–112). The lover who disdains heaven's light in favor of the lamp of physical beauty has therefore failed to refine his own lamp-flame. Spenser discriminates between false lovers and true lovers, between those who regard "such lamps" as the lady not in love but in lust, and those whose "refyned mynd" also refines the be-loved's lamp of beauty "Vnto a fairer form," "the mirrour of . . . heauenly light" (HL, ll. 192–196). Thus lightened of the "dirtie drosse" of false or lustful love, and alert to the "flaming light of . . . celestiall fyre," the true lover can "mount aboue the natiue might / Of heauie earth, vp to the heauens hight" (HL, ll. 183–189).

In the second hymn, the lover is lifted above this earthly lamp, which is at best the idea of feminine beauty, to a second lamp, the idea of beauty itself.[7] Accordingly, the image of the lamp is also refined and redefined: the face, which was itself the lamp of the first hymn, is here kindled by the soul's inter-nal lamp of beauty. Spenser foreshadows his own use of this lamp at the open-ing of the hymn: he must, he argues, "refyne" his former lamp by "Doing away the drosse which dims the light / Of that faire beame" (HB, ll. 47–49). His two references to the lamp in the hymn follow this intention. Venus's beam of beauty

> . . . is the thing which giueth pleasant grace
> To all things faire, that kindleth liuely fyre,
> Light of thy lampe, which shyning in the face,
> Thence to the soule darts amorous desyre.   [HB, ll. 57–60]

That Spenser intends the lamp shining in the lady's face to be light kindled by the soul, not the body, is clearer in his second passage. The fire in the lady's face, her "goodly hew of white and red," even her eyes that sparkle like "stars so bright," shall "loose their goodly light" and "turne to dust":

> But that faire lampe, from whose celestiall ray
> That light proceeds, which kindleth louers fire,
> Shal neuer be extinguisht nor decay,
> But when the vitall spirits doe expyre,
> Vnto her natiue planet shall retyre,
> For it is heauenly borne and can not die.   [HB, ll. 99–104]

As Spenser immediately explains in the following stanza, this lamp is the immortal soul, itself enlightened by "that great immortall Spright," Beauty itself.

We might pause at this point to observe that Spenser's treatment of the various lamps returns to strategies already described. To the "faithfull" or "refyned" mind, the place of any given lamp opens onto other places of other lamps. Such a mind understands that its task is "to reade enregistred in euery nook" how "All ioy, all blisse, all happinesse" there "haue place" (HHB, ll. 131, 243). That reading is accomplished only by remaining faithful to the metaphoric nature of all places. To the unrefined mind, a mind closed or blind to the metaphoric nature of lamps, place is also closed and enclosing. The site of the lady's body is dis-placed from the site of her soul just as the site of earthly love is dis-placed from that of heavenly love. Such false reading is again bound to literal dichotomies. But these dichotomies are exactly what a right reading of place denies. The conflicting, antagonistic forces of earth, air, fire, and water—elemental dichotomies—are resolved in the metaphoric view of love which "place[s] them all in order" (HL, l. 87). More provocatively, Spenser's own meditation on this issue involves how the lover perceives the lady's eyes. Does he see that they represent a site fashioned by both body and soul, or does he separate physical and spiritual places? The site such lovers see is therefore a product of the sight by which they see: "the image of their eye." Again the implications for Spenser's poetic strategies are far-reaching. The openness of every place becomes a defense against semantic closure, against the literalizing that encloses all spaces.

We can bring the issue of place into relation with our Sidneyan terms by looking more closely at the operations of the "faithfull mind":

Such is the powre of that sweet passion,
That it all sordid baseness doth expell,
And the refyned mynd doth newly fashion
Vnto a fairer forme, which now doth dwell
In his high thought, that would it selfe excell;
Which he beholding still with constant sight,
Admires the mirrour of so heauenly light.

Whose image printing in his deepest wit,
He thereon feeds his hungrie fantasy,
Still full, yet neuer satisfyde with it,
Like *Tantale*, that in store doth sterued ly:
So doth he pine in most satiety,
For nought may quench his infinite desyre,
Once kindled through that first conceiued fyre.   [HL, ll. 190–203]

Correct sight of the lady's lamp of beauty—the site of her eyes—leads to an insight of the site within—the "fairer forme" which "dwells" now in the lover's thought. But that internalized image (a conceit "first conceiued") still does not satisfy and must be raised to a higher site / sight: it "makes him mount aboue the natiue might / Of heauie earth, vp to the heauens hight" (HL, ll. 188–189). Here, in broadly sketched and figurative terms, is the Sidneyan process by which a reader moves from a text to fore-conceit to Idea. As we described in the Introduction, the reader opens the semantic places of the text to the increasingly higher forms those places metaphorically imitate.

That process duplicates not only the poet's act of making, but also the greater Maker's creation. Spenser opens his own terms to this larger model by analyzing the mimetic principles of creating and re-creating forms. "Soule is forme," he tells us in the second hymn (l. 132), and that form "frames her [earthly] house, in which she will be placed, / Fit for her selfe" by adorning it with "th'heauenly riches." The enlightened soul, that is, "tempers so trim," enlightens, the light of the physical body in order more nearly to approximate the lamp of beauty which is the soul's source and site. Spenser develops this notion of dual enlightenment by describing the processes by which the soul's place can be either deformed or reformed.

Yet oft it falles, that many a gentle mynd
Dwels in *deformed* tabernacle drownd,
Either by chaunce, against the course of kynd,
Or through vnaptnesse in the substance fownd,
Which it assumed of some stubborne grownd,
That will not yield vnto her *formes* direction,
But is *perform'd* with some foule imperfection.
                              [HB, ll. 141–147, my italics]

To guard against such a spiritual deformation, the reader is urged to "still preserue your first *informed* grace," first by selecting a love-object "the which your *formes* first sourse may sympathize," and then by "*comforming* it [the "more refyned forme" of the beloved] vnto the light, / Which in itselfe it hath remaining still / Of that first Sunne" (HB, ll. 167, 192, 214, 218–220). The processes of reforming forms,[8] refining lights, and opening metaphoric places here converge to define not only each other, but also the poet's strategies of proper mimetic and metaphoric making, as well as the reader's task of mimetic and metaphoric reading.

Following this process Spenser returns, in the third hymn, to his image of the lamp, "conforming" it "vnto the light" of divine love. Purging himself of "th'heat of youth," he calls upon the "most blessed Spirit, pure lampe of light, / Eternal spring of grace and wisedome trew" (HHL, ll. 43–44), to teach him the ultimate source of love. The light of the Holy Spirit is "pure" light because it enlightens without poisoning or heating, but Spenser suddenly complicates the seemingly constant refinement of his image by reminding us of the fallen angels, who had been a "thousand lamps of burning light" until misled by Satan, "the Child of light" (HHL, ll. 59–83). Even at the level of heavenly lamps, the potential for deformation is present. More important, we are warned of the danger of spurning that lamp which kindles all: if we mistake a lesser lamp for the ultimate one, we may kindle "the flame of [God's] consuming yre" (HHL, l. 86), and deprive ourselves of the possibility of redeeming and reforming grace.

The concept of redemption evokes Spenser's next image of the lamp:

> O blessed well of loue, O floure of grace,
> O glorious Morning starre, O lampe of light,
> Most liuely image of thy fathers face,
> Eternall King of glorie, Lord of might,
> Meeke lambe of God before all worlds behight,
> How can we thee requite for all this good?   [HHL, ll. 169–174]

Christ is the ultimate unfolding and refinement of the idea of the lamp, the purity, effectiveness, and glory to which all other lamps in the poem aspire. Furthermore, it is precisely the paradox and mystery of Christ that allows Spenser to portray Him as the source and site of all light, for Christ's lamp does not derive from the "fathers face," but is identical to and coeternal with that face. He is the only lamp that is not kindled from a source, but burning with the source, the sole lamp whose one place is an everywhere. Christ is also, therefore, the only truly portable lamp, a guide that can be carried with man and so carry man in turn, the lamp in which producing and receiving light are made one continuous act.

In the fourth hymn, Spenser uses the image of the lamp only once. Looking back from the enlightenment granted by the lamp of Christ, the poet focuses on his own refined perception:

> And that faire lampe, which vseth to enflame
> The hearts of men with selfe consuming fyre,
> Thenceforth seemes fowle, and full of sinfull blame.
>
> [HHB, ll. 274–276]

We might be led to see in these lines a rejection of lamps altogether, and certainly a rejection of the lamp of the "Hymne in Honovr of Love." But that is not Spenser's intention. Each lamp is "darkened" by succeeding lamps, but this does not mean they are rejected. Instead, we must understand how Spenser urges a continual transcendence by use of each lamp in its turn. Each is valuable, that is, for the light it sheds in its place, and valuable for lighting our way to the next lamp and the next place. In this sense, we see that any one lamp serves as a metaphor for all lamps, the lamp of Cupid as metaphoric of Christ's lamp as Christ is a metaphor for Cupid. All lamps, like all places, "speak metaphorically." But here we confront an obvious problem, for the metaphoric relationship between the lamp of Cupid and that of Christ is not the same as the relationship between Christ's light and Cupid's spark. By refocusing our attention away from lamps themselves and to the process of enlightening, we can define the metaphoric nature of lamps more exactly. We can also begin to understand why Spenser's most perfect lamp appears in only the third hymn and how he takes us beyond even that glorious image.

Thus far we have used the word "enlighten" to designate the process by which one lamp is kindled from another. But Spenser himself never uses this term in *The Fowre Hymnes*, preferring instead "illuminate." His choice is the more significant because illuminate does not imply the uplifting sense of enlighten and does not, etymologically, contribute to the ascending movement through places in the poem. Spenser's first use of the word appears in the Hymn of Love, where man is "enlumind with that goodly light" of beauty (HL, l. 108). This passage occurs in the midst of Spenser's distinction between the fire infused in animals, which leads only to the desire "to quench the flame," and the heavenly fire infused in man, which leads him to aspire towards the immortal flame of pure beauty. Initially, therefore, Spenser does conceive of illumination as a process of ascent, a questing motion which seeks greater forms of itself. Man's "enlumind" light aspires to yet brighter light.[9]

At the opening of the second hymn, the poet calls upon Venus "T'illuminate" his "dim and dulled eyne" with her "loue-kindling light" (HB, ll. 20, 19). Like the true lover in the first hymn, Spenser has used Cupid's illuminating spark of desire to aspire to greater illumination. Later in the same hymn, the poet warns the ladies of the court not to let their lamps of beauty "be dimd, and . . . darkned quight" (HB, l. 165). Instead, they are urged to seek greater light through love:

> But gentle Loue, that loiall is and trew,
> Will more illumine your resplendent ray,
> And adde more brightnesse to your goodly hew,
> From light of his pure fire.   [HB, ll. 176–179]

Again Spenser conceives of illumination as a quest: the lover who remains content with Cupid's spark chooses merely to quench his flame; similarly, the lady who chooses simply to be beautiful, "enshrines" her light and assures her ultimate "darknesse." Only by moving outside the closure of the self to seek further illumination is present illumination worthy of praise.

At the very end of the third hymn, Spenser envisions the ascent of one who has been inflamed by zealous love of the ultimate lamp, Christ. In the presence of that glorious light, the physical eyes are blinded and the spiritual "eyes" illuminated; the site of this lamp turns "sight" to "insight":

> [Those] glorious beames all fleshly sense doth daze
> With admiration of their passing light,
> Blinding the eyes and lumining the sprite.   [HHL, ll. 278–280]

> And thy bright radiant eyes shall plainely see
> Th'Idee of his pure glorie present still,
> Before thy face, and all thy spirits shall fill
> With sweete enragement of celestiall loue,
> Kindled through sight of those faire things aboue.
>   [HHL, ll. 283–287]

Certainly we are very close here not only to full recognition of Christ, but even to full participation in Him and His site. And in these terms, we might recall that Spenser's previous address to the court ladies continues a few lines more than we quoted above:

> But gentle Loue, that loiall is and trew,
> Will more illumine your resplendent ray,
> And adde more brightnesse to your goodly hew,
> From light of his pure fire, which by like way
> Kindled of yours, your likeness doth display,
> Like as two mirrours by opposed reflexion.   [HB, ll. 176–181]

Love and beauty illuminate and are illuminated by each other. But this illumination is by means of a mirror, an opposed reflection, a metaphoric relationship. Presumably, for the soul "face to face" with Christ, such a mirror or metaphor is inconceivable. Yet it has not totally vanished, either, as Spenser's reference to the "Idee of his pure glorie" attests. In some form or another, that Idea is still a reflection and a dis-placement, not a full participation. Illumination has been "reformed," but it has not yet "conformed" unto the lamp of purest light. Thus, the process of illuminating must continue into the fourth hymn.

The ascent in the "Hymne of Heavenly Beavtie" takes us through a series of refined spheres of heaven, all of them "vnmouing, vncorrupt, and spotlesse bright," and each of them "illuminated" by "their own natiue light" (HHB, ll. 68–70). We ascend, in other words, to sites of light where once again the kindled cannot be distinguished from the kindling, illuminated from illuminator. In fact, it is precisely the simultaneity of light that assures the full participatory glory of this illumination.

At this point Spenser records his final image of that condition. Exhorting us to cease ascending now in order to "lowly fall" before Christ's throne, he describes the glorious light of Truth:

> His seate is Truth, to which the faithfull trust,
> From whence proceed her beames so pure and bright,
> That all about him sheddeth glorious light.   [HHB, ll. 159–161]

Spenser manipulates the syntax here to allow multiple readings of the lines. Christ's throne illuminates truth, which in turn illuminates Him; the light of truth is kindled by the trusting faithful, and both then illuminate Christ. Either way, Spenser has fundamentally altered the earlier conception of the lamp. Here it is the mutual illumination of all lamps that creates the "glorious light." Love and beauty, illuminated and illuminator, kindled and kindling, all resolve into the process of illumination itself. Immediately, Spenser adds these intriguing lines:

> Light farre exceeding that bright blazing sparke,
> Which darted is from *Titans* flaming head,
> That with his beams enlumineth the darke
> And dampish air, wherby all things are red.   [HHB, ll. 162–165]

The light of truth, of Christ, of the faithful, even of the appropriately diminished Titan, converge in the illumination "wherby all things are red." The poet and his audience also converge in this text, for the illumination granted the poet is assured only if it illuminates the reader, who in turn further illuminates Christ himself. The process of illumination, spreading ever outward throughout the four hymns, has here announced its ultimate end. The poet who has constantly sought the kindling lamp of illumination, here becomes that lamp himself, illuminating not only the lamps of his readers and the lamp that is the poem, but even in his lesser light illuminating the most glorious lamp of light, Christ.

In order to see how conscious Spenser is of the fullness of illumination at this point, we may return to the soul's entrance into Christ's presence:

> Thence gathering plumes of perfect speculation,
> To impe the wings of thy high flying mynd,
> Mount vp aloft through heauenly contemplation,
>
> . . . .
>
> And like the natiue brood of Eagles kynd,
> On that bright Sunne of glorie fixe thine eyes,
> Clear'd from grosse mists of fraile infirmities.   [HHB, ll. 134–140]

In altered form, Spenser here reiterates the image of refining the lamp-light, but which lamp is refined? Certainly the soul is cleansed of infirmities so that it can behold Christ's full illumination. But the illuminated observer or reader also illuminates Christ: the "bright Sunne" is Himself "clear'd from" the mists through which man usually perceives Him. The soul and the object of its contemplation are illuminated at the same time and by the same illuminating process. In such a process of continual illumination, the poet's function is clearly defined: by displaying his own illumination, he enlightens the reader, whose reformed vision teaches him how to "conform" his own light to the source of all light. That act of "conforming" increases anew the glory of the heavenly lamp.

Spenser's use of the image of the lamp and the process of illumination are deeply rooted in his conception of Christ. The paradoxes of light in the poem all stem from the central paradox of Christ, the "lamp of light" whose purity exists in its coequality with God the Father. But the glory of Christ resides less in the purity of his light than in the communicability of that light. Christ's sovereign flame, Spenser writes in the fourth hymn, "from whose pure beams al perfect beauty springs, / . . . kindleth loue in euery godly spright." The patterns of ascent and descent in the poem are here resolved into one movement, the perfect circle in which the divine light is forever descending down through the cosmos and forever leading the human soul up through the cosmos to the source. In that movement, even the dialectic of love versus beauty is resolved, for the one but illuminates the other. The love of Christ is the beauty of creation. What seemed paradoxical to the seeker in the hymns is not so at all when seen rightly in its full and logical manifestation as the power, glory, and communicability of God.

The incarnation of Christ, then, perfectly defines the process of illumination as Spenser perceives it, and it is for this reason that he alters the scheme of his poem at the end of the third hymn by calling directly upon the reader to meditate upon the paradoxical nature of that incarnation:

> Beginne from first, where he encradled was
> In simple cratch, wrapt in a wad of hay,
> Betweene the toyleful Oxe and humble Asse.

> Through meditation of his endlesse merit,
> Lift vp thy mind to th'author of thy weale,
> And to his soueraine mercie doe appeale.
>
> [HHL, ll. 225–227; 255–257]

In fact, the third hymn ends by reconstructing a full preparatory meditation in the conventional Loyolan form.[10] Lines 225–245 are a dramatic composition of place; lines 246–266, an exercise of the understanding; and lines 267–287, an emotional redirection of will. This three-part conclusion, deliberately patterned to give identical length to each part, implies through its very form a broader symbolic movement in the *Hymnes* beyond the metaphoric structures of the first two to a higher level of faith and belief. In colloquy with the Word fully revealed, the word which is a lamp, the reader will himself be illuminated with the glory of Christ and will be led to illuminate Christ in turn. He becomes one of the faithful who shed their light on Christ's throne by full recognition of the divine Truth.

Spenser has here altered not only the progression of his poem, but its metaphoric nature as well. The languages of love and beauty serve throughout the poem as metaphors both for each other and for divine Christian truths. But once those languages address the incarnational mystery of Christ, they, like the terms of the *Amoretti*, are wholly transformed. Their original metaphoric meaning derived from the literal act of the incarnation and the paradox of that act has a profoundly literalizing effect now on the languages themselves and on the poem which uses them. The enlightenment granted by Christ and then returned to Him is a literal participation in the unfolding Word of divine illumination. The poem suddenly becomes not Spenser's, but God's, who, "with the force of a divine [light] . . . bringeth things forth far surpassing" man's nature. This is not to say that the poetic Christ is the literal Christ, of course, but that the act of illuminating His illumination is a direct participation in that illumination, a process of imitation which does not metaphorically distort but literally refines.

Obviously, we have shifted our focus away from the parallels and contrasts within Spenser's text to the broader system behind that text when we name the final stanzas of the third hymn as a meditation. And it is equally clear that neither neo-Platonic ascent nor Christian mysticism is a particularly visible pattern here, for the mere presence of a formal meditation calls these systems into question. The real issue, however, is why Spenser should turn to the meditation at all. We can answer this question by looking once more at the fourth hymn.

The hymn of heavenly beauty is the only one for which Spenser seems to use an external pattern, here the formal spiritual exercise elaborated in Bonaventure's *Itinerarium Mentis in Deum*.[11] Lines 1–28 comprise a "bestirring of self" and a preview of the entire meditation; lines 29–105 are devoted to polishing the mirror of the created universe; lines 106–182 polish the mirror of the mind in order to reflect clearly the truth of Christ; lines 183–287 define the essential attributes of divine Wisdom; and lines 288–301 constitute a withdrawal from intellectual pursuit and an anticipation of repose. It is not, however, the similarity of structure, or even similarities of focus—patterns of ascent and descent, images of light and fire, mirrors of perception, and so on—that draw our attention to the *Itinerarium*. All of these individual elements were available to Spenser in countless meditational manuals. But Bonaventure's work provides the most useful example of the aesthetic wedding of form, structure, and substance that Spenser himself desires in his own vision.

Contemplating the Seraph that appeared to Saint Francis on Mount Alverna, Bonaventure argues that its six wings represent "the six stages of illumination that begin from creatures and lead up to God, whom no one rightly enters except through the Crucified"; or again, the Seraph symbolizes "the six levels of illumination by which, as if by steps or stages, the soul can pass over to peace through ecstatic elevations of Christian wisdom."[12] Illumination to wisdom, Cupid's spark of illuminating desire to Sapience—here is Spenser's scheme in its barest form. But what is especially clear is that Bonaventure's method provides a model to ensure the *performance* of what the meditative quest has taught. The stages themselves, in other words, and the particular images the movement through those stages reveals, are not as important as the process the meditation sets to work, the direct participation in the illumination "wherby al things are red." By engaging the reader directly in a literal performance of illumination—the meditation itself—both Spenser and Bonaventure try to engage him as well in the glorious exaltation of man, in the paradoxical and literal truth that the reader's own illumination illuminates the ultimate "lamp of light."

The Fowre Hymnes is Spenser's most optimistic poetic effort. It is also an affirmation and demonstration of a Sidneyan poetic, for Spenser's Christ is the Idea of illumination which both poet and reader must imitate in order to be illuminated and in order to illuminate in turn. By "conforming" their mental and spiritual forms "vnto the light" of Christ, they preserve their "first informed grace" and "reform" their "deformed" earthly tabernacles. No less than Sidney, Spenser here exalts the power of poetry not only to instruct man but also actually to set in motion the ethical performance by which he can, through God's informing grace, transcend the metaphoric strictures of a fallen language to enter a full participation in the literally unfolding Word.[13]

Part II. *The Faerie Queene*

Chapter 6. "Writing" the Proems

Throughout the minor poems, Spenser's desire to announce himself as a Sidneyan Right Poet is inseparable from his need to defend himself against a variety of wrong, or false, poets. Rightly to proclaim is made to depend upon the ability to disclaim, and praise of right speaking requires the blame of wrong speaking. As a result, Spenser traps himself in a defensive paradox: the more he tries to affirm his own voice, the more he is committed to giving voice to the very false poets he wishes to silence. This narrative effect is also evident in *The Faerie Queene*, where, as modern scholarship has shown, "wrong-speakers" and "faultfinders" abound. In the present chapter, we shall look more closely at why Spenser needs these abusers of the poetic word and what specific problems arise because of that need.[1]

That the proems to the six books of *The Faerie Queene* announce Spenser's subjects and intentions is self-evident. Equally obvious, though less discussed, is the fact that the proems announce the poet himself. More particularly, the proems seek "rightly to define" the metaphor that expresses the poet's presence in the poem. As we might expect, a large portion of that expression is devoted to discriminations between the poet's own right speaking and various kinds of misspeaking. But unlike those in the minor poems, the discriminations here are not reducible to a simple literal-metaphoric dichotomy, and instead of defending the poet, they constantly betray him. As we progress through the proems, we see Spenser's growing awareness of how thoroughly he is himself implicated in and even dependent upon the misrepresentations of the fictional false poets, of how both his manner and his matter duplicate theirs. Similarly, as Spenser comes to understand the extent to which any literary text distorts the Idea from which it arises, the comfortable Sidneyan distinctions between right and wrong poets he has used in the minor poems become increasingly tenuous. The drama of the proems, then, is the clash between Spenser's attempts to forestall misuses of his text and his developing consciousness of problems inherent in his own defensive and proclaiming postures.[2]

The seriousness of such problems to Spenser is also evident in the extent to which he feels compelled to devote portions of each book to addressing the literary questions raised in its proem. Not shaped solely or even significantly by the unfolding definition and demonstration of a titular virtue, these narrative moments are directly conditioned by Spenser's need to defend both himself and his text. By isolating such passages within the books and by clarifying their relationship to the challenges articulated in the proems, we can learn much about Spenser's fears concerning his greatest literary task..

Of course, so narrow a focus cannot presume to comprehensive treatment of any single book, and the critical risks in isolating parts from poetic wholes are evident. But neither the whole of *The Faerie Queene* nor the whole of any one of its books is our present concern; rather, we want to reveal the ways in which Spenser's consciousness of false speaking and false reading shapes particular sections of the poem. What narrative demands, in other words, do the questions raised in the six proems exert upon the books that follow them?

i

Like Book I itself, Spenser's first proem is an optimistic announcement of a mission and an intention. Beneath the conventional self-effacements of the *humilitas* tropes, Spenser's narrative voice not only asserts his guidance by Clio and Cupid, Venus and Elizabeth, but even presumes his song is fit matter for the education of the Queen. He intends, the proem argues, to "blazon broad" the gentle deeds of knights and ladies which have for too long "slept in silence"; to lament the "vndeserued wrong" suffered by the "most noble Briton Prince," Arthur; and to delineate Elizabeth herself by drawing "that true glorious type" of her, Gloriana. Both the invocations and the designated subjects imply a progression from the fictional to the historical realms, from the broadly mythic and archetypal to the specific and the present, focusing finally on the figure of Elizabeth the Queen.[3] Equally clear is the self-consciousness of the Sidneyan humanism which motivates this attempt to recover the past in such a way as to inform and reform the present.

A number of subsidiary strategies assist Spenser's initial announcement, but it is just at this point that complications arise. At the moment, the narrative voice is unaware of the problems, too self-confident to realize the risks he is taking. The reader, however, may sense that under the seemingly frank admission of the work's plan lie troubling implications for the poet's own position. Some of these are discernible in the opening stanza:

> Lo I the man, whose Muse whilome did maske,
>> As time her taught in lowly Shepheards weeds,
>> Am now enforst a far vnfitter taske,
>> For trumpets sterne to chaunge mine Oaten reeds,
>> And sing of Knights and Ladies gentle deeds;
>> Whose prayses hauing slept in silence long,
>> Me, all too meane, the sacred Muse areeds
>> To blazon broad emongst her learned throng:
> Fierce warres and faithfull loues shall moralize my song.

As every reader of Spenser knows, the poet here alludes to and aligns himself with the career of Virgil in order to enunciate his own claim to being England's moral poet.[4] But his adaptation of the opening lines to the *Aeneid* ("*Ille ego, qui quondam gracili modulatus avena / carmen . . . at nunc horrentia Martis*") introduces a crucial and problematic difference. Virgil's "I" asserts a literal and personal identity: I, Virgil, who earlier wrote pastorals, am now writing epic. Spenser's "I" is metaphoric: it does not identify a literal person but a generic role and progress. Spenser's assumption of the Virgilian mantle is intended, therefore, to reveal a general and metaphoric definition of the Poet; but insofar as this particular poet presents himself as a metaphoric imitation of Virgil, his own identity as Edmund Spenser has been to some extent concealed. We might wonder about such a strategy. Is the masking of an individual identity required to unmask the metaphoric one? In a book which is going to focus on various maskings and unmaskings of truth, on appearances which only "seem" versus realities that "be," this question is a crucial one. When, later in Book I, Spenser has poet-Archimago imitate Redcross by assuming the knight's clothing, he clearly intends us to be struck by the apparent similarity between guise and disguise, between imitations that reveal and those that conceal.

Once the status of the poet's metaphoric identity is opened to question, other of his strategies become problematic. When Spenser comes, in the middle of the stanza, to name his subject, he brings his text into metaphoric relation not with the martial Virgil but with the romantic Ariosto, not with "arms and the man" but with "*Le donne, i cavallier, l'arme, gli amori / le cortesie, l'audaci imprese io canto.*"[5] The initially doubled identity is here redoubled, and the possibilities of duplicity such metaphoric doubling gives rise to is evident when we bring Spenser's own intention to sing of "fierce warres and faithfull loues" into relation with the deceptive minstrels of Lucifera's House of Pride, who beguile men from their quests by delightful tales of "Old loues, and warres for Ladies doen by many a Lord" (I.v.3). Since the strategies of metaphoric imitation accommodate both the poet's right speaking and his antagonists' false speaking, metaphor itself would seem to be an unreliable measure of the ethics of speech.

We should pause over this similarity between Spenser's own song and that of Lucifera's minstrels. One of the persistent themes of *The Faerie Queene* is the danger of rest, that most human of desires to escape awhile the rigors of the quest. Such rest is precisely the ethical action intended and represented by the minstrels' songs. The characters in the House of Pride are lulled into rest by these songs, and the songs themselves are respites from the reformative obligations of the true poet. By relating his poem to theirs, Spenser identifies two potential dangers he will have to defend against. At the very end of the poem, in Book VI, we can see Spenser still concerned with these issues as

he wonders momentarily whether his own return to the pastoral is not a surrender to the desire for rest, a retreat from the arduous and dangerous quest
for communal reform into the securer world of literary artifice. This is perhaps one of the most troubling questions Spenser will ask of his text, and it is
revealing that he anticipates it at the very beginning of the poem.

In the second stanza of the proem, Spenser calls upon Clio to "lay forth out
of thine euerlasting scryne / The antique rolles, which there lye hidden still."
As Giamatti and others have taught us, the urge to reach back and to include
all history, even prehistorical myth, is a primary motive of the humanist
romance-epic, and Spenser commits himself to this responsibility immediately.[6] Yet again the conventional and laudatory intention of subjecting
the frequently chaotic past to the ordered form of present discourse is announced through a potentially ambiguous phrase. The poet calls upon Clio to
"sharpen my dull tong." Later in Book I, Spenser describes Archimago:
"For that old man of pleasing wordes had store, / And well could file his
tongue as smooth as glas" (I.i.35). Although the passages insist upon a distinction between poetic voices (dull versus smooth tongues), the poet's plea is
to be made like Archimago. He too must find "pleasing wordes" and he too
must "forge true-seeming" images. Again the similarities between the narrating voice and the poet's arch-antagonist—who is further designated as the
father of lies (I.i.38)—raise important questions not only about how the poet
defines himself, but also about the claims he might make to speaking the
truth.

The reader's experience of the proem, of course, is not sullied by these implications: at this point in his reading, he is probably as innocent as the narrative voice, willing to see only the optimism of high and noble argument. But
like everything else in *The Faerie Queene*, the images and issues raised in the
proem are repeated again and again, gradually accruing darker implications
which call into question some of the assumptions of the proem's narrator.
This process of continually repeating formulae in differing contexts is Spenser's basic strategy; with it he not only lays clues for the interpretation of future passages, but also suggests inadequacies in the reader's understanding of
previous passages.[7] Our experience of the initial proem, therefore, follows the
poet's; and just as he uses the subsequent true and false poets of Book I to
define further his own poetic voice, so we continuously revise our understanding of that voice and his assumptions as we encounter the later poet-
figures. Both the false poets—Archimago, Duessa, the minstrels, Despair—
and the right poets—Merlin, Fidelia, Heavenly Contemplation—teach us
the artistic problems Spenser himself is formulating and facing. The opening
proem, then, alerts us to one thread of Spenser's concern in the book to follow and defines one lens through which we can view that book.

The most obvious extension of this issue in Book I is Spenser's portrait of Archimago. Initially, Archimago is fashioned by the same defensive strategies and the same self-defensive needs we observed in the minor poems. Right speaking is defined by the narrative antithesis of wrong speaking. As we have noted, however, the poet himself is already a metaphor, expressed by metaphoric and mimetic relation to Virgil and Ariosto; now the poet is reexpressed by metaphoric and mimetic relation to Archimago. The metaphor that defines Spenser-in-the-poem can be situated in a mediating position between the metaphoric Virgil-Ariosto and a metaphoric Archimago; and if Virgil and Ariosto represent the Idea the poet sets out to imitate, Archimago represents the text he might become. Archimago, then, is both Spenser's textual exploration of the kinds of duplicity that inhabit all metaphoric imitation, and his attempt to limit that duplicity to the text itself. An Archimago bound in the text cannot disgrace the conceit of the poet who shapes that text.

The problem is that Archimago refuses to be bound or limited: he continually escapes the fictional role of a simple antagonist, and his duplicitous creations threaten constantly to contaminate the poet's. Even his name is witness to Spenser's inability to contain him. For Archimago is precisely the same kind of doubled metaphor as the poet. He is both arch-image and archemagus, both literal antithesis and metaphoric origin, both text and conceit.[8] He is thus not susceptible to the kind of discriminating judgment which binds because it accurately names such false poets as Colin, Verlame, or Alcyon. Archimago's nature encroaches more directly on the poet's own. The potential analogy between the two figures, as Nohrnberg correctly notes, "offers to equate Archimago's activity with the imagination concurrently shaping Spenser's poem."[9] Nohrnberg consistently interprets this equation positively. Archimago is a poet manqué, and conversation with him inevitably discloses the truth because even evil words, by parodying the true Word, bring that Word to light. So Archimago, creating a false Una, unwittingly abets the purposes of Spenser in defining the "troth-ful" Una.[10]

The paralleling of poet and antagonist, however, is fraught with peril. The very event which Nohrnberg isolates, the metaphoric naming of the book's heroine, is the effect of a fictional displacement from which we never really recover. Cut off from the truth, we inhabit only metaphoric approximations of it. In fact, both Una and Redcross are named in the narrative only after their feigned doubles are created. The semantic duplicity which allows metaphors to arise and be expressed brings those metaphors into direct relation with the lie rather than the truth. Again Spenser seems to be reassessing his earlier distinctions between conceit and deceit, revealing and concealing, truth and falsehood. The mind faithful to metaphor here seems to require additional awareness of the lie inhabiting any expression of truth.

Narratively, the same effect can be seen. Archimago's division of his "guests" into "double parts" is not simply a dramatic incident complicating the plot of Book I, but a necessary cause of the very presence and continuation of that narrative. Without Archimago, Spenser has nothing to do; Archimago provides the narrative dilemmas which the poet must then solve. "Who now can saue" Una or Serena or Florimell? The poet can, and does. He introduces new characters and is able to carry forward his own narrative precisely because his poetic antagonist keeps trying to interrupt and stop it.[11] One consequence of this thought is that Spenser underscores his true poet-false poet dichotomy with a secondary opposition: the false poet seeks always to draw the story to premature conclusion, to stop the poet's tongue; the true poet, realizing that conversion depends upon conversation,[12] must keep the narrative going. He must, that is, continuously offer his antagonist opportunities to speak, even to disseminate lies, for any attempt to silence him may represent a false desire for final rest or ending. Such desire is false, of course, because it denies man's basic condition as a rest-less sojourner, questor, between the world of Nature and that of Grace.

The more important question at the moment is how Spenser's creation of Archimago as his own double duplicates the strategies of Archimago himself. Is this coincidence of poetic manner a means of surrounding and defeating the false poet or an admission that the usual distinctions between true and false speaking are not convincing? If truth is constantly privileged for its naked simplicity, does not Archimago's duplicity implicate the poet as well? At the very least, Spenser's treatment of Archimago shows how alert he is to the potential dangers of his own literary task. Furthermore, if his own poetic image (e.g., Una) inevitably distorts a purer Idea (Truth), as the Sidneyan poetic implies, then the difference between Spenser's creations and Archimago's is measured only by degree, not by kind. The presence of the false-speaking Archimago, originally determined by necessities of self-defense, paradoxically increases rather than decreases the need for such defense.

Looking more closely at one of Archimago's key actions, we can see how problematic he becomes for Spenser. In the opening canto of Book I, Archimago fashions a "fit false dreame" for the sleeping Redcross. Fantasizing of "loues and lustful play," Redcross imagines that Venus brings Una to his bed while the Graces, "dancing all around," sing *Hymen iö Hymen*. The knight's heart, we are told, "did melt away, / Bathed in wanten blis." This dream, metaphorically figuring forth a parodic betrothal, also prefigures the knight's narrative end. In Canto xii, Una's father presents her to the knight and ties the betrothal knots, while "sweete musicke" crowns and surrounds the now-blessed pair. Redcross, completing the parallel, finds "his heart did seem to melt in pleasures manifold" and himself "swimming in that sea of blisfull ioy." Obviously, Spenser has here converted Archimago's false story into a true one, redeemed the deforming dream into a reforming reality. But his own narrative depends upon the counterfiction for its effect. Our recognition, that is, of the metaphoric nature of this final union is dependent in part upon our awareness of its relation to the earlier version. As a result, Archimago— the duplicity that inhabits all metaphors—intrudes upon the celebratory moment even as he is bound in prison, and his story intrudes upon Spenser's even as it is being rewritten and discredited. In short, it is the metaphoric accommodation of true and false narratives that ensures our progression to the poetic conceit and precludes our taking the text of Canto xii as a final or literal truth. The poet is neither willing nor able to silence all strains of his opponent's song.

The mere fact that all subsequent false-speakers in *The Faerie Queene* grow directly out of the arch-magus affirms that Spenser found himself unable to mount a successful defense against his antagonist. And while the later poetic imitators of Archimago may be understood and dealt with more easily than their progenitor, the persistence with which they rise against the poet testifies both to the threat he feels and to the need he has of them. Even in Book I, Archimago invokes poetic followers, principally, of course, Duessa. As Waters and Nohrnberg have shown us, Duessa's identification with the Whore of Babylon immediately involves her in deformative false speaking. *The Geneva Bible* explains in the Argument to Revelation: the "strompet [shall seek] vnder colour of faire speache and pleasant doctrine to decieue the worlde."[13] When Duessa enters the narrative in Canto ii, her first act is to create a fictional tale about her past. Born of an emperor, betrothed to a mighty prince, and bereft of his "blessed body" before their "spousall" day, Duessa-Fidessa is now condemned to wander through the world seeking her lost lord. Although her "faire speache" participates directly in Archimago's false dream and obviously parodies the narrative condition of the true Una, it easily deceives Redcross. Even after Fradubio warns him that Duessa is a false "author" and a "false sorceresse," Redcross cannot see through either her appearance or her metaphors. Hoping himself to win her hand, he acts so as to bring her tale literally to life. In fact, until he is captured by Orgoglio in Canto vii and Duessa rewrites her own tale by accepting the giant as her proper "leman," Redcross's ethical actions are determined by her fable. And only when he is finally able to interpret her correctly in Canto xii is he rightfully betrothed to Una. Redcross's success in the quest is thus both imperiled and achieved by his reading of Duessa's false fiction.[14]

The second poetic follower of Archimago in Book I is Despair.[15] He too offers Redcross a narrative of his own life, and he too tries to induce ethical action by means of that narrative. His tale, of course, is not so much false as inadequate or incomplete: he omits the Pauline assurance of heavenly mercy and leads Redcross to attempt his own life. Una saves her knight by supplying the biblical corrective:

> In heauenly mercies hast thou not a part?
> Why shouldst thou then despeire, that chosen art?
> Where iustice growes, there grows eke greater grace,
> The which doth quench the brond of hellish smart,
> And that accurst hand-writing doth deface.   [I.ix.53]

Once more, Spenser defines the success of his own heroes as a process of "defacing" the false fictions created by his poetic antagonists. And once again, we see that process as one shaping the poet's own text as well.

Against the seductive internal fictions of Archimago, Duessa, and Despair, Spenser sets the right speaking of Merlin, Fidelia, and Heavenly Contemplation. His portraits of these three figures are clearly meant to affirm a Sidneyan faith in the effectiveness of the true poet, but even here difficulties arise. Fidelia, who carries "A booke, that was both signd and seald with blood, / Wherein darke things were writ, hard to be vnderstood" (I.x.13), acts initially as a positive corrective to the "dark" magic of Archimago. As both poet and interpreter-reader, Fidelia is the ideal humanist teacher, the purveyor of divine instruction, "celestiall discipline," as Spenser calls it, to Everyman. But she is also, significantly, a magus:

> For she was able, with her words to kill,
> And raise againe to life the hart, that she did thrill.

> And when she list poure out her larger spright,
>   She would commaund the hastie Sunne to stay,
>   Or backward turne his course from heauens hight;
>   Sometimes great hostes of men she could dismay;
>   Dry-shod to passe, she parts the flouds in tway;
>   And eke huge mountaines from their natiue seat
>   She would commaund, themselues to beare away,
>   And throw in raging sea with roaring threat.
> Almightie God her gaue such powre, and puissance great.

> [I.x.19–20]

It could be argued that not until the portrait of Fidelia does Spenser adequately define his own poetic lineage in terms which defend him against the charge of an Archimago-like creation of "feigned" images. Whatever Fidelia may represent for the educative growth of Redcross—she teaches him how the "faithfull mind" reads the human condition—she represents even more to Spenser's defense of his own narrative voice. By setting Archimago loose in the fiction, Spenser creates the necessity for a counterforce. His fictional strategies are so close to his antagonist's that he must derive a positive source for his own transforming powers, both to reveal what is dark and hidden and to "raise againe" what is low and fallen. Fidelia provides, in short, a divinely-sanctioned authority for Spenser's narrative presumptions.

It should be noticed, however, that Spenser's narrative strategy again mirrors Archimago's: both create "feigned images" by metaphoric and parodic doubling. As Archimago himself parodies Una and Redcross, Fidelia parodies Archimago and Despair.[16] The result is that Spenser finds himself in a peculiar position, for his false-speaking antagonists are bound to the truth, whereas he is contracted to the lie. Not only is the narrative strategy called into question, but so too is the source of the poet's material. Archimago provides Spenser with both method and matter, and again what seemed a simple self-defense becomes increasingly problematical. How exactly is right speaking to be distinguished from false speaking?

Even more troubling, in the instance of Fidelia, is the effect her right speaking has upon Spenser's hero:

> By hearing her, and by her sisters lore,
>
> . . . .
>
> That wretched world he gan for to abhore,
> And mortall life gan loath, as thing forlore,
> Greeud with remembrance of his wicked wayes,
> And prickt with anguish of his sinnes so sore,
> That he desirde to end his wretched dayes.   [I.x.21]

Fidelia's instruction, which begins as the attempt to correct Despair's false teaching, leads to the same anguished result. Rather than evoking a proper ethical response, Fidelia's words must themselves be further clarified and buttressed by Speranza's. Again Spenser suggests the necessities of conversation: to stop conversing is to stop converting. However unintentionally, Spenser has here injected a new and serious question into the Sidneyan paradigm. For Sidney, right speaking provokes right acting, and where the one stops the other begins. For Spenser, the distinctions between speech and action are not so sharp. To anticipate a bit, this unwillingness on Spenser's part to draw a clear line between his poetic speaking and a reader's ethical action will require him to move the reader's sphere of action inside the poem itself. Ethical action will not be subsequent to the text, but concurrent with it.

The holy hermit, Heavenly Contemplation, is another Spenserian attempt at self-definition. Like Merlin, who both precedes and follows him, the hermit is an instructor who illuminates in Spenser's own epic manner: by providing their individual "students" with metaphoric images of their private and public pasts, such poet-figures direct present and future actions to purposeful ends. This poetic ideal is perfectly Sidneyan and humanistic. As the disseminators of ancient wisdom to present societies, these poets ensure continuous communal reform.

Within this optimistic portrait, however, Spenser again sows some troublesome seeds. When Redcross is first brought to the hermit, Spenser tells us:

> Who when these two approching he aspide,
>   At their first presence grew agrieued sore,
>   That forst him lay his heauenly thoughts aside;
>   And had he not that Dame respected more,
>   Whom highly he did reuerence and adore,
>   He would not once haue moued for the knight.   [I.x.49]

Why, we might ask, is Heavenly Contemplation so reluctant to teach Redcross? Do we not sense a danger in his apparently total commitment to "heauenly thoughts"? We may be reminded of Colin Clout, who is similarly "agrieued sore" at having his contemplations interrupted on Mount Acidale and who is also reluctant to instruct the intruding student. The poetic danger that Spenser is trying to articulate here becomes clearer when we see the effect of the hermit's teaching:

> O let me not (quoth he) then turne againe
>   Backe to the world, whose ioyes so fruitlesse are;
>   But let me here for aye in peace remaine,
>   Or streight way on that last long voyage fare,
>   That nothing may my present hope empare.
>   That may not be (said he) ne maist thou yit
>   Forgo that royall maides bequeathed care,
>   Who did her cause into thy hand commit,
> Till from her cursed foe thou haue her freely quit.   [I.x.63]

Redcross again succumbs to the desire to rest, to withdraw from the arduous tasks of the timely quest in order to "for aye in peace remaine." This ethical choice is once more the effect of a misreading. Redcross perceives the hermit's vision in literal terms and thus fastens onto the false dichotomies attendant upon such literalizing: here versus there, earthly versus heavenly existence, temporal versus eternal, quest versus pilgrimage. He does not see, and Spenser may imply that the hermit does not sufficiently reveal, the metaphor that resolves these dichotomies. Neither poet-teacher nor reader-pupil seems to identify the precise way in which the knight's earthly end metaphorically speaks his heavenly end.

But if the encounter with the hermit fails in some respects to instruct Redcross, it does instruct Spenser, and when he gives us our vision of the final end he defines with considerable care its metaphoric status. The battle be-

tween Redcross and the dragon is Spenser's metaphoric equivalent of the hermit's vision of the New Jerusalem, and our task in reading this metaphor
is clarified by Redcross's misreading of his. As noted most comprehensively
by Kellogg and Steele and by Nohrnberg, Spenser heightens this battle by
implying a number of apocalyptic parallels.[17] Redcross reverses the Fall,
reclaims Eden, and bruises the serpent's head. As the capstone to his own recreated vision of a recovered paradise, Spenser has Truth stand forth unveiled,[18] and further sanctifies the occasion with communal dancing, sports,
and merriment. This brief moment of joyous festivity (xii.3–9) is unlike anything else in *The Faerie Queene*, and certainly the freest, most spontaneous
moment in all of Book I. Something grand has been achieved.

In the midst of the festivity lies the dead dragon and these provocative
stanzas:

> And after, all the raskall many ran,
>   Heaped together in rude rablement,
>   To see the face of that victorious man:
>   Whom all admired, as from heauen sent,
>   And gazd vpon with gaping wonderment.
>   But when they came, where that dead Dragon lay,
>   Stretcht on the ground in monstrous large extent,
>   The sight with idle feare did them dismay,
> Ne durst approch him nigh, to touch, or once assay.
>
> Some feard, and fled; some feard and well it faynd;
>   One that would wiser seeme, then all the rest,
>   Warnd him not touch, for yet perhaps remaynd
>   Some lingring life within his hollow brest,
>   Or in his wombe might lurke some hidden nest
>   Of many Dragonets, his fruitfull seed;
>   Another said, that in his eyes did rest
>   Yet sparckling fire, and bad thereof take heed;
> Another said, he saw him moue his eyes indeed.
>
> One mother, when as her foolehardie chyld
>   Did come too neare, and with his talants play,
>   Halfe dead through feare, her little babe reuyld,
>   And to her gossips gan in counsell say;
>   How can I tell, but that his talants may
>   Yet scratch my sonne, or rend his tender hand?
>   So diuersly themselues in vaine they fray;
>   Whiles some more bold, to measure him nigh stand,
> To proue how many acres he did spread of land.   [I.xii.9–11]

The surest clue to Spenser's control in these stanzas is the playful "Drago-
nets"; the humor of the entire incident is remarkable.[19] After working so hard
in the preceding canto to suggest allegorical equivalences, Spenser suddenly
and wittily strips his metaphors of all simplistic equation. The dragon, as a
result, both is and is not Satan or the serpent; Redcross is and is not Christ
bruising the serpent's head; and the garden he regains both is and is not
Eden. The provisionality of these metaphors requires us, like the curious
onlookers, to "measure" the distance between the metaphoric vehicle and its
various apocalyptic and everyday tenors, to discriminate likenesses from unlikenesses. Such measuring, Spenser implies, is the beginning of the reader's
ethical action. For this reason, Spenser must not allow his fiction to reach a
condition of presuming "euerlasting" rest; he must un-figure his metaphors
by calling them into question. As the hermit must bring Redcross back to his
given task, so Spenser must bring us back from the apocalyptic vision of
Canto xi to the human experience of Canto xii. Only then, as we try to understand the relationship between our "ending end" and the narrative's end, can
we set about the work of refashioning our lives.

As we see by the failures of Archimago and Duessa at the end of Book I,
Spenser weights the moral scale of the opening legend toward figures of the
Right Poet. The narrator, like Fidelia and Heavenly Contemplation, sketches
an optimistic portrait of what man can achieve. Although Spenser qualifies
the ultimate meaning of Redcross's fight with the dragon, he certainly intends
the battle to represent man's ability, with God's grace and proper instruction,
to regain some of his prelapsarian stature and excellence. The battle validates
and affirms the poetic vision given Redcross by Heavenly Contemplation.
The optimism and idealism of Book I as a whole thus occasion an equally
optimistic view of the poet and his function. At the end of the book, with
Archimago apparently defeated, the moral integrity of the Sidneyan Right
Poet remains intact. This is not to say, of course, that that integrity is free
from challenge. Archimago is not vanquished but forestalled; he remains free
to create more seductive fictions which Spenser will have to anticipate and
correct.

ii

The proem to Book II opens with a confession that "this famous antique history" can be read as either a lie or the truth, as either "th'aboundance of
an idle braine / . . . and painted forgery" or as "matter of iust memory."
Spenser pointedly challenges the reader to "measure" his understanding of
the preceding book. If he has read it "aright," his recovery of the poetic conceit should have enriched his memory, and his re-cognition of the poetic Idea

should have reminded him of the *imago Dei* out of which he was originally bodied forth. The reader is asked, in effect, to affirm both the rightness of the poet's words and his own acceptance of the Christian condition by acknowledging that the terms of the poetic text figure forth his own Ideas.

But although Spenser is addressing problems of right reading, and thus warning his audience to use "better sence" instead of "witlesse[ly] . . . misween[ing]," it is also clear that the similarities between Archimago's lies and his own truths have given rise to another narrative problem. Despite Sidney's assertion that "the poet never affirmeth," Spenser recognizes that in the face of his antagonist's false-speaking he must justify the poem's claim to truth. Yet even though he may "vaunt" and "vouch" for that truth, he can never definitively "show" it, can never make it "manifest in such excellency as he hath imagined" it. The need to defend the text thus forces Spenser to try to affirm the truth in order to save himself from the potential charge of an outright lie.

We may anticipate, therefore, that while Book II continues the poetic defense of right speaking, it will not focus on a true poet-false poet dichotomy. Instead, Spenser broadens the question to address the epistemological status of the poetic language:

> Why then should witlesse man so much misweene,
> That nothing is, but that which he hath seene?   [II.Pro.3]

The capacity of the spoken word to reveal ontological truth even in defiance of "ocular proof" is here both asserted and questioned. To deny the assertion or to affirm the question would put the reader in the untenable position of presuming that the poetic text is a mere castle in the air. But if the poem is not an ontological lie, is it necessarily the truth?

After two stanzas of sophistic defense of his "vnseene" faerieland, Spenser again challenges both his audience and his Queen:

> Of Faerie lond yet if he more inquire,
>> By certaine signes here set in sundry place
>> He may it find; ne let him then admire,
>> But yield his sence to be too blunt and bace,
>> That n'ote without an hound fine footing trace.
>> And thou, O fairest Princesse vnder sky,
>> In this faire mirrhour maist behold thy face,
>> And thine owne realmes in lond of Faery,
> And in this antique Image thy great auncestry.
>
> The which O pardon me thus to enfold
>> In couert vele, and wrap in shadowes light,

> That feeble eyes your glory may behold,
> Which else could not endure those beames bright,
> But would be dazled with exceeding light.   [II.Pro.4–5]

Although this defense fulfills conventional expectations by identifying the words of the text as poetic metaphors, Spenser adopts a disturbing perspective. The reader, he argues, can find the true "Faerie lond" only "by certaine signes here set in sundry place." The poem, in other words, is not so much metaphor as deliberately contrived riddle. Such a description initially presumes the poet's full control over both the text itself and the reader attempting to understand it; but whereas most riddles applaud the reader's wisdom once he unravels the clues, this poem seems to deny the reader any share in determining the meaning of the text. His senses, rather than "better" for having understood, are still "blunt and bace." So radical a separation of poet and audience is surely problematic in a work seeking to educate and reform the reader. It is precisely that separation that Spenser is calling into question, for, as we have seen, he wants to insist upon the reader's active presence within the text. The process of attributing both meaning and truth to the poem is a cooperative action of poet and reader, of right speaking and proper reading. We may assume, then, that the apparent separation of poet and reader in the present proem is conditioned by the unique nature of Book II and by Spenser's need to challenge further the reader's passive acceptance of the faerie fiction.

Spenser's narrative posture becomes additionally troubling in the final stanza as the traditional defense for writing allegory is given in terms that by now are fraught with negative connotations. We have just ended Book I by unveiling Truth, by allowing Una to stand forth and become betrothed to Everyman in "The blazing brightnesse of her beauties beame, / And glorious light of her sunshyny face." Yet immediately the poet "enfold[s]" her again in "couert vele, and wrap[s her] in shadowes light." [20] Have we—the real Everymen—been suddenly divorced from Truth again? And is this not the same "narrative" strategy that the false-speaking Duessa adopted in order to "disgrace" the "shining ray" of Fradubio's lady (I.ii.38–39)? We are invited to question a poetic method that so willingly adopts the strategies of its announced antagonists in order to defend itself against those antagonists. As the poet seems deliberately to distance himself and the truth from his own readers, he seems to draw closer to his fictional enemies. The reader, in turn, might well wonder what attitude he is to take towards the narrative voice and towards the ostensible truth that voice speaks.

In this second proem, Spenser brings to the narrative surface issues that were only implied in Book I. He subjects his own text to the kinds of dichotomies that "measure" literal-mindedness. The literary perception that sees absolute disparity between the lie and the truth, seen and unseen, veiled and unveiled, fictional lands and real lands, reader and poet, measures a mind unfaithful to the metaphoric nature of the text. The proem challenges both poet and reader to void such dichotomies by understanding how the text speaks metaphorically.

But while the questions Spenser raises here return us to the implicit issues of Book I, we need to understand why Spenser suddenly feels compelled openly to invoke them. Since the reader has already accepted the groundplot of the faerieland quest as both the structural and imagistic foundation of the poem, why does Spenser need to defend that particular "invention"? Why, in short, does faerieland become problematic at this point? We could say that Book II, of all the legends in *The Faerie Queene*, is the most distanced from the historical contingencies of Elizabeth and her realm; so Spenser takes the only narrative opportunity available to him to remind the Queen that she is indeed the poem's metaphoric tenor, no matter how "dark" the conceit.[21] Although this answer may be true in part, it conceals the real issue. Spenser seems clearly to recognize that Book II presents interpretive problems that are quite different from those of Book I, and that these problems concern the unique way the book speaks metaphorically.

In the former book, the status of faerieland was not an issue. Redcross, the metaphoric *miles Christi*, seeks Una, the metaphoric Truth which Faith grants, across an obviously metaphoric landscape. The conceits shaping these images are carefully controlled by "matter of iust memory"—by the biblical and historical texts lying behind Spenser's own. In Book II, however, the metaphors are not directly dependent upon a prior truth, and their status as metaphors is consequently less discernible. Guyon is not readily interpretable *in imitatio Christi*, or even as a classical model, and his realm of faerie seems far removed from the metaphoric *locus* of the sojourning Christian exile. In the absence of a prior truth—or what Maureen Quilligan has recently called a "pre-text"[22]—according to which Guyon and his faerieland can be read metaphorically, we could, Spenser seems to fear, misread them as merely "painted forgery."

The problem Spenser conceives here is clarified by noting that the two poetic texts within the legend mirror the relationship between Spenser's own two books: *Briton Moniments* is to Book I as *Antiquitie of Faery Lond* is to Book II. That Spenser intends these parallels is evident in the fact that the two fictional texts reveal the basic historical and mythic resources of *The Faerie Queene* itself, and we are meant to see Spenser's own poem as both drawing from and dependent upon these two fabrics of collective human memory.

Briton Moniments is a chronicle of error, war, and bloodshed, of mostly failed kings and constant factions, of human weaknesses rather than human strengths. Yet Arthur is ravished by this bloody history, joyous over what it reveals, and dutifully thankful for all his country has accomplished. What does Arthur read in the *Moniments*, asks the most perceptive critic of Book II,[23] to justify such responses? And he answers that Arthur sees in the Briton history the gradual and steadily unfolding course of divine Providence. He reads metaphoric concord behind the narrative discord by understanding that the history of England recapitulates and carries forward both the universal history of human civilization and the darkly revealed plot of redeemed Christian time. Perhaps we are meant to see Arthur's perception as one afforded by the "Saveours Testament" given him by Redcross in Book I, for what he sees is clearly a Christian subtext behind the historical narrative. Arthur reads his text, in other words, as we read Book I, unfolding the metaphoric narrative to disclose the providential givens of human existence. Equally clear is the fact that both texts record human struggles: the actors in those texts are real human beings who fall into error and frequently fail, but for whom an ultimate Christian triumph is prophesied. To Arthur, *Briton Moniments* is an optimistic affirmation of what sinful man can achieve when he recognizes and acts according to the will of God. It is the same view Book I presents to us.

Antiquitie of Faery Lond records no such failure and no such redemption. The elves and faeries, as "goodly creature[s]" of the garden, have no history at all—at least no history that can be measured or understood in human or Christian terms. Here there is no Fall, no sin, no suffering, and Berger rightly concludes that the chronicle shows why Guyon must battle foes of human excellence rather than those of human existence.[24] This is a telling remark, but one that has never been taken quite seriously enough. Guyon, despite his notorious faint, is not a human being. He is an elf, a mythic figure of the human imagination who is excluded from the humblest of human conditions—existence. The fiction that Guyon reads, therefore, is analogous to the fiction he is in. Each is a literal fantasy behind which stands no factual subtext affirming a higher truth, but only the poetic imagination itself.

The two chronicles allow Spenser to shift somewhat the terms of his argument. The disparities identified in the proem—veiled and unveiled, seen and unseen, lie and truth—here reach out to further disparity between myth and history, ideality and reality, elves and humans, fantasy and fact. It is also clear that these extensions bear directly upon the nature and the situation of the poem itself insofar as it frames the disparate chronicles registered within it. As noted before, it is precisely the function of Spenser's own book to subsume into metaphoric relationship the literal books it records and thus to void their dichotomies.

At the same time, the presence of the two chronicles in the text occasions literal disparity. When we think of Book II as a whole, we see that most of its significant incidents are arranged to display these dichotomies. The first narrative action of Guyon's quest is his discovery of Ruddymane. Both Guyon and the Palmer explicate the bloody babe as if he were an emblem of the human condition, an icon of the sad state of mortality. However nearsighted their "reading" may be in terms of Christian salvation or the promise of redemption opened in Book I, it is absolutely correct in terms of man's inescapable entanglement in sin. And by those terms, Guyon is once more set apart: because he inherits no sin, he does not share Ruddymane's nature or situation and is consequently powerless to help him.[25] In this confrontation, Spenser reverses the reader's problem: whereas the mythic ideal observes and judges, but cannot participate in, the historical reality, we observe but cannot participate in the ideal. Guyon and the reader are both forced to come to terms with a situation and a nature from which each is excluded by literal disparities of place.

The same situational discrimination separates Guyon and Arthur, as well as the double description of Alma's castle. Guyon is an image of perfection, and rather than seeking a virtue, like the poem's other heroes, he is a virtue. His condition, therefore, is not available to the sinful Everyman who is reading the text. Nor is his domain. Guyon can inhabit faerieland because faerieland is also granted a perfection unavailable to fallen earth. The faerie vehicle, which in Book I was used to reveal human possibilities, to disclose an image of what man can become and a place he might inhabit, is here used to reveal human limitations, to disclose an image of what man cannot become and a garden from which he is forever exiled.[26] The presence of Arthur in the narrative testifies to this lesson. As the continuing Everyman from Book I, Arthur's place is not faerieland but a site beyond and outside it. He is made, therefore, to do battle with anomalies in faerieland, like Maleger, the human condition itself, whereas Guyon is sent after Acrasia, a faerie fantasy. The struggles of reality have been narratively differentiated from those of ideality.

This lesson is repeated in the descriptions of Alma's castle. It is first presented, in II.ix.22, as a pure geometric shape, an abstract glorification of an imaginary perfection. It is immediately re-presented, in stanzas 23–26, in a physical allegory that takes its meaning and its metaphoric method from the definition of the human condition given in the haunting death-in-life song of Ecclesiastes 12:1–8. Throughout the book we find an ideal of perfection set beside a real imperfection, and this disparity is aligned with the faerie fiction on the one hand and historical reality on the other.

We must ask why Spenser would want to do this when his very poem is dependent upon our association with its narrative. We, after all, are both origin and end of the narrative, the site that calls it into being and the site in which it will be put to ethical work. Clearly, Spenser is trying to discriminate among the variety of ways by which we measure this association. In Book I, we easily and readily align ourselves with Redcross—even when his actions embarrass us and thus betray us—but here every offered alignment is subverted. Inhabiting neither Alma's castle nor the Bower of Bliss, we are quite literally dis-placed from the narrative. Unwilling to be the bloody babe, we are forbidden to be Guyon. The question, then, is where and how the reader situates himself among the disparate sites of the text, and again the answer offers a lesson in how the text speaks metaphorically.

A partial solution to the reader's problem is provided by the relationship between Redcross's recovery of the Garden in Book I and Guyon's destruction of the garden in Book II. The actions of the two heroes, like the gardens themselves, are disparate versions of the same metaphoric activity. The festivity that surrounds the dead dragon finds a parallel in the freeing of Verdant, and the completion of both acts is made possible by the binding of an antagonist. More interesting than these parallels, however, is the fact that Spenser subjects both incidents to significant qualification. The recovery of Book I in no way guarantees habitation in the Garden; the destruction of Book II does not affect Gryll or deny habitation in his kind of self-imposed and imprisoning garden. What we are given in both actions, and particularly in the structural and thematic relations between them, is the "groundplot of a profitable invention." But the invention, in this case, is ours, a space in which ethical activity is freed from the literal terms of disparity to embrace a metaphoric imitation. The situation of the reader is thus a metaphoric site which accommodates mimetically the literal texts of imperfection and perfection, Redcross and Guyon, garden and bower, *Briton Moniments* and *Antiquitie of Faery Lond*.

When viewed in these terms, Guyon's destruction of the Bower of Bliss is the most important and the most ironic passage in the two books. The Bower is the quintessential garden of the imagination, the poetic paradise par excellence, and an obvious analogue to the poet's own faerieland. It is one of the few "perfect" places—and perhaps the only perfect place—left to us when the Garden is withdrawn. But unlike the Garden, which has a pre-text, the Bower is a pretext: it exists only in the "golden world" of poetic making as an attempt to body forth in literal terms the condition of atemporal nonsuffering described in Guyon's history. In effect, Spenser has here "read" the *Antiquitie of Faery Lond* into the kind of enclosure made possible by the literalizing intelligence. When Guyon enters the Bower, he ironically acts in our stead, encountering the poetic fiction from within the narrative and teaching us that even here it has and is no privileged place. The Bower, like Guyon and Acrasia, like *Antiquitie of Faery Lond*, and like the poet's portrayal of them all, is "perfectly" beautiful; but the beauty is a perfection that can only be imagined and a perfection so beautiful that it tempts to literal nonaction. The Bower, like all poems, must be destroyed if life is to be freed. Ethical action,

the ending end of poetry and the metaphoric site of our being, requires ultimately the effacement of the very groundplot that propels action. As in Book
I, but in more direct relation to the fiction itself, the life of the reader begins
when the poem's metaphors are "measured" and ultimately set aside. Such
poetic truth is glimpsed in the fact that the hero and the site of this book are
ushered into the narrative by a character named Mortdant; they are ushered
out by one named Verdant.

The false speaker of Book II is Spenser himself. Guyon's history, like the
Elfin chronicle, like *The Faerie Queene* itself, is a fiction within a fiction. Ad-
mittedly, it is quite different from the perverse tales of Archimago, Duessa,
and Despair, but it is not less dangerous. Misused or misread, it is equally
capable of cutting off ethical action and thus open to the charge of directly
misleading. Spenser tries to defend himself against potential abuses and
"abusions" of his word by turning the fiction back upon itself, by creating
himself the inadequate literal legend against which the metaphoric one must
be measured. Without that false tale, he would have no foil to validate his
own ethical lesson and would run the risk of having his story confused with
human history, or of having the Elfin chronicle mistakenly read as the history
of England. Spenser needs, that is, a countertext, an overt veil through
which, and only through which, we can perceive the covert truths of human
existence. Perhaps he was aware that, as the Bishops Bible tells us in suitably
Sidneyan terms, truth is apprehendable only "through a dark speaking" (1
Corinthians 13). False speaking, Book II assumes, is seducing the reader into
debilitating fantasies or forgetting that the fiction must be set against, and
then accommodated with, the background of human fact. The tension between Guyon's story and the poet's, between vanquishing mythic foes of human excellence and providing the practical lessons for human existence, controls much of our reaction to Book II. By means of that tension, Spenser
assures us that his poetic call is not to fictional ideals but to human potentials,
that his commitment is not to myth but to man. The defense of the text,
therefore, has resulted in calling the text into question, which is, paradoxically, an affirmation of its provisional, relational, and metaphoric truth.

We can corroborate this interpretation of Spenser's defense in Book II by
looking briefly at its principal false poets, Phaedria and Acrasia. Whatever
else these two damsels may represent in the narrative, the fact that Spenser
depicts them singing particular songs which move their audiences to specific
actions identifies them as poet-figures. Phaedria sings "a loue lay" with which
she charms the "careless" Cymochles. The song, of course, is a perverse parody of Christ's Sermon on the Mount (Matthew 6:25–34),[27] and it urges the
literal futility of earthly labors and the purer pleasures freely granted by nature. Spenser defines exactly the strategy of Phaedria's "skilful art": ". . . she
had his eyes and sences fed / With false delights, and fild with pleasures

vaine" (II.vi.14). Here is an art which seeks only to delight, to be beautiful, an art whose intentions and effects are identical to those of Lucifera's cunning minstrels, and one whose powers to turn *carmina* into charms ultimately derive from Archimago himself.

In Canto xii, while Acrasia hangs greedily over her sleeping lover, "some one did chaunt [a] louely lay." Although the singer is identified as a "he," it is clear that the song is Acrasia's device. Equally clear is the song's inversion of Phaedria's "moral": instead of counselling retreat, it urges boldness; instead of letting nature provide, it calls for gathering while there is time. Yet the intention is again simply to be beautiful, and the effect is exactly the same as Phaedria's: like Cymochles, Verdant has hung up his warlike arms and given himself over to the "pleasing wordes." It is perhaps not too farfetched to argue that Spenser sees in these two songs the same literary danger that Book II itself presents, for both songs offer their audiences an imaginative vision of human success, a vision which denies the necessities of sin, suffering, or struggle by playing upon the pleasures and desires of the human fantasy to render life as perfectly beautiful. So long as the poet accepts the task of pleasing his audience as a legitimate part of his own literary responsibility, the temptation to sing such songs must constantly be faced. But such an art, Spenser asserts, is life-denying; it enervates human will and severs itself from all moral obligation. In fact, such poetry has proved unfaithful to its very nature by presuming a dichotomy between aesthetic pleasure and ethical instruction. And the danger this poetry gives rise to is not simply failing to reform its audience, but actually deforming that audience by lulling it into a false security and deflecting it from proper ethical action.

Book II is as much a prologue to *The Faerie Queene* as Book I, but rather than defining human possibilities it explores human limits. The situation of the reader, and of the faerieland to which he is called, is a metaphoric site which accommodates the visions of Books I and II and avoids the disparities of either. To bring the ideal into relation with the real, the beautiful into relation with the true, is to perceive the seam between one imitation and another. The right reader is he who understands the relation, then, between myth and mimesis, who understands that the myth is not an answer but a challenge to mimesis, and who sees that the mimesis which makes the myth is the same mimesis by which the myth can be remade. For the poet, the same result obtains. By calling the mythic terms of Book II into question, Spenser establishes the boundaries of his ethical concerns and frees his metaphoric faerieland from the literal dichotomies that would restrict it to either a falsely contrived answer to human problems or a mere castle in the air. For him, no less than for the reader, the question of the poem's truth has been answered in Sidneyan terms: the fiction, as fiction, is neither lie nor truth, but "the groundplot of a profitable invention."

iii

At first glance, the proem to the Legend of Chastity seems to return to the kind of self-effacing rhetoric of poetic inadequacy we saw in Book I, but Spenser alerts us to newer issues by confessing, for the first time in the poem, not that he is unfit for his literary task, but that he may actually deface his text in the process of writing it. In the opening stanza, Spenser identifies the appropriate "speaking picture" for his sought virtue as the human heart, but he immediately wonders about where to find a suitable "ensample" and about his ability to portray such a heart:

> It falles me here to write of Chastity,
> > That fairest vertue, farre aboue the rest;
> > For which what needs me fetch from *Faery*
> > Forreine ensamples, it to haue exprest?
> > Sith it is shrined in my Soueraines brest,
> > And form'd so liuely in each perfect part,
> > That to all Ladies, which haue it profest,
> > Need but behold the pourtraict of her hart,
> If pourtrayd it might be by any liuing art.

As in the proem to Book II, Spenser questions the propriety of the faerie fiction as a vehicle for his ethical lesson, but only to affirm by the end of the stanza the mediating and metaphoric nature of that fiction. It is, he tells us, a "liuing art" [28] which draws both "forreine ensamples" and "my Soueraines brest" into accommodating relation with "all Ladies" that profess to honor chastity. But even as he proclaims the right speaking of such an art, Spenser raises a telling disclaimer—the portrayal may not be possible:

> But liuing art may not least part expresse,
> > Nor life-resembling pencill it can paint,
> > All were it *Zeuxis* or *Praxiteles*:
> > His daedale hand would faile, and greatly faint,
> > And her perfections with his error taint:
> > Ne Poets wit, that passeth Painter farre
> > In picturing the parts of beautie daint,
> > So hard a workmanship aduenture darre,
> For fear through want of words her excellence to marre.   [III.Pro.2]

Regardless of how "liuing" the art may be, or how "life-resembling" the tools that it employs, the literary representation of an image may taint or mar the human reality behind that image. As in the minor poems, Spenser here wonders how "mortall tongue [can] hope to expresse" the Idea he has in mind. The issue now is not an antagonistic or false speaker, but the simple fact that the poet cannot manifest his sought virtue "in such excellency as he hath imagined it." To body forth that Idea in a verbal text is inevitably to subject it to limitation and distortion.[29]

This point is reiterated in the third stanza where even the "choicest wit" of Gloriana's realm "cannot [her] glorious pourtraict figure plaine." How, then, can Spenser's apprentice pen presume to "shadow it" in "coloured showes," or in "antique praises"? Rhetorical "colours," the very instruments of the poet's trade, cast a shadow over the "plaine" subject rather than clearly revealing it. The overt veil which was posited in the proem to Book II as a defensive necessity has again become a literary threat which must itself be defended against. Thus Spenser, like all poets who presume to address historical figures or to affect human conditions, must once more denigrate his own text by supposing a "mirror"—not the perfect likeness of a living art, but a distortion, a glass through which we see but obscurely, a "dark" rather than a right speaking. The proem, therefore, issues a warning in addition to its self-questioning: it challenges the reader not to expect accurate human reflections, but to read human realities through or behind the poetic shadows—to be as alert, that is, to unlikenesses as to likenesses, and to be faithful to the metaphoric but distorting nature of the portrait the poet draws.

In the proems to Books II and III, the poet's defense of his own text has become increasingly dependent upon the abilities of his readers. The affirmation of his own voice and his own vision requires the poet to "add faith" in the perceptions of his audience, especially in their willingness to correct whatever errors mar his speaking picture. No longer is the poetic defense a simple matter of distinguishing right speakers from false speakers, for the speech-act embraces both poet and reader in a mutually dependent relationship. The task of right speaking thus enlarges to include instruction in right reading, not, from this perspective, for the purpose necessarily of educating the reader ethically, but in order to ensure his approval. Potentially, then, the drama of self-defense involves not only antagonistic false speakers but antagonistic misreaders.

Although Book III is populated with a variety of misreaders and although their faulty interpretations constantly occasion narrative predicaments they either escape from or succumb to, such characters are not yet antagonists of the poet himself. Nonetheless, their common inability to read correctly a particular text-within-the-text has obvious implications for the poet himself and, consequently, for his responsibility to ensure that his text does not lead to similar error. Whether he consciously organized the book around this issue or simply realized in the process of writing it that the issue was becoming more insistent, Spenser defines the interpretive hazards of his own audience by dramatizing the failures of readers within the narrative. The "text" for these internal readers is the conventional literary myth of Cupid, a text Spenser records, in bits and pieces, throughout the book. In the final chapter we will look more closely at the way the myth operates in the book, but we can anticipate that analysis by suggesting how Spenser learns, by observing his characters' responses to Cupid, his own poetic difficulties in ensuring that his text speaks correctly and metaphorically.

Cupid first appears as an undescribed figure summarizing and emblematizing the principal activity of Malecasta's castle. Coming immediately after Spenser's depiction of the costly arras portraying the destructive love of Venus for Adonis, Cupid defines Castle Joyous as a secular temple of lusty pleasures:

> So was that chamber clad in goodly wize,
>   And round about it many beds were dight,
>   As whilome was the antique worldes guize,
>   Some for vntimely ease, some for delight,
>   As pleased them to vse, that vse it might:
>   And all was full of Damzels, and of Squires,
>   Dauncing and reueling both day and night,
>   And swimming deepe in sensuall desires,
> And *Cupid* still emongst them kindled lustfull fires.   [III.i.39]

Midway through the book we find Cupid again, this time in the Garden of Adonis, "sporting him selfe in safe felicity." Having laid "his sad dartes / Asyde," he is now reconciled and wedded to Psyche, living "in stedfast loue and happy state" (III.vi.49–50). Obviously, the Garden is an antithesis of Malecasta's arras, and Cupid is similarly rewritten as a positive, beneficent figure. Finally, at the end of the book, Spenser describes the statue of Cupid as the symbolic center of Busyrane's palace of perversion:

> Blindfold he was, and in his cruell fist
>   A mortall bow and arrowes keene did hold,
>   With which he shot at randon, when him list,
>   Some headed with sad lead, some with pure gold;
>   (Ah man beware, how thou those darts behold).   [III.xi.48]

This final appearance of the god of love returns us to the Cupid of Castle Joyous and gives us, for the first time in the book, the full range of conventional Cupidean terms: blindfolded, cruel, mortal, shot, random, wounds, hideous, remediless. In fact, the very conventionality of the portrait has disturbed some readers. After waiting almost eleven full cantos to see Cupid, we somehow expect more than literary clichés. But Spenser has no intention of making his Cupid unique or original; instead, he wants to emphasize how familiar this speaking picture is to us and how automatic and unthinking our response to it has become. It is no accident, therefore, that all the characters struck by Cupid's dart in Book III "read" their love-wounds in the conventional literary terms. Even when they do not realize the dart has struck, their commonplace Cupidean phrases betray their subjection to the stereotype.

Yet Spenser's own descriptions of Cupid call the conventional terms into question. If Cupid can be both wanton and wedded, sad and happy, lecherous and steadfast, destructive and beneficial, then the traditional icon is a literal distortion, a misleading interpretation by characters who do not understand the human reality resident in the literary metaphor, or how that metaphor voids the kinds of dichotomies with which they invest it. Spenser makes this point again and again in Book III. Britomart "reads" her love-wounds as tyrannical, bitter, unlucky, and woeful. Timias "reads" his wounds as luckless, cruel, ill, and dishonorable. Amoret "reads" hers as transfixing, consuming, deadly, despoiling, and cruel. Even Paridell and Hellenore, who obviously have no fear of a wanton Cupid, still see love's darts as empoisoned, wicked, wounding, and painful. But all of these terms are wrong, the effects of literalizing misinterpretations. As Merlin teaches Britomart and as Amoret herself learns, Cupid-as-Vice is a textual image masking and distorting the human reality of love in the process of moving from inception to action. And if Cupid is misread in this fashion, the action a character subsequently takes is likely to be destructive.

It is precisely this point that Spenser makes with his telling parenthesis in the climactic portrait of Cupid in Canto xi: "Ah man beware, how thou those darts behold." The truth and falseness of Cupid are in the interpretive eyes of the beholder. And falseness is here defined, as it is throughout the book, as the presumption that the literal image of Cupid correctly expresses his human significance. The question of how the poet rightly speaks of Cupid's meaning, therefore, is shown to depend upon how his audience rightly reads that meaning. Unless the reader realizes the distortions which obtain in the fictional image—reads unlikenesses as well as likenesses—he will be led into false disparity rather than metaphoric accommodation, and to destructive actions rather than productive ones.

In the case of Cupid, the responsibilities for misreading seem mostly to lie on the viewer's or the reader's side. But Spenser says, in the proem, that such defacing and marring of human realities is also his risk. His exploration of this side of the literary act can be seen in his treatment of Amoret and Belphoebe, for the differences between these two spectacular damsels reveal Spenser's careful discrimination between a "liuing art" that encourages metaphoric extension and imitation and an essentially static art that encourages premature and literalizing closure.

Our first introduction to Belphoebe comes not in Book III, but in what Harry Berger has wittily called a moment of "conspicuous irrelevance" in Book II.[30] Braggadochio is wandering in "a forrest greene" when he is suddenly confronted by "a goodly Ladie clad in hunters weed" (II.iii.21). For ten stanzas the narrative stops as Spenser affords Belphoebe one of the longest and most marvellous descriptions in his poem. Yet every image of this description is perfectly conventional; indeed, Spenser uses almost all of them in the *Amoretti*. Cheeks which "shew / Like roses in a bed of lillies shed"; eyes "Kindled aboue at th'heauenly makers light"; a forehead "Like a broad table"—each of these images is traditional sonnet material. As a portrait of "womanhood," Belphoebe is a prime example of what Rosalie Colie calls an unmetaphored character, a character quite literally created out of the stock literary metaphors. Or rather, Spenser has taken the standard metaphors of the idealized sonnet lady and literalized them in a particular character. No stanza of the description is more revealing of Spenser's method than the penultimate one:

> Her yellow lockes crisped, like golden wyre,
>   About her shoulders weren loosely shed,
>   And when the winde emongst them did inspyre,
>   They waued like a penon wide dispred,
>   And low behinde her backe were scattered:
>   And whether art it were, or heedlesse hap,
>   As through the flouring forrest rash she fled,
>   In her rude haires sweet flowres themselues did lap,
> And flourishing fresh leaues and blossomes did enwrap.   [II.iii.30]

As A. C. Hamilton suggests, this description might well serve as a gloss on the first panel of Botticelli's *Primavera*.[31] Zephyr is here, the flight, even the metamorphosis into flowers. What must be emphasized is that the parallel affirms, and line 6 of the stanza underscores, the artifice of Belphoebe. She is an abstraction, a perfection whose origin is not human existence but the artistic imagination. This is why she first appears in the legend of the equally perfect Guyon. She is as removed from the concerns of men and women as Guyon is, and her enclosed status is confirmed by everything she does in the poem. Even the humor of Braggadochio's foolish attempt to ravish her derives from her special nature: imaginary images cannot be embraced physically or held in hand.

Amoret shares much of Belphoebe's separate and special condition. Her twin by the miraculous conception and delivery of Chrysogonee, her sister in education because she is brought up by Venus as Belphoebe is raised by Diana, her equal in inhabiting a paradise of unfallen splendor and innocence, and her type in virtue since both are mirrors of "perfect chastitee," Amoret is nonetheless fundamentally different from Belphoebe.[32] Whereas the latter remains firmly enclosed in her forest green, Amoret is forced to make her way through various settings. In fact, her movement through the narrative recapitulates in general terms universal human history, and her "exile" from the Garden of Adonis is thus a "fall" into humanity. As a consequence, her tale is dramatic, unlike the static fable of Belphoebe. She wanders, searches, fears, suffers, learns, and finally succeeds, emerging at the end of the book as the perfectly human embodiment of the steadfast and gentle heart. She grows, in other words, into the very metaphor Spenser announces in the proem as his task to express. Belphoebe, spared all of Amoret's pain and suffering, is also forever excluded from her joy.

It may be objected that this distinction between the artifice of Belphoebe and the humanity of Amoret is misleading, for both are purely fictional characters. Of course, this is true, but only in a sense which we can define by recalling the particular kind of chastity Spenser accords each figure. Amoret, as we have learned from Williams,[33] Roche, and Alpers, is Spenser's most profound psychological study of the complexities of feminine sexuality. She is also, as the final chapter will show, an equally profound study of active, creating love, of the strengths of the human heart, of the total commitment of lover to beloved. None of these descriptions could be applied to Belphoebe, and we might well ask what a reader learns from her portrait. Her narrative chastity is life-denying, her honor bought at the price of exclusion from the world and from experience. Nothing in her actions suggests she is a contemplative who has forsaken the world for higher spiritual values; she is simply an uncompromising and unaccommodating ideal. Like Guyon, she exists in the narrative to help Spenser delineate his human values: however "perfect" these figures are, they teach the reader to glory in his simple and elemental humanity, a condition from which both figures are excluded. Spenser's creation of Belphoebe, therefore, can be seen as a narrative necessity to defend his portrait of Amoret from error. As in Book I, the alter-image defines the human lesson of the privileged model. But whereas the false Una is precisely that, Belphoebe is, in effect, too good. The poetic truth can be misspoken in two clearly different ways.[34]

The distinctions between the two figures again provide a lesson in Spenser's own metaphoric speaking. Both ladies clearly originate in textual metaphors. But where Spenser continually opens the metaphor of Amoret to further metaphoric extension and accommodation, he withholds such extensions from Belphoebe and keeps her metaphor closed to additional accommodations. And this difference in the two ways of speaking a metaphor articulates a discrimination between ways of reading the metaphors. The narrative use to which Amoret is put, the accommodations her metaphor is made to perform, serve as a poetic lesson in how to remain faithful to the metaphoric nature of the text. The poetic use of Belphoebe is a lesson in how the textual metaphor may be closed to literalizing stasis even though it intends to speak a kind of perfection.

That Spenser is thinking of the relation between his speaking and a reader's reading can be seen in a passage in which he addresses his audience directly concerning Belphoebe. After the presumed "death" of Timias, Spenser praises Belphoebe's inviolate flower of chastity and turns abruptly to the ladies of the court:

> To youre faire selues a faire ensample frame,
>   Of this faire virgin, this *Belphoebe* faire,
>   To whom in perfect loue, and spotlesse fame
>   Of chastitie, none liuing may compaire:
>   Ne poysnous Enuy iustly can empaire
>   The prayse of her fresh flowring Maidenhead;
>   For thy she standeth on the highest staire
>   Of th'honorable stage of womanhead,
> That Ladies all may follow her ensample dead.   [III.v.54]

Spenser works hard in this stanza to explain the ways in which Belphoebe both is and is not a "liuing" portrait, and his rhetorical tensions are testimony to the literary difficulties he perceives. The perfect and spotless chastity which Belphoebe represents is a literal condition from which the reader is excluded, to which "none liuing may compaire." And yet, "this faire virgin, this *Belphoebe* faire," can be framed to the reader's own "faire selue." The "ensample dead" may be recreated and reformed into a "faire ensample" "that Ladies all may follow" only by subjecting it to the kinds of metaphoric accommodation Spenser himself exploits in the portrait of Amoret. "Liuing art," as Spenser calls it in the proem, is the mimetic process by which both poet and reader join in freeing the textual metaphors from the mythic sites in which they may be literally imprisoned and putting them to work in their own ethical actions.

iv

If Book III tries to defend the poetic text against the mimetic abuses which may mar or taint the poet's verbal portrait, and against as well the reader's assumption that the literal textual image offers literal terms for human action, then the proem to Book IV implies that such a defense has failed. In fact, the very book in which that defense is made is now subject to the charge that it has mislead its readers:

> The rugged forhead that with graue foresight
>   Welds kingdomes causes, and affaires of state,
>   My looser rimes (I wote) doth sharply wite,
>   For praising loue, as I haue done of late,

> And magnifying louers deare debate;
> By which fraile youth is oft to follie led,
> Through false allurement of that pleasing baite,
> That better were in vertues discipled,
> Than with vaine poemes weeds to haue their fancies fed.   [IV.Pro.1]

This is the same "crime" that Spenser ironically imputes to his own "lewd" lays of earthly love and earthly beauty in *The Fowre Hymnes*. And although the charge grows out of the issues Spenser has explored in Book III, the focus has obviously changed. In the first three proems, Spenser questions the internal strategies and capacities of his art—its necessary duplicity, its tendency to literalize its own metaphors, its veiling of truth, its inability rightly to express the human reality it would reform, and its potential to create ideals which are incapable of assuming human form. Here the charge is against the external effects of art: does it actually mislead or deform the reader? Does it lead him, like the songs of Phaedria and Acrasia, to commit immoral actions by the very qualities that render its depictions charming or delightful? In Sidneyan terms, Spenser has here turned his self-analysis and defense away from the problems of writing poetry to those of the "ending end" of poetry—moving the reader to virtuous action.[35] At issue is still the distinction between right speaking and wrong speaking, but the standard for evaluating speech has become its listener, the poet's own reader.

By adjusting his focus from internal problems of mimesis to external poetic effects, Spenser aligns his own defensive progress through the six proems with the broader progression of *The Faerie Queene* itself. The drama of the proems, therefore, both contributes to and is shaped by the overall movement in the poem from private virtues in the first installment to public ones in the second. The poet must first do battle with his own individual weaknesses—his poetic powers and choices—and with weaknesses inherent in his craft; then he must confront public antagonists, readers of various kinds, before he can establish his full identity and mission as a poet. The announcement and affirmation of the New English Poet, therefore, does not precede the poem, but develops continuously with the narrative and becomes a significant portion of the narrative as the poet learns, by overcoming internal and external challenges to his art, how to translate his private vision into public action.[36]

Spenser responds to the charge of misleading "fraile youth" by attacking the "rugged forhead" who raises that charge. Such a critic "ill iudge[s] of loue," and cannot himself either love or "feele [the] kindly flame." Such a reader should look back to former times to learn that all brave exploits, indeed "all the workes of those wise sages" whom we most admire, "In loue were either ended or begunne." It will be noticed that this *apologia* avoids direct response to the charge that has been raised. Nor is the poet's answer likely to be accepted, for it requires an intelligence willing and able to see the metaphoric relation between "louers deare debate" and "kingdomes causes, and affaires of state." To the mind that cannot feel the kindly flame, praising love can only be antithetical to disciplining in virtue, and the poet is thus subjected to a familiar litany of condemnations: "looser rimes," leading frailty into folly, "false allurement," "pleasing baite," "vaine poemes" and "fancies." These, in fact, are the same charges Spenser himself levels against Lucifera's minstrels, Phaedria, and Acrasia: the grave forehead confuses the words of the poet and the songs of his foils. Against such a misreading, Spenser has little defense. He tries to argue that "to such therefore I do not sing at all," but this defense is untenable. If the poet can speak only to those who already know and practice love, like his "soueraigne Queene," of what educative or reformative value is the lesson he provides? Is he not obligated to sing precisely to those who "ill iudge of loue"?

As in the other proems, we need to remind ourselves that it is Spenser himself, not some external voice, who criticizes the poem. What is most interesting about such a strategy is the apparent but paradoxical need to conceive of the reader as antagonistic to the poet. The poet, who writes only to reform the reader, fashions a reader who deforms his writing. In fact, the fictional reader does even more, for by attacking the words of the poet he becomes a competitive speaker, an interpreter of the text challenging the poet's manner and his matter. It is tempting to argue that Spenser has so completely defined his own voice in terms of hypothetical enemies that he cannot speak in any other terms. So deeply does he feel the need to defend himself that he has to create antagonists to defend against. This is surely a curious narrative dilemma for a humanist poet trying to bring his fellow man to "as high a perfection" as he "can be capable of." Book IV tends to support this line of argument, for Spenser here again commits large portions of his narrative to giving voice to false interpreters of his own tale, interpreters whose words, in turn, become the false speaking of antagonistic poets.

The first and most threatening false speaker of Book IV is Ate, "mother of debate, / And all dissention," an obvious follower of the duplicitous poetic of earlier false poets—Archimago, Duessa, Despair. Like Spenser himself, and as he has just urged in the proem, Ate looks to the "monuments of times forepast" for guiding principles—conceits—of present action. But she does not see the glorious effects of love there displayed; rather, she sees the "sad effects of discord sung" (IV.i.21). Is she, then, a bad reader of antiquity? In a way she is, not because discord is absent from history but because she fails to perceive the mimetic relationship between the surface discord manifest in history and the providential concord manifested by history. As an interpreter of the past, Ate suffers from the same nearsightedness as Mutability, and both are like Sidney's *mysomousoi*, who try to correct textual verbs before they understand the nouns by which the texts were made. Reading their historical texts literally, Ate and Mutability try to develop definitions of existence directly from the historical contingencies. Like the poet, they attempt to express abstracted conceits, but their minds are closed; and rather than accommodating disparities, they fix and arrest them.

Despite her blindness to the larger order of existence, Ate is far from a mere faultfinder or foolish wrong-speaker, and the fact that her literalizing view of history is wrong does not diminish the power of her verses. Around her hell-gate house she cultivates

> The seedes of euill wordes, and factious deedes;
> Which when to ripenesse due they growen arre,
> Bring foorth an infinite increase, that breedes
> Tumultuous trouble and contentious iarre,
> The which most often end in bloudshed and in warre.   [IV.i.25]

Ate herself is as duplicitous as her words: "Her lying tongue was in two parts diuided"; "And as her tongue, so was her hart discided / That neuer thoght one thing, but doubly stil was guided"; "Als as she double spake, so heard she double" (IV.i.27–28). Again, the literal mind shapes itself by the dichotomies it perceives. Like her poetic doubles, Ate challenges even the divine Maker:

> So much her malice did her might surpas,
>   That euen th'Almightie selfe she did maligne,
> Because to man so mercifull he was,
>   And vnto all his creatures so benigne,
>   Sith she her selfe was of his grace indigne:
> For all this worlds faire workmanship she tride,
>   Vnto his last confusion to bring,
>   And that great golden chaine quite to diuide,
> With which it blessed Concord hath together tide.   [IV.i.30]

Throughout Book IV Ate rides, sowing her seeds of dissention and discord: between Scudamour and Blandamour, between Blandamour and Paridell, among all the knights and ladies at the tournament of Satyrane, even between Artegall and Britomart. Her success at moving men to action with her fictions is striking when considered in relation to the poet's own difficulties, expressed in the proem, even in making himself understood. In a sense, Ate might be taken to represent Spenser's bitterness over his poetic failures and his growing awareness that the Sidneyan ideals for poetry are too dependent upon a perhaps unwarranted faith in the good will of its readers.

His poem tries to inculcate virtue, but that quest suddenly seems futile. Or worse, he is accused by those he sets out to reform of inculcating vice and breeding social dissention. The false speakers seem to have all affective poetic power on their side.

That Spenser identifies Ate, the false interpreter and poet, with his own potential misreaders, those Stoic censors who attacked Book III, is suggested by his description of a second Ate-figure, the "foule and loathly creature" of Sclaunder:

> Her nature is all goodnesse to abuse,
> And causelesse crimes continually to frame,
> With which she guiltlesse persons may accuse,
> And steale away the crowne of their good name;
> Ne euer Knight so bold, ne euer Dame
> So chast and loyall liu'd, but she would striue
> With forged cause them falsely to defame;
> Ne euer thing so well was doen aliue,
> But she with blame would blot, and of due praise depriue.
>
> Her words were not, as common words are ment,
> T'expresse the meaning of the inward mind,
> But noysome breath, and poysnous spirit sent
> From inward parts, with cancred malice lind,
> And breathed forth with blast of bitter wind;
> Which passing through the eares, would pierce the hart,
> And wound the soule it selfe with griefe vnkind:
> For like the stings of Aspes, that kill with smart,
> Her spightfull words did pricke, and wound the inner part.

> > [IV.viii.25–26]

In the first stanza, Sclaunder is a willful misreader; in the second, she makes her distortions manifest exactly in such terms as she imagines them. We should hear in this second stanza a parody of the mental processes Spenser describes in *The Fowre Hymnes* and which we there noted for the resemblance to Sidney's mimetic assumptions. Sclaunder's words are not infused "with the force of a divine breath," and rather than enriching or improving the mind they pierce and wound it. But while Spenser subjects Sclaunder to outright censure, both he and his narrative are sorely threatened by her verbal force.

When we first encounter Sclaunder she is serving as unwilling and temporary hostess to Aemylia, Amoret, and Arthur. As she scolds and rails at the three, they patiently talk among themselves, oblivious to her defamations. But Spenser hears her and suddenly conceives a danger:

> Here well I weene, when as these rimes be red
>> With misregard, that some rash witted wight,
>> Whose looser thought will lightly be misled,
>> These gentle Ladies will misdeeme too light,
>> For thus conuersing with this noble Knight;
>> Sith now of dayes such temperance is rare
>> And hard to finde, that heat of youthful spright
>> For ought will from his greedie pleasure spare,
> More hard for hungry steed t'abstaine from pleasant lare. [IV.viii.29]

Although Spenser has explicitly named and described her, and even refused to give us her exact words, he still feels threatened by Sclaunder's power to mislead and is forced to stop the poem for six full stanzas in order to defend his own characters from a reader Sclaunder might have "wounded." Ironically, his defense rests upon the "simple truth" and "blamelesse" concord of antiquity, when the lion and the falcon consorted with the lamb and the dove, when treachery was unknown. Spenser momentarily forgets, of course, that his own narrative belies any such literal golden age. Sclaunder already exists in his own "antique world," just as false readers and false poets have always existed to undermine the true meaning of the Right Poet's speech.

It is a provocative narrative moment in which a simple act of conversation, an exchange of words, is caught between two opposing readers, Sclaunder and the poet, each striving to make a third reader believe his interpretation. Sclaunder's words suppose a disparity between what the conversation seems and what it is; but so too do Spenser's, although the disparity he locates is a temporal one, whereas Sclaunder's is an intentional one. The poet has been trapped by his own fictional antagonist into posing the kind of literal dichotomy it is his task to avoid. Presumably, in the innocence of antiquity, all readers could see virtue for what it was; now, in a fallen present, the depiction of virtue must assume the same duplicity that vice does. After the attacks on his poem in the proem, and the attack on his characters here, Spenser seems to have lost some of his faith in the capacities of a right reader.

That Spenser's optimism is severely strained in Book IV is also evident on those occasions when he tries to portray the true reforming poets. His major attempt occurs in Canto ii as an answer to the challenge raised by Ate's deformed and deforming language:

> Firebrand of hell first tynd in Phlegeton,
>> By thousand furies, and from thence out throwen
>> Into this world, to worke confusion,
>> And set it all on fire by force vnknowen,
>> Is wicked discord, whose small sparkes once blowen
>> None but a God or godlike man can slake;

Such as was *Orpheus*, that when strife was growen
Amongst those famous ympes of Greece, did take
His siluer Harpe in hand, and shortly friends them make.

Or such as that celestiall Psalmist was,
   That when the wicked feend his Lord tormented,
   With heauenly notes, that did all other pas,
   The outrage of his furious fit relented.
   Such Musicke is wise words with time concented,
   To moderate stiffe minds, disposed to striue:
   Such as that prudent Romane well inuented,
   What time his people into partes did ruie,
Them reconcyld againe, and to their homes did driue.   [IV.ii.1–2]

Spenser here contrives a mythic answer to the challenges raised against him:
the Right Poet can, and does, effect private and communal reform. Orpheus
and David, of course, are conventional figures in such a myth; those who follow in their line, like Agrippa, presumably inherit their powers. Yet in this
particular narrative incident, the myth betrays the poet. Glauce, an unlikely
poet-figure to begin with, but who is named by Spenser as another such divine maker, tries to pacify the dissenting Blandamour and Paridell. However,
she is remarkably ineffective, as Ate once more stirs "vp strife, twixt loue and
spight and ire" (IV.ii.11). Even the powers of Orpheus and David seem unable to contain the affective "pricking" of the false poets.

Book IV concludes with another myth, a marriage, and a betrothal. As recent studies have shown, the wedding of Thames and Medway is a grand
showpiece for Spenser, and he masterfully accomplishes what he keeps insisting is impossible.[37] No two cantos of the poem treat matter more prosaic or
intractable; yet Spenser weaves his poetic magic with a grace and ease that
convincingly attest to his talent. More important, he demonstrates that the
poetic urge to catalogue, to create metaphoric order out of literal disorder,
can indeed be fulfilled. After the narrative chaos of the preceding ten cantos,
the ending of Book IV would seem to ensure right poetry its victory over the
slanderous, discordant poetic of such figures as Ate. Myth here informs a
"natural" marriage, which in turn will instruct the human lovers and lead
them to virtuous and creative imitation. The earth itself seems suddenly re-
vitalized, and the poet's part in this reformation is by no means insignificant.
Furthermore, if Giamatti is correct in arguing that the central mythic type
of the false poet is Proteus, the fact that this re-creation occurs within his
very walls would seem to imply a final exorcising of dissention, discord, and
double-speaking. Language itself is tamed, purified, and redeemed.

Yet we must ask what price Spenser pays for this apparent poetic victory.
In effect, does Spenser achieve his artistic success at the expense of his hu-

manistic vision? It is significant that the wedding of Thames and Medway excludes man from its celebration: Marinell and Florimell are present—though displaced—only as mythic emblems; they do not emerge as human beings until the following book.[38] Nor does the marriage, or the rewriting of the natural world, sufficiently address the view of existence proposed by Ate and Sclaunder. The world of man, it seems, is exactly where Spenser left it, controlled by destructive and deforming forces. And in that world, as the tournament of Satyrane clearly demonstrates, even the unveiling of truth is no longer adequate to fend off discord, envy, and dissention. Is, then, the poetic affirmation of these two cantos a genuine accommodation or a self-consolation?

This question assumes greater importance when we notice that the effect of the wedding is to force myth and mimesis back into literal disparity. The myth of Cantos xi and xii stands in stark contrast to the mimesis of Cantos i to x, in the same way that nature suddenly contrasts with man. Nor are these the only disparities the myth gives rise to, for the success of the final cantos is all Spenser's; the reader bears no significant part in determining their meaning. In no other passage of the poem does Spenser so rigorously insist upon divided and distinguished worlds; in no other narrative does he fail to provide the terms of a metaphoric accommodation. Freely ranging in his own golden world, the poet seems to have turned away from the brazen one to which his poetry has previously been directed.

V

As many critics have observed, the proem to Book V is one of the bleakest, most pessimistic moments in *The Faerie Queene*. Usually, Spenser's vision of a world "quite out of square" is seen as a reaction to the political failures of Elizabeth's Irish policies and a failure on his own part sufficiently to distance his narrative of Justice from the particular historical dilemma in which he found himself.[39] In part, this reading of Book V is probably correct; but only in part, for the conditions exhibited in the book are a direct consequence of the issues raised in Book IV. The wedding of Thames and Medway is the last wholly successful moment of the faerieland myth in the poem, and, as we have seen, even it is curiously out of place in the context of the human society depicted in that book. It is not Book V that darkens Spenser's vision, but Book IV.

If it is correct to see the educative progress of the poet through the proems as parallel to the situations of his heroes, then Spenser's current problem can be characterized by recalling Artegall's condition. The hero of Book V, armed with conceptions of Justice formulated in a golden age of pre-fallen virtue, is forced to make his way in an obviously fallen world. The poet, similarly armed with the literary ideals generated by his nostalgic recreation of a mythical realm of faerie, must now confront the bleaker historical reality which lies outside his poem. Both hero and poet face a serious challenge: how to preserve some mimetic relation between outmoded ideals and a real world without simply fleeing that world in despair or giving it up to the chaotic forces of envy and detraction.

The literary challenge has been set for the poet by his own narrative in Book IV. Having created there two poet-figures of apparently invincible destructive force and seemingly accurate perceptions of the dissention and discord dominating the present time, Spenser is powerless to reaffirm his optimistic humanism. Ate's and Sclaunder's interpretations of man's nature and conditions are too real, too close to what Spenser sees around him. The visions of the false poets call his own faerie metaphors into question.

In the face of that challenge, Spenser is forced to contrive a new defense. Now it is not enough simply to reiterate Sidneyan ideals of a reformative art; the poet here is called upon to recognize how limited the effects of that art are and to define more clearly its practical ends. In a world seemingly controlled by processes of entropy, a world which "growes daily wourse and wourse," where all is "transformed" and "degendered," and where the regression towards dissolution has so accelerated that it threatens a "last ruinous decay," the Sidneyan intention of reforming society through poetry becomes increasingly less tenable.

In characteristic fashion, Spenser contrives his new defense of literature out of the very charges raised against it. The false poets of Book IV have argued, in part, that poetry fails to reflect the "course of common life," that its view of man's state is so blatantly wrong that it is merely building castles in the air. The charge, of course, is directed at the very heart of the poetic enterprise—the claim that poetry speaks metaphorically, that its fictions reveal the mimetic principles by which man acts in his world. In Book V, Spenser seems to concede the point: by urging the world of man to imitate the world of the poem, he has failed to make the latter a metaphor of the former. He has "made" the fiction, in other words, an antithesis to rather than an imitation of human fact and human experience.

Spenser makes this concession in the opening stanza of the proem, where he dramatizes himself at what has been, to this point in the poem, his most characteristic activity:

> So oft as I with state of present time,
>   The image of the antique world compare,
>   When as mans age was in his freshest prime,
>   And the first blossome of faire vertue bare,
>   Such oddes I finde twixt those, and these which are,

As that, through long continuance of his course,
Me seemes the world is runne quite out of square,
From the first point of his appointed sourse,
And being once amisse growes daily wourse and wourse.

If we take Spenser quite literally for a moment, it is precisely his own poetic strategy that occasions the bleak vision recorded in the remainder of the proem. By definition and design, *The Faerie Queene* is a comparison of two distinct things: "the state of present time," which is (reality), and an "image of the antique world," which is not (fiction). "To compare" has thus implicitly become "to contrast," and metaphoric parity has become once more a literal disparity. It is not, therefore, the condition of reality that causes the poet's despair and pessimism, but the discrepancy he perceives between that reality and an imagined past of unequalled glory. By accepting the poetic fiction as the standard of excellence, the poet can only conclude that the world has gone awry.

The problem Spenser is addressing here involves a rethinking of his Sidneyan premises. As we have observed several times in this study, the poet is both a maker and a reader. As a maker, his text is a metaphoric bodying forth of an abstract Idea; and insofar as he envisions the mimetic process as concluding with a text, the text itself is a final act of closing and enclosing, a particularized distortion or limitation of the multiple options of the abstract Idea. As a reader, however, his text is a metaphoric opportunity to abstract an Idea. In this case, the mimetic process concludes with the Idea and the text is an initial act of opening and disclosing. Thus, while the metaphoric nature of that text does not change, its use does, depending upon which of his roles the poet chooses to emphasize. The same double perspective defines the poem's relation to the world. As the conceit mediating between God's Idea and a created reality, the poem offers a perceptual threshold. If the poet stresses his status as a metaphoric maker, nature is a final and distorted closure; if he stresses his role as a reader of God's Book, nature is revealing and disclosing. The condition of reality, in short, like that of the poem, is dependent upon which direction we perceive the mimesis as progressing. And while it is clear that the mediating positions of text and poet require an accommodation of both stages and roles, it is all too likely that only one will be emphasized.

To bring these thoughts back into relation with our present text, we could suggest that to this point in the poem Spenser has conceived of himself primarily as a poet-maker and the reality he addresses as the final distortion of the divine Idea. The metaphoric comparison of the "antique world" and "present time" thus occasions a prospect of mimetic decline. To correct this potential misuse of the poem, the poet needs to invert the mimetic emphasis. He needs, in short, to become a poet-reader and to demonstrate that his "antique world" is a metaphoric opening of the "present time." In this way, he can draw the disparity between fact and fiction back to metaphoric relation.

The whole of Book V is designed to effect this inversion. The transparency of the historical allegory forces both Spenser and us to be highly conscious of what he calls, in Canto xi, the "course of common life," or, in the proem, "the common line / Of present dayes." And we are asked continuously to "measure" the adequacy of the poetic forms and metaphors to clarify the historical and human problems. Such testing of the literary conceits occurs even within individual characterizations. Artegall, constantly compared to figures of myth, is finally judged by the way those figures accommodate him rather than how he accommodates them. His success, that is, does not arise from his becoming literally or even metaphorically a second Astraea or a Hercules, but from the way in which those figures disclose his own human dilemmas. Even his virtue is subjected to this redirected perspective: the literary ideal of Justice is judged by its mimetic confirmation of earthly expedience rather than having the narrative of such expedience expose a distortion of the fictional ideal.[40] In fact, it is precisely Artegall's titular virtue that poses the shifted perspective in its clearest terms, for Justice, as purely abstract ideal, is inconceivable. Justice is called into being and hence into operation only as a solution to problems of historical contingency. Its status, therefore, is not an Idea, but a conceit. Like Astraea, the fixed Idea flees the text.[41]

The uniqueness of Book V, then, consists in Spenser's restructuring of his own poetic enterprise and his own textual accommodations.[42] The focus is established early in the book and reiterated throughout. In the proem, Spenser argues that he will not draw his concept of Justice from present use but from past ideals—

> Let none then blame me, if in discipline
>   Of vertue and of ciuill vses lore,
>   I do not forme them to the common line
>   Of present dayes, which are corrupted sore,
>   But to the antique vse, which was of yore,
>   When good was onely for it selfe desyred,
>   And all men sought their owne, and none no more;
>   When Iustice was not for most meed outhyred,
> But simple Truth did rayne, and was of all admyred—   [V.Pro.3]

but this announced intention does not survive the fifth stanza of the opening canto. Astraea, mythic Justice personified, flees a world already fallen from imagined perfection "Into all filth and foule iniquitee." Artegall is thus from the beginning placed in an ironic situation: trained by Astraea in "all the discipline" of perfect Justice, he is abandoned by her to make his way in a very imperfect world. Artegall's dilemma is the same one confronting another would-be reformer, Raphael Hythlodaeus. But whereas Raphael refuses More's advice to fashion his ideals in terms of the actual "play in hand," to accommodate his "academic philosophy" to the real demands of a political commonwealth, and finally flees society altogether for his imaginary island, Artegall learns to temper the literal demands of ideal Justice to the metaphoric requirements of a real world. It is a lesson Spenser himself has learned and he refashions his literary task accordingly.

In Canto x, for example, the poet recalls that there is some debate over the components of his sought virtue:

> Some Clarkes doe doubt in their deuicefull art,
>   Whether this heauenly thing, whereof I treat,
>   To weeten *Mercie*, be of Iustice part,
>   Or drawne forth from her by diuine extreate.
>   This well I wote, that sure she is as great,
>   And meriteth to haue as high a place,
>   Sith in th'Almighties euerlasting seat
>   She first was bred, and borne of heauenly race;
> From thence pour'd down on men, by influence of grace.
>
> For if that Vertue be of so great might,
>   Which from iust verdict will for nothing start,
>   But to preserue inuiolated right,
>   Oft spilles the principall, to saue the part;
>   So much more then is that of powre and art,
>   That seekes to saue the subiect of her skill,
>   Yet neuer doth from doome of right depart:
>   As it is greater prayse to saue, then spill,
> And better to reforme, then to cut off the ill.   [V.x.1–2]

These stanzas chart the great distance Spenser has travelled from Books I–III. No one doubted the ideals of Holiness, Temperance, or Love, and even the false speakers within the narratives seem clearly to accept the unquestionable status of the virtues they assault or abuse. Now, however, both status and definition occasion narrative and extra-narrative dissention. The simple fact that the reader here is outside the text argues Spenser's concern to set his poem in active dialogue with the world he would reform. It is a sign that he is alert to and openly addressing the problems of his real readers. Spenser has, of course, been doing this throughout the poem, but never before has that intention assumed major control of the fictional narrative.

So Spenser now finds himself in the curious position of qualifying his own virtue. It is not, he implies, a static Idea or a dogmatic fiat, but a metaphoric instrument which both produces and is produced by larger accommodations. The process by which the divine Maker "speaks metaphorically" the word of

Justice merges with the process by which the lesser maker "reads" that word out of his experience. Justice, in short, is itself a metaphor that voids the dichotomies that often conflict in historical expedience, namely retribution and forgiveness, justice and mercy. "Rightly to define" or "t'expresse" that word is thus a process of simultaneously speaking as a poet and interpreting as a reader. And it is only in this fusion of disparate processes that the full sense of the metaphoric word can be seen.

Spenser's accommodation in these stanzas is even more impressive when we notice that by the end of stanza 2 the word Justice has, in effect, been effaced. In its stead, Spenser writes a succession of infinitives intended to disclose the broader lessons that he is attempting to express by means of the word: to preserve, to save, and to reform. The metaphor of Justice is here unfolded to reveal the multiple ethical activities it both engenders and accommodates. We might even hear in these verbs the completed lesson of the second installment of *The Faerie Queene*. And if we can align preserving friendship, saving justice, and reforming courtesy with the ethical activities of Books IV, V, and VI, we may begin to understand how, even on a grammatical level, the virtues of each book resolve into and are metaphorically subsumed by each and all of the others.

At the opening of Canto iv, Spenser again suggests the error of conceiving Justice as an absolute Idea:

> Who so vpon his selfe will take the skill
>   True Iustice vnto people to diuide,
>   Had neede haue mightie hands, for to fulfill
> That, which he doth with righteous doome decide,
> And for to maister wrong and puissant pride.
> For vaine it is to deeme of things aright,
> And makes wrong doers iustice to deride,
> Vnlesse it be perform'd with dreadlesse might.
> For powre is the right hand of Iustice truely hight.   [V.iv.1]

Unlike Book I, where it seemed enough merely "to deeme of things aright," enough to let truth stand forth unveiled for all to see, here the presence of Justice does not guarantee its practical implementation. The Idea, in and of itself, is simply not enough; it must accommodate a method of activating itself, of metaphorically bodying itself forth. Again these questions arise not only because of the nature of Justice, but also because it seeks to address and thus depends upon society as a whole for its effectiveness. So long as the virtues remained individual and private, Spenser did not have to confront the largest issue of humanistic reform—namely, the unwillingness of most people to be reformed or to reform themselves. In Books IV through VI, the problematic nature of society itself increasingly complicates the reformer's task. That truth is not lost on the poet, for the same people who dismiss mythical Justice are also likely to misread his mythical text. Again the issue of right speaking becomes dependent upon and thus inseparable from the problems of right reading.

The characteristic action of Book V is judgment, the careful weighing of antithetical disparity to find an accommodating parity. Justice, therefore, is like the moral side of Guyon's Temperance, a conceit of virtue which arises out of the need to mediate between dooms exacted on high and the exigencies of "common life"—a conceit, in short, that is "made" rather than an Idea that is given. This is the significance of Duessa's trial in Canto ix. It affirms the fact that Justice cannot be prescribed, but occurs only in accommodation with the reformative expedience of the "common wele." Yet, in this case, that concession creates literal narrative problems for the poet. He must record both the judicial outcry against Duessa and the advocates for her innocence without prejudicing the lawful case. The reader's surrogate within the text, Prince Arthur, is first led to condemn Duessa, then to pity her, and then to condemn her again. Narratively, such wavering on Arthur's part severely strains his fictional heroic role; and while it does faithfully reflect the historical dilemma confronting Elizabeth-Mercilla, it also deflects the issue from matters of judicial fact to the effects of judicial rhetoric.[43] Thematically, the problem is even more complicated. Spenser ends Canto ix by granting mercy the last word, unwilling, apparently, to force Justice to any rigid conclusion. Even in Canto x, which begins, as we have seen, by arguing that it is better mercifully to reform than judicially to kill, Spenser finds the accommodating mean difficult to attain or sustain. This can be seen in the tortuous syntax with which he records Mercilla's final decision:

> Much more [Mercilla's mercy] praysed was of those two knights;
> > The noble Prince, and righteous *Artegall*,
> > When they had seene and heard her doome a rights
> > Against *Duessa*, damned by them all;
> > But by her tempred without griefe or gall,
> > Till strong constraint did her thereto enforce.
> > And yet euen then ruing her wilfull fall,
> > With more then needfull naturall remorse,
> And yeelding the last honour to her wretched corse.   [V.x.4]

One might well wonder whether the moral principle of mercy is not here confused with simple compassion as the judicial action would seem to violate the thematically asserted goal. Like Mercilla herself, Spenser is "constrained" by the historical contingency to choose between mutually exclusive demands which preclude the desired accommodation of reform. But Spenser's rhetoric so loads the case against Justice, so convinces us of Mercilla's merciful "tempering" of the damnation all heap upon Duessa, that the fact of Duessa's death can be slipped into the stanza only covertly, lest it shatter the rhetorical pretense. Accommodation is never actually achieved, and, with "the last honour" paid, the narrative hastens on to other matters.

The pressure of the historical moment clearly controls Spenser's fictional presentation in this incident, and while this may also be true of passages earlier in the poem the presence of that pressure has never seemed so overt. That is, Spenser here makes the pressure a tangible element of his own text. We feel the fiction being adjusted to and accommodated with the particular political experience. It seems that the poet no longer trusts the reader to make the historical connection—as he does, say, with Timias and Belphoebe—but makes the necessity of connection a condition of the narrative itself. There is no surer sign of the altered strategy of his poem than the reader's consciousness of this historical straining.

In this regard, it is worth recalling that we enter Mercilla's court via the character of a poet—the only explicitly named poet in all of Book V. Even that fact is important: as the fictional realm comes ever closer to that of historical expediency, the poet seems more and more an outsider. But one poet is here, a would-be servant of Mercilla:

> There as they entred at the Scriene, they saw
>   Some one, whose tongue was for his trespasse vyle
>   Nayld to a post, adiudged so by law:
>   For that therewith he falsely did reuyle,
>   And foule blaspheme that Queene for forged guyle,
>   Both with bold speaches, which he blazed had,
>   And with lewd poems, which he did compyle;
>   For the bold title of a Poet bad
> He on himselfe had ta'en, and rayling rymes had sprad.
>
> Thus there he stood, whylest high ouer his head,
>   There written was the purport of his sin,
>   In cyphers strange, that few could rightly read,
>   BON FONT: but *bon* that once had written bin,
>   Was raced out, and *Mal* was now put in.
>   So now *Malfont* was plainely to be red;
>   Eyther for th'euill, which he did therein,
>   Or that he likened was to a welhed
> Of euill words, and wicked sclaunders by him shed.   [V.ix.25–26]

Who has judged Bon Font? We are told that he is "adiudged so by law," and presumably the law is Mercilla's. But when viewed from the perspective of the proem to Book IV or the ending of Book V, Bon Font could as easily have been judged by the forces of Envy and Detraction, those malevolent "fault-finders" whose seditious effects Spenser has already chronicled. In a book which argues that Justice is only a conceit for action, even a Right Poet could legitimately be silenced if his poem occasions, as the proem to Book IV suggests it has, active dissention and discord. Once the virtue is rendered relative to the common good, the poet faces the risk of all would-be reformers: the law might misjudge him or even accurately judge him as a socially disruptive influence.

Did Bon Font actually write "lewd poems," or were his verses, like Spenser's own Book III, simply misread? Did he actively seek evil or was he merely "likened . . . to a welhed / Of euill words"? Anyone who is so "bold" as to take upon himself the title and obligations of a Poet runs the risk of having his good name similarly effaced. Once again, Spenser confronts that risk directly. He realizes that by his very aims the poet places himself at the mercy of his readers, who can either applaud him as Bon Font or accuse him as Malfont, either praise him for combatting Sclaunder or charge him with being Sclaunder.[44] It is significant that Spenser raises these optional responses immediately before he enters his own most politically dangerous incident. However ambiguous the trial of Duessa may seem, we are urged not to abuse the poetic word by turning it into a blasphemy against the Queen or a well-head of "wicked sclaunders." To do so, the emblem of Bon Font implies, is to indict not only the poet's speaking but also our own reading. The presence of the emblem is a testimony to the fears Spenser has and a gauge of how concerned he is to mount an adequate defense of himself. It is also, of course, a principal means by which he brings into the open the historical contingencies of his own narrative and thus prepares us for the pressures we have seen at work in the trial which immediately follows.

At the conclusion of Book V, Artegall completes his appointed task by freeing Irena from the tyranny of Grandtorto and by restoring her to "her kingdom's seat." His success is immediately qualified, however, when Spenser suggests again that judicial restoration is not an end in itself:

> During which time, that he did there remaine,
>   His studie was true Iustice how to deale,
>   And day and night employ'd his busie paine
>   How to reforme that ragged common-weale:
>   . . . .
> But ere he could reforme it thoroughly,
>   He through occasion called was away,
>   To Faerie Court, that of necessity
>   His course of Iustice he was forst to stay.   [V.xii.26–27]

The freeing of Irena is only a preliminary step; reforming her community is both more important and more difficult. The conceit of Justice is further opened to that of reformation, and the implication is that only by approaching the issue of justice from a "readerly" perspective can we keep that metaphor open to larger accommodation. Although Spenser shapes the present fiction to reflect the history of Grey's problems in and his recall from Ireland—thus again forcing us to feel the narrative pressure of historical contingency and precluding any idealistic conclusion to the public problem—that is not the significant factor of the incident.[45] Rather, it is that Spenser chooses exactly this point of interrupted communal reform to bring the Blatant Beast, tool of Envy and Detraction, into the fiction. Braying at the passing Artegall, the Beast functions as a complex symbol of Spenser's growing doubts about communal reform. Although the beast does not bite Artegall, the only actions we see in Irena's realm as the hero and the narrative withdraw from it are slander, rage, and "fell contention." That Artegall is not injured by the Beast clarifies the creature's public role: having completed his private quest, Artegall is safe; but the public effects of his actions are now "read" as foul treacheries. The Blatant Beast thus serves as the sole surviving public voice of the very community in which Artegall's reforms are to be carried out. Irena, we recall, speaks not a word.

Because the Blatant Beast is both a wrong-speaker and a faultfinder, it represents Spenser's most fearful anticipation of the potential abuse of the poetic word.[46] As a false speaker, the Beast effects an absolute inversion of the poet's initial design. From the opening of the poem, at least part of his task has been to silence false speaking in order to generate right speaking, to foster a conversation of Truth which would incite a conversion of Faith. But although he has learned, by Book V, how to accommodate his fiction to accomplish that end, he suddenly finds that his own reforming speech is itself silenced by the din of "bitter words" poured forth by the deforming forces of Ate and Sclaunder. Even more significant is the fact that it is precisely the chronicle of Artegall's moral success that gives rise to such envy and detraction. By thus projecting the Beast as a public misreader of both Artegall's accomplishments and his own political fiction, Spenser has reinvoked in a more threatening form the charges leveled against him in the proem to Book IV.[47] This historically accommodated fiction, which sets out only to reform, has itself created the negative reaction which acts against such reform. Instead of encouraging ethical action, the poetry has called forth dissention; instead of effecting communal concord, it has created public discord. Whether he realizes it or not, by the end of Book V Spenser has combined his two most feared antagonists—the wrong speaker and the false reader—into a single figure whose "welhed / Of euill words, and wicked sclaunders" he is powerless to stop. As his earlier emblem had anticipated, the *bon* that "once had written bin" is now effaced, and "*mal* is now put in."

vi

Spenser's retreat, in Book VI, from the hazardous world of political expedience to a peaceful haven of pastoral myth is, in part, a reaction to his inability to predict reform in the public sphere. But as modern criticism has amply demonstrated, and as the poet's own heroes are forced to learn throughout the poem, no retreat is safe, no haven secure. Spenser, of course, knows this truth as well as we do, and we seriously underestimate his integrity if we presume Book VI is a simple poetic escape. That Spenser encourages such an assumption, indeed entertains it himself, is testimony to the rigor and the honesty of his self-examination in this book.[48] If he cannot provide an adequate public defense of his own right words, he can at least assure himself that he has not misspoken; and if he cannot silence the detractions of the slanderous Beast, he can at least be certain that the lies spread about him contain no truth.

There are two problems singled out in the book's proem: the poet's own motives for writing the legend and the source of the sought virtue. In order to address the first problem, Spenser raises the possibility that he is seeking in the imagination the support and consolation apparently denied him by "the course of common life":

> The waies, though which my weary steps I guyde,
>   In this delightfull land of Faery,
>   Are so exceeding spacious and wyde,
>   And sprinckled with such sweet variety,
>   Of all that pleasant is to eare or eye,
>   That I nigh rauisht with rare thoughts delight,
>   My tedious trauell doe forget thereby;
>   And when I gin to feele decay of might,
> It strength to me supplies, and chears my dulled spright.   [VI.Pro.1]

Seemingly lost within the "spacious and wyde" ways of his own poetic maze, Spenser wonders again, as he had in the proem to Book IV, whether he has committed himself more to "vaine poemes" and "fancies" than to virtuous discipline. Like Redcross in the Wandering Wood, Cymochles on Phaedria's wandering Isle, or Mortdant in the Bower of Bliss, he seems to have been seduced by the alluring temptation to rest. The worldly ways are "tedious trauell" and have made him "weary."

Later in the legend, Spenser shows Calidore similarly entranced by the "delightfull land" of Melibee's arcadia, and the dangers he perceives in his own ravishment are revealed by his treatment of Calidore's.

> Who now does follow the foule *Blatant Beast*,
>   Whilest *Calidore* does follow that faire Mayd,

Vnmyndfull of his vow and high beheast,
Which by the Faery Queene was on him layd,
That he should neuer leaue, nor be delayed
From chacing him, till he had it attchieued?
But now entrapt of loue, which him betrayd,
He mindeth more, how he may be relieued
With grace from her, whose loue his heart hath sore engrieued.

That from henceforth he meanes no more to sew
His former quest, so full of toile and paine;
Another quest, another game in vew
He hath, the guerdon of his loue to gaine:
With whom he myndes for euer to remaine,
And set his rest amongst the rusticke sort,
Rather then hunt still after shadowes vaine
Of courtly fauour, fed with light report
Of euery blaste, and sayling alwaies on the port.

Ne certes mote he greatly blamed be,
From so high step to stoupe vnto so low,
For who had tasted once (as oft did he)
The happy peace, which there doth ouerflow,
And prou'd the perfect pleasures, which doe grow
Amongst poore hyndes, in hils, in woods, in dales,
Would neuer more delight in painted show
Of such false blisse, as there is set for stales,
T'entrap vnwary fooles in their eternall bales.   [VI.x.1–3]

It does not matter, at this point, that Calidore's retreat is as necessary to his quest as the descent into Despair's cave is to Redcross's quest. At issue here is Calidore's motive, his willful forsaking of his sworn task in a misdirected desire for release from the risks and the toil of an active pursuit of public virtue. Although that desire is humanly understandable (the poet faces it too) and therefore not "greatly" to be blamed (because Calidore's situation is the poet's), Calidore's motives are judged. Calidore is right not to delight in the "painted show" of the court, but he is clearly wrong to presume that he can justifiably relinquish his communal obligations. As always in *The Faerie Queene*, private retreat, such as Aldus's or Melibee's, must patiently and arduously be earned by public action.

By thus aligning himself with his hero, Spenser reexamines his own motives for withdrawing into the fictional realm of faerie. Is he really trying to fashion reformed and reforming gentlemen, or is he seeking a golden world he can control, in which the heroes win because they are good and the villains lose because they are evil? By criticizing Calidore's motives, Spenser purifies his own.[49] His retreat—as Calidore's also will eventually prove to be, despite the hero's intentions—is not a private withdrawal from his announced public quest, but a continuation of it. By thinking of his poetic choices in terms of such dichotomies, Spenser already assures the kind of accommodating answer we have come to expect. He must withdraw, he argues, to find the "sacred noursery / Of vertue" which lies hidden from the "view of men, and wicked worlds disdaine":

> Reuele to me the sacred noursery
>   Of vertue, which with you doth there remaine,
>   Where it in siluer bowre does hidden ly
>   From view of men, and wicked worlds disdaine.
>   Since it at first was by the Gods with paine
>   Planted in earth, being deriu'd at furst
>   From heauenly seedes of bounty soueraine,
>   And by them long with carefull labour nurst,
> Till it to ripenesse grew, and forth to honour burst.
>
> Amongst them all growes not a fayrer flowre,
>   Then is the bloosme of comely courtesie,
>   Which though it on a lowly stalke doe bowre,
>   Yet brancheth forth in braue nobilitie,
>   And spreds it selfe through all ciuilitie.   [VI.Pro.3–4]

We are not wrong to hear in these lines a reformulation of the Sidneyan process by which the Idea implanted in the mind of man eventually is bodied forth in particular ethical action. James Nohrnberg provides a valuable Plotinian commentary on this process, and on the relationship between contemplative withdrawal and public reform:

> Begetting originates in contemplation and ends in the production of a form, that is, a new object of contemplation. In general, all things as they are images of their generating principles produce forms and objects of contemplation. . . . Moreover, animals generate due to the activity within them of seminal reasons. Generation is a contemplation. It results from the longing of pregnancy to produce a multiplicity of forms and objects of contemplation, to fill everything with reason, and never to cease from contemplation. Begetting means to produce some form; and this means to spread contemplation everywhere.[50]

Plotinus's words are especially relevant to a poet whose task is to enrich the memory and to provide the reader with "a new object of contemplation" in order to "spread contemplation everywhere." And by these terms, Spenser assures himself of both the purity and the necessity of his own inward retreat.

Why he should retreat now, at the end of his poem rather than at its beginning, remains to be seen.

The final lines of the proem address Spenser's second question, the source of the sought virtue. Is courtesy private or public, "deepe within the mynd" or manifest "in outward shows" which spread "through all ciuilitie"; is it a country virtue or a courtly one, an ideal from antiquity or a present reality? Such oppositions identify a different kind of virtue than we have met in the preceding books. Never before has Spenser been particularly troubled to locate a source for his virtue, and never before has the sphere of the virtue's action been called so conspicuously into question. What does that questioning mean, and what does it tell us about courtesy?

The proem draws four speaking pictures of the virtue. It is a heavenly seed, planted in a separate and sacred nursery, brought to perfect ripeness, and then sent forth to flower and branch "through all ciuilitie." It is an antique ideal still cherished in present society despite its currently diminished forms. It is an internal attitude of mind which is manifest in, though not defined by, external actions. And it is a special grace imparted by a virtuous sovereign to her loyal and loving subjects and dutifully returned by them to honor her. The four images share a basic symbolic pattern—a circular movement outward from a source and a subsequent return. As many scholars have noted, the book itself participates in this movement.[51] The poet's courtesy will be derived from the Queen, spread over and through the realm of faerie, then returned as tribute to the Queen. The progression of heroes (Calidore-Calepine-Calidore) and settings (faerieland-arcadia-faerieland) within the book duplicates the pattern, as does the visionary dance of the Graces on Mount Acidale: *emanatio, transformatio, remeatio.*[52]

Our recognition of this persistent pattern yields one reason for Spenser's focus on the source of the virtue. Since courtesy is an action which emanates, embraces, and returns (or, in slightly altered alignment, gives, transforms, and receives), the source is critical in order to define accurately the symbolic movement. And although that source is variously identified as the Queene, the poet's lady, and Venus, each of these metaphors is clearly shaped by and in imitation of the only ultimate source, the divine Maker. The symbolic motion of courtesy is an analogue for the pattern of Christian charity flowing outward from God, causing all men to love and thus transform one another in love, and then returned to God as fit honor and tribute. Spenser's courtesy can be defined, then, as the first and second commandments as Jesus explains them to the Pharisees, the Old Testament law and its New Testament fulfillment: honor God and love thy neighbor as thyself (Matthew 22:34–40). Once this submerged metaphoric tenor of love is understood, it is easier to explain the presence of figures like Mirabella in the narrative; to justify Calidore's pastoral retreat, since in learning love he learns the source of courtesy; and to explain why the purified Venus is an appropriate figure for the fourth and central Grace on Mount Acidale. The biblical lesson also clarifies the giving-receiving pattern seen in the concentric circles throughout the book.

But as important as the circular progress of courtesy is, Spenser devotes more time to one phase of its movement than to the others. Hence, although courtesy transforms and frequently converts evil figures in the poem, and although it is often repaid to Calidore and Calepine in kind when they act courteously, Spenser is more interested in the initial movement of courtesy from a source to an object. "Vertues seat is deepe within the mynd," the proem argues; but virtue, as an action, as a force ethically moving and directing men, must be bodied forth in social behavior and manners: "the gentle minde by gentle deeds is knowne" (VI.iii.1); it must make its courtesy manifest in such excellency as it has imagined it. Similarly, while the queen's virtue may be seen in the mirror of her "pure minde," it must be sent forth, figured forth "into the rest, that round about [her] ring" in order to be manifest as true courtesy.

In each phase of the movement of courtesy, but especially clear in the initial one of giving, courtesy is depicted as a transfer of virtue from one place to another. The terms of this transfer are even more precise. In the first formal definition of courtesy given in Book VI proper, Spenser argues that it is the ground "of all goodly manners" and the "roote of ciuil conuersation" (VI.i.1). This association of manners and conversation had been standard courtesy doctrine at least since Castiglione's *Courtier*. Spenser's further designation of the Graces as the specific benefactors of courtesy implies, as C. S. Lewis noted long ago, that he envisions courtesy as "the poetry of conduct," sent from an "author" to a "reader" who can learn and profit from that conversational and hence converting "text."[53] That this implied metaphor is not merely incidental is confirmed by the frequency with which Spenser, like Castiglione before him, defines courteous behavior in poetic or aesthetic terms. The following description of the decorum of manners, for example, depends upon accommodating artistic principles to ethical activity:

> What vertue is so fitting for a knight,
>   Or for a Ladie, whom a knight should loue,
>   As Curtesie, to beare themselues aright
>   To all of each degree, as doth behoue?
>   For whether they be placed high aboue,
>   Or low beneath, yet ought they well to know
>   Their good, that none them rightly may reproue
>   Of rudenesse, for not yeelding what they owe:
> Great skill it is such duties timely to bestow.   [VI.ii.1]

The significance of the poetic metaphor, of the analogy between social manner and artistic conversation, is that for perhaps the first time in the poem poetry itself serves directly in the ethical process. The bodying forth of poetic examples of courtesy is, like courtesy itself, a movement from one place to another—from the poet's mind to his text, and from his text to a reader. Not only does the poet thus teach the method by which the virtue is transferred from one place to another, but he actually begins that process. The poet himself, in short, is the source that Spenser sets out to identify. He himself initiates the public movement of courtesy as he sends forth the private Idea to be taken up by the community of readers, set to work now in their own public lives. The poetic metaphor is here reversed: since the ethical actions of courtesy are poetry, Spenser's own poetic activities are courteous.

We asked earlier why Spenser turns inward at the end rather than the beginning of his poem. We can now see that his retreat here signals not a withdrawal into the fictional realm but an escape from it, a turning outward toward the actual reader by paradoxically returning to himself. It is therefore significant that Spenser abandons, in Book VI, the Virgilian persona he had adopted at the opening of the poem and speaks, in the proem at least, in a voice more nearly approximating his own. And while it may be impossible to distinguish in any exact sense the voice of the first proem from that of the final one, the very fact that Spenser questions his own motives here and invites us to question them implies a more intimate, more personal stance.[54] The Virgilian narrator is not susceptible to the fears or dangers that prey upon Spenser himself. This shift in voice is maintained throughout the book—Spenser's use of his own earlier persona, Colin Clout, is another indication that he here relinquishes the Virgilian mantle—but perhaps nowhere as dramatically as at its very end.

When the Blatant Beast escapes from Calidore's iron chains in Canto xii and rages again through "each degree and state," we expect that, like Archimago and Duessa at the conclusion of Book I, the monster will slip quietly away to lurk in the darker folds of the narrative. But Spenser has a bolder plan in mind. Instead of hiding the beast in rocks and caves to await new fictional antagonists, he has it leap out of the narrative to attack the poet who is writing it. And it is clearly Spenser himself who is attacked, not a fictive narrator.[55] That the Beast subjects him and his poem to the same slanderous charges raised at the opening of the poem's second installment only increases the poet's genuine fears of being misread and misinterpreted. Again Spenser uses the Beast as a speaking picture of a faultfinding reader who defaces the poet's *bona carmina* by accusing the text of being *mala carmina*.

As I have argued elsewhere,[56] Spenser is very deliberate in setting his fictional beast at large in the real world to attack his own poem. For once he is unleashed, the Beast becomes more than a false reader: he becomes as well a false speaker whose slandering voice silences the poet's own. Civil conversation, the originating source of the courtesy of "commun wele" and the root of all ethical conversion, is deformed into simple detraction and incivility. The effect of the Beast's attack is thus to issue a direct challenge to the reader, for while the fictional heroes cannot chain the beast, we can. By correcting the Beast's misreadings and by defending both the poet and his poem, we return to him the courtesy he first extends to us. Significantly, our action is not bound by the limits of the fiction—the "ending end" of the poem, for us, is not the end of the poem. Our defense of the poet is an ethical act of courtesy conducted now in life itself, an actual public reform which accepts and acts upon the virtuous obligations to which the poet has called us.

Only at the end of Book VI does Spenser close the gap between art and life, fiction and reality. And he does so precisely because he learns through his consistent attempts at self-defense that this is the one thing he cannot do. Defense of the text ultimately rests with us.[57] If we are called upon to defend it, then the text is good; if we are not, then it is not. Right speaking is finally the poet's ability to "add faith" in his audience's right reading. And our right reading is initially a right speaking about the poet's text, our ability to "add faith" in him as he has in us.

It is easy to underestimate Spenser's achievement in the six proems because the conventional self-effacements disguise a more profound one. The understandable urge to defend his own voice conditions, in the proems, a variety of semantic closures which attempt to protect the poet's words from the abuses of those who would misspeak or misread them. Thus Spenser assumes, as we have seen, the mantle of Virgil, the magic of Fidelia, the pipe of Colin. But all such fictive roles are potential enclosures, trapping the poet in literal options which deny the full metaphoric opportunities of his art. Spenser has to learn, therefore, to open the metaphor of Poet to the same extensions granted his other poetic words. To speak metaphorically even of himself, the poet must remain faithful to the mimetic accommodations his own semantic and narrative places allow. For this reason, Virgil is no more— nor less—important than Archimago, Fidelia than Fidessa, Colin than Malfont. The courtesy of language which gives rise to the metaphor of the poet is a courtesy which denies no one because that metaphor accommodates everyone. And this is true as well for the apparent dichotomy between Spenser and his reader. Self-defense, in these terms, would be a blatant act of discourtesy, an attempt to exclude and condemn us rather than to include and reform us.

The characteristic activity of the Right Poet, then, is finally to cease speaking, to relinquish the literal poetic guises that falsely constrain him, so that others may join their voices to his. We could, of course, accuse the poet of succumbing to the desire for rest, but our faith in him must meet his faith in us at this point. Only by stopping the poem does Spenser free the metaphor of "Poet" from its literal place within the semantic borders of the fiction and open it to ethical imitation. And this courtesy to the metaphor is itself a metaphor for the courtesy we owe the poet. The conversion to which he calls us requires a conversation among all men, good poets and bad, right readers and wrong ones. And here we locate Spenser's most profound self-effacement, for he has learned that regardless of how many speakers he creates in the narrative, the poem is still a solitary voice, still only an incentive to the conversation that occasions conversion, and at best a mere groundplot of more profitable inventions.

Chapter 7. The Poem's "Wise Rede"

As *The Faerie Queene* continuously tests Spenser's notions of poetic making by trying "t'expresse" various metaphors of the Right Poet, so it constantly challenges his faith in poetic interpretation by fashioning metaphoric right readers. And just as Spenser puts the former metaphors to work in order to dramatize his own act of writing the poem, so he uses the latter to dramatize our act of reading it.[1] Spenser's insistence, moreover, that our reading is both a literary and an ethical activity conditions many of the principal terms of the narrative. One of the poet's earliest decisions was to call his six fables "legends" (L. *legere*: to read, to pass through, to follow the footsteps of).[2] By that etymological pun, Spenser refuses to allow the reader a passive role in the fiction-making process: his reading is a metaphoric quest which imitates those of the poet and his heroes. And insofar as this mimetic relation obtains, it follows that reading must remain open to the activity of writing in the same way that we have seen writing accommodate reading. Both poet and reader bear equal and concurrent responsibility to speak and to read the metaphors that "make" the text. Again Spenser argues that defense of the poem is not his task alone.

When the necessities of defense are brought to bear upon the problems of right reading, however, additional troubles arise. The poet's concern over the difficulties of reading his text are voiced, as we have seen, in the dedicatory epistle.[3] This "discovery" of the "general intention and meaning" of the poem is "annexed" to the work in order to give "light to the Reader, for . . . better vnderstanding." The first sentence of the epistle worries about "how doubtfully all Allegories may be construed" by "gealous opinions and misconstructions." Even here we can see Spenser opening the metaphor of reading to include tasks normally reserved for writing: the measure of something wrongly construed (misread) is a misconstruction (a miswriting or mismaking). Once Spenser admits the reader's participation in the process of making the text, he must also admit the possibility of his abusing the text by wrongly re-creating it. In so doing, the metaphoric reader-poet would then become an antagonistic wrong-speaker and faultfinder. As we have come to expect, what begins as a strategy of defending the poem ends by itself requiring further defense.

That broader defense depends upon two important assumptions: first, that the reading process follows the same linguistic model as the speaking process; and second, that the provisionality which inhabits all right speaking also governs all right reading. Although the two presumptions are difficult to separate, let us explore them singly as far as we can. By means of another ety-mological pun, this time on the Anglo-Saxon *ræd* and Middle English *rede*, Spenser sets forth his poem as a "wise rede" or counsel capable of fashioning noble and virtuous gentlemen.[4] Each legend, or book, is a particular textual "reading" of that abstract Idea. Analogously, individual poet-figures within the legends offer "wise rede" to various sojourning characters whose subse-quent actions are presented as instances of their particular "readings." In both cases, we are to recognize the process by which these readings are fig-ured forth—a mimetic imitation conducted along the stages of Sidney's ver-bal pattern. Hence, the relationship between each Idea and its subsequent reading ought to reveal the fore-conceit "to read." This lesson addresses not only the narrative speaking, but also our own interpretive reponses, for the poet's "wise rede" is presented to us as an abstract noun which we must body forth in our own ethical "readings." By using the same verb to define and express his own, his characters', and his reader's activities, Spenser enforces the Sidneyan lesson that poetry teaches the art of mimetic imitation; it teaches us, in brief, how "to read."

As our earlier discussions have emphasized, however, each stage of the mimetic process provides an occasion for distortion. The only real defense the poet has offered against such distortion is a negative one: as long as the imitation remains aware of its status as a metaphor and thus open to further metaphoric extension, it avoids the literal closures that identify distortion. In effect, this defense means that all speech is provisional. The same provi-sionality must obtain in all readings, and we may therefore expect that just as Spenser has called his own capacities for right speaking into question, so he will now question the reader's ability to read correctly.

To some extent, the provisionality of all readings is a rhetorical attempt on Spenser's part to align his literary microcosm with the larger world of signs which it reflects. If that world is hard to read aright, so too must its poetic imitation. What makes nature so difficult to read is neither God's writing nor nature's text, for both speak clearly and accurately—

> For day discouers all dishonest wayes,
> And sheweth each thing, as it is indeed:
> The prayses of high God he faire displayes,
> And his large bountie rightly doth areed.   [III.iv.59]

But man, of course, has fallen away from clarity and accuracy. And if he must therefore guard against presumptuous readings of the Maker's Poem—"But let the man with better sence aduize, / That of the world least part to vs is red"—then he should also guard against arrogant or complacent readings of the lesser maker's text. Spenser here twists Sidney's analogy between God and the poet into a self-defensive equation between man as reader of God's

Book and man as interpreter of his book. The new analogy makes the reader's obvious problems in reading nature speak metaphorically of his trouble understanding the poem. Conversely, the analogy urges that the right reader should be as responsible to the poetic text as he is to the divine one it metaphorically re-presents.

The difficulty in correctly reading either text or nature issues a clear warning to the poet's audience; yet Spenser also faces this danger. In a startling moment of prophecy and self-defense, Spenser emphasizes that he hazards his own reputation and name as much on right reading as on right speaking. As Arthur and Artegall enter Mercilla's castle, they encounter, as we have seen, a figure who, like Spenser,[5] "on himselfe had ta'en" "the bold title of a poet":

> Thus there he stood, whylest high ouer his head,
>   There written was the purport of his sin,
>   In cyphers strange, that few could rightly read,
>   BON FONT . . .   [V.ix.26]

If Bon Font is displayed for some sin he has committed, why is the "purport" of that sin written in unreadable cyphers? Or is it his name that is cyphered and which few can rightly read? Spenser hardly allows us time to puzzle out his meaning before adding:

>   but *bon* that once had written bin,
> Was raced out, and *Mal* was now put in.
> So now *Malfont* was plainely to be red.

Whatever Bon Font was or did, the fact that few could rightly read it contrasts sharply with the ease with which Malfont is read. The contrast implies not only two radically different interpretations, or readings, of a single poet, but opposing judgments of his poetry: a *bona carmina* which is written in cyphers and hence hard to understand, and a *mala carmina* which is read plainly and openly. Hard to read versus easy to read, cyphers versus plain speech, metaphoric readings versus literal ones, *bona* versus *mala carmina*: like the metaphor of writing, the metaphor of reading introduces and expresses disparities resident in the poetic word. But these disparities are themselves a sign of the closure they figure forth—namely, the literal separation of writing and reading into two discrete acts. Once that is allowed, it is a short step to see that even a Right Poet's writing can be "raced out" by a reader's wrong reading.

Spenser's general awareness of the problems of reading finds other means of expression. In the procession of the deadly sins drawing Lucifera's chariot we find Idleness, who carries a well worn, but little read, breviary (I.iv.19). Apparently, reading is to be understood here as an antidote to spiritual sloth;

reading itself is a positive and beneficial act. In *Mother Hubberd's Tale*, however, Spenser shows that this is not always the case. When the Ape and the Fox encounter "a formall Priest," they show him their "pasport" or license to beg:

> Which when the Priest beheld, he vew'd it nere,
> As if therein some text he studying were,
> But little els (God wote) could thereof skill:
> For read he could not euidence, nor will,
> Ne tell a written word, ne write a letter
> Ne make one title worse, ne make one better.   [ll. 379–384]

A modern reader, more likely than not bringing to this passage some suspicion of Spenser's Puritan leanings, will probably anticipate a satiric portrait of this priest. But that is not Spenser's intention at the moment, as implicit in the final line and made explicit when he continues:

> Of such deep learning little had he neede,
> Ne yet of Latine, ne of Greeke, that breede
> Doubts mongst Diuines, and difference of texts,
> From whence arise diuersitie of sects,
> And hatefull heresies, of God abhor'd:
> But this good Sir did follow the plaine word,
> Ne medled with their countrouersies vaine;
> All his care was, his seruice well to saine,
> And to read Homelies vpon holidayes.   [ll. 385–393]

That Spenser does go on to satirize the priest at some length[6] does not alter the fact that reading itself is not a privileged action here. Too much reading, too much glossing upon the text, is as dangerous as no reading at all. Spenser makes the same point in the dedication to *Virgils Gnat*:

> But if that any *Oedipus* vnware
> Shall chaunce, through power of some diuining spright,
> To reade the secrete of this riddle rare,
> And know the purporte of my euill plight,
> Let him rest pleased with his owne insight,
> Ne further seeke to glose vpon the text.   [ll. 5–10]

Reading, Spenser implies, is an ethical action which must be undertaken seriously and responsibly in order to cultivate an appropriate mean between the slothful non-reading of Idleness and the deceptive glossing of the Ape and the Fox.

Proper reading, in these cases, is a metaphor which voids the literal dichotomies of rote repetition on the one hand and sophistic exegesis on the other.

When individual readings are limited to either of these extremes, they can be judged as unfaithful to the accommodating options of the infinitive (to read) they body forth. We may again anticipate, therefore, that Spenser's repetitions of the verb *read* throughout *The Faerie Queene* attempts a twofold mimetic lesson: how right reading is ensured and how wrong reading is determined.[7] Above all, the literal narrative activities of reading—activities of widely differing contexts and meanings—provide the groundplot out of which the properly metaphoric conceit of "to read" may be invented.

The simplest and most abundant use of *read* occurs in passages where one character asks another to "read" (i.e., to tell) his name or fortune. Roughly similar, and about as numerous, are instances in which a character "reads" another a plan of action, advises him, in other words, on an ethical course. Our initial interest in such passages stems from Spenser's decision to use the verb "read" for activities which "speak." Already he calls our inclination to discriminate into question by warning us against the kinds of dichotomies the two verbs give rise to: speaking versus reading, writer versus reader. He also, of course, tries to expand our usual presumptions about what reading is by demonstrating that any apparently simple communication (giving one's name or directions) involves interpretation, both on the part of the speaker and on the part of the auditor. Literal "telling" and "advising" become metaphoric "readings," and Spenser thus lays the semantic foundation for his own accommodating metaphor. Only after establishing this mimetic relation between speaking and interpreting can he go on to show how susceptible to error such interpretations are—how often, that is, characters do not "read" correctly even their own names and how frequently they "read" bad advice.

In the two literal activities we also glimpse Spenser's larger designs, for the analogies between speaking and listening, writing and reading, telling and advising reach out to include the relationships between perception and judgment, literary fact and ethical value. Indeed, the very force of poetry's instruction depends upon these relations, for the processes of literary perception (reading) teach us the mimetic processes of moral action (also a reading). The poem itself makes this point again and again by shaping the literally discrete activities of narrative "reading" so as to disclose the conceit ("to read") which they metaphorically imitate.

Another relatively simple use of the verb occurs as Spenser has one character "read" or "read through" another. The savages "read" Una's sorrow in her countenance (I.vi.11); Orgoglio "reads" his end in Arthur's crystal shield (I.viii.21); all goodness and honor can be "read" on Belphoebe's forehead (II.iii.24); Arthur, chancing upon the fainted Guyon, "reads" magnanimity in his face (II.viii.23); Calidore and Artegall catch sight of each other, "knew them selues, and both their persons red" (VI.i.4). Reading here means discerning, a fundamental act of re-cognition or attributing meaning to a concrete particular which demonstrates by narrative analogy the method of read-ing the "continued allegory" of the text itself. In Books I and II, such readings are frequently isolated from any ethical actions a character might take or from any further knowledge he may achieve. In later books, however, this form of reading increasingly assumes moral commitment and higher wisdom.[8] The palmer "reads" the relics of the Rock of Reproche in order to teach Guyon the moral effects of shame (II.xii.35); Redcross and Britomart "read" superfluous riot beneath the rich show of Malecasta's inner room and are thereby put on their guard (III.i.33); Ate's infernal origins can easily be "read" by her monstrous shape, thus warning the observer how to approach her (IV.i.26); Envy's bones can be "read" through her cheeks, teaching the reader how empty and death-like she is (V.xii.29). When characters "read aright" in this fashion, Spenser implies, they are using both their senses and their rational powers properly to confront a present event and to prepare for a future one. Again, however, it is Spenser's decision to use the verb *read* that makes these instances revealing: since each of the actions could be rendered more objectively and literally by the verb *see*, Spenser again warns us that all observations are metaphoric acts of reading—adjustments of past to present, present to future, outsides to insides—whether we are conscious of the inter-pretive process or not. Furthermore, in a world in which we are saved or lost by the moral choices we make, we must be reminded of the fact that every perception potentially dooms us to such a choice. We do not simply see an-other person or event; we "read" them. And unless we do read them, we are likely, literally, to misread them. The analogy between reading and ethical action is here totally collapsed. Perception is a moral activity.

Characters who cannot read or who misread others are nearly as common in *The Faerie Queene* as those who correctly read.[9] Indeed, such instances are merely the inverse of those just described, but they are often rendered more dramatically as Spenser tries to intensify the difficulties reading occasions. That Spenser here complicates the act of reading is also clear from the fact that both good and evil characters are involved. Morality, in other words, ensures neither the capacity to read aright nor the ability to read at all. Scudamour cannot "aread a right" what has become of Amoret (IV.vi.35); no one can "read" the Salvage Knight who enters Satyrane's tournament (IV.iv.39); Timias lets himself grow so disheveled in the forest that he cannot be "read" (IV.vii.40); Marinell's mother cannot "read" the root of his malady (IV.xii.22); Britomart cannot reach a full understanding of Isis Temple be-cause she has never seen or "read" its like (V.vii.5); and Burbon "cannot read aright" why Flourdelis has forsaken him (V.xi.49). At times Spenser height-ens the character's inability to read by increasing the irony involved in his attempt. Britomart, "oft and oft" "ouer-read[ing]" the phrase *Be bold* in Busyrane's castle, still cannot "find what sence it figured" (III.xi.50). And

Arthur, despite having "rightly read" Belphoebe's name carved in the forest trees, still does not know what the name means or whom it signifies (IV.viii.46).

In most of these passages, Spenser dramatizes the conditions which both call for and hinder right reading. The various readers "see" a given fact—a figure, an illness, a temple, a word—but cannot "read" its meaning, cannot penetrate the veil the fact itself erects between surface and depth, outside and inside, signifier and signified. Such disparities are felt by all the characters, but they are neither understood nor resolved. Hence the activity of accommodating the disparities into metaphoric relation—the business of "reading"—is restricted to literal observation. In each of these instances, Spenser's use of the verb is ironic, for reading is precisely what the characters fail to do.

Misreadings are also dramatic and ironic. Scudamour "reads" the fact that many knights have fallen before her spear as evidence of Britomart's treachery (IV.vi.7); and Turpin argues that he will be "read" as base if he aids Serena (VI.iii.31). A more striking example occurs at the end of Book I when Archimago thrusts Duessa's letter into the hands of Una's father. The letter itself is framed by Spenser's reference to the sire's interpretive act:

> Then to his hands that writ he did betake,
> Which he disclosing, red thus, as the paper spake.   [I.xii.25]
>
> When he these bitter byting words had red,
> The tydings straunge did him abashed make.   [I.xii.29]

Despite having been witness to the grand battle between Redcross and the dragon, despite having given his lands and his daughter over to Redcross and hearing of the knight's commitment to serve the Faerie Queene, and despite the presence of Una in her unveiled state of troth-fulness, the father still misreads the letter. He looks on Redcross now "with doubtfull eyes," a formulaic lack of faith already witnessed several times in the book, one reminding us of "how doubtfully all Allegories may be construed" and "misconstructed." Obviously, part of Spenser's point here is the seductive power of Archimago and Duessa; equally important, however, is his insistence that even in this instance of clear and evident truth misreading can occur. Later, in Book II, Duessa contrives a fictional account for Guyon concerning Redcross; Guyon, like Una's father, hastily misjudges. Again Spenser uses his key verb: "False traytour certes (said the Faerie knight) / I read the man" (II.i.17). When Guyon later tells Redcross that a false knight "red" a complaint of outrage falsely against him, the irony reverberates: Guyon himself has been the false-reading knight.

These instances of either misreading or nonreading are reasonably straightforward. That is, we either realize the characters' mistakes as they occur, or we usually know the information they are unable to "read." Hence we remain at some ironic distance from them and are not really implicated (save as potential "readers") in the processes of their reading. Yet in both contexts, Spenser forces us to recognize that the characters' actions are readings and to be aware of how inadequate those readings are, either in generating the proper ethical action or in leading them to the truth. We are asked, in other words, to understand that reading is a process of inventing mimetic metaphors; when such invention does not take place, reading degenerates into literal dichotomies and falsely conceived ethical options. Having established and forced us to judge improper acts of reading, Spenser can go on to show us that our own observations of reading are also acts of reading and thus susceptible to the same difficulties and the same judgment.

One strategy for involving the reader directly in the reading process[10] is Spenser's use of the verb *to read* as a sign of knowledge shared by poet and reader. Nilus's brood, we are told, consists of more ugly monsters than man could elsewhere read (I.i.21). We are invited, in this line, to complement and complete the poet's description by recalling other descriptions of monstrous shapes and to perceive their mimetic relation to the poet's own metaphor. When Redcross falls beside the Tree of Life, we are asked to supply out of our communal knowledge the "great vertues" which "were redd" into the metaphoric fruit of that metaphoric tree (I.xi.46). In Book III, Spenser describes Merlin's looking glass by twice appealing to our own reading:

> Who wonders not, that reades so wonderous worke?
> But who does wonder, that has red the Towre,
> Wherein th'Aegyptian *Phao* long did lurke.   [III.ii.20]

A slightly different strategy is used in the narrator's "prologue" to Canto iv of Book III. Invoking the medieval formula of *ubi sunt*, the narrator asks where all the glorious women-warriors have gone. In the following stanzas, he gives us the answer—they have become part of our literary heritage, our reading:

> For all too long I burne with enuy sore,
> To heare the warlike feates, which *Homere* spake
> Of bold *Penthesilee*, which made a lake
> Of *Greekish* bloud so oft in *Troian* plaine;
> But when I read, how stout *Debora* strake
> Proud *Sisera*, and how *Camill'* hath slaine
> The huge *Orsilochus*, I swell with great disdaine.   [III.iv.2]

Spenser multiplies ironies here, of course, by perhaps unwittingly reducing the historical Deborah to the same fictional status as Virgil's Camilla; but his purpose clearly is to urge the reader to recall famous women he has met in his reading. As before, Spenser uses the strategy to force the reader to flesh out the poetic portrait: Britomart metaphorically incorporates and accommodates all previous women-warriors, both those the poet names and those the reader recollects. Additionally, the reader is asked to see that the process by which the textual heroines give rise mimetically to the metaphor the poet has "made" is the same process by which the reader "reads" the metaphor that Britomart is. In fact, it is precisely because both poet and reader share the creative process that the text can speak metaphorically. The reader is thus again invited to participate directly in the activity of the poet, recreating by means of his past reading the contextual significance of the present moment in the poetic narrative. Both poet and reader, we might say, "read" the literary ancestry of the metaphoric heroine and thus simultaneously "speak" it.

Spenser also uses this strategy to direct his reader where to read—to other passages in his own poem or to other works altogether. At the end of his description of the Garden of Adonis, Spenser identifies its chief inhabitants and sorts them by pairs: Venus and Adonis, Psyche and Cupid, Amoret and Scudamour. Scudamour is essential to this series as the final human embodiment of the Venerian principle defining the Garden and the six mimetic figures. Yet Spenser cannot stop here to tell his story; so he enjoins the reader to expect it later: "As ye may elsewhere read that ruefull history" (III.vi.53). At the end of Book III, Spenser returns to an earlier narrative of Britomart, "Who with Sir *Satyrane*, as earst ye red," is riding forth from Malbecco's house (III.xi.3). Both passages, looking forward and backward in *The Faerie Queene* itself, again put the reader in the position of "construing" and "re-constructing" the poet's text. By relating one passage to another, accommodating one context to a later or an earlier one, the reader's reading metaphorically imitates the poet's writing and "makes" the text itself speak metaphorically. Such active participation in the fiction-making process privileges the reader's memory of prior incidents, characters, descriptions, even single words, and it defines the tremendous demands Spenser puts upon the reading process.[11] It also suggests the obligations of that process, for unless the reader does accommodate the narratively discrete passages, his reading of any one forces it into literal disparity.

The reader's reading of external texts is also required by the poem. In a simple example, Spenser directs us to Alain de Lille to "read" how Nature is dressed (VII.vii.9). In a more complex instance, Spenser begins his description of the wedding of Thames and Medway by directing us to their lengthy wooing, "as we in records reed" (IV.xi.8). He then attempts to catalogue the attendant rivers, but hedges his list by humbly protesting that he cannot recount them all, "nor read the saluage cuntreis, thorough which they pace"

(IV.xi.40). Finally, pretending to be overwhelmed by the sheer number of rivers he has described, he pleads:

> Witnesse th'exceeding fry, which there [in the sea] are fed,
> And wondrous sholes, which may of none be red.
> Then blame me not, if I haue err'd in count
> Of Gods, of Nymphs, of riuers yet vnred.   [IV.xii.2]

This particular sequence of "readings" is masterfully controlled. Fully aware of the narrative difficulties in making his catalogue encyclopedic, Spenser first invokes the assistance of our reading to complete it. But by Canto xii, he is so confident of his success that he can challenge our reading directly: if he has not named a river, it remains "vnred." [12]

All of the instances we have treated here force the reader to acknowledge that his participation in the poet's text involves more than his current attention or simple observation. Because Spenser repeatedly calls upon what the reader has read elsewhere, he challenges him to perform the act of accommodating all past readings to the present text. And in this fashion, we should note that the repetition of the verb *read* aids Spenser in his broader encyclopedic designs. Not content merely to subsume preceding epics and romances, he wants the poem to subsume all prior and to direct all future readings. As we have seen in *The Shepheardes Calender*, even the formal genres of the work contribute to the opening of the textual metaphors and of the metaphor that is the text. The metaphor that is the poet's "wise rede" accommodates any and all particular generic "readings." The same point is made even when Spenser inverts his stance: this "reading" is all readings, for all else is "yet vnred."

As we have been emphasizing, the strategies that enlist the reader's active participation in creating the poem also force upon him a measure of responsibility for the poem. The text is not simply the poet's "wise rede" to a reader; it is equally a reader's "wise reading" of the poet. "To read," therefore, defines the semantic space in which poet and reader share in the literary task and become responsible to each other. And just as Spenser has articulated his own obligations to read aright to us, so he demands that we read him aright. As our Sidneyan paradigm has taught us, the reader's imitation imitates the poet's imitation, and reader and poet must join in the same verbal act of speaking-reading metaphorically.

So far we have focused on a few of the narrative *readings* out of which Spenser conceives the metaphor *to read*. And while he has used the disparities between good readings and bad ones, faithful readings and doubtful ones, to create that metaphor, he has not seriously questioned whether right reading can actually be performed. He has not, that is, made even right reading provisional. It does not take Spenser long, however, to do so. In Book I, Prince Arthur tells Una that "Full hard it is . . . to read aright / The course of heauenly cause" (I.ix.6). By itself, Arthur's statement could be interpreted as nothing more than his humble acknowledgment of the greater mysteries of God which are beyond human understanding. But the phrase "full hard it is" becomes formulaic in the poem, a figure constantly reminding us that right reading of all kinds is inevitably problematical and provisional.

In Alma's castle we meet Fidelia, who carries a sacred book which "none could read, except she did them teach" (I.x.19); her text is comprised, moreover, of "darke things," "hard to be vnderstood" (I.x.13). In the Bower of Bliss, we are told that "Right hard it was, for wight, which did it heare, / To read, what manner musicke" was made there (II.xii.70). Florimell tells the old fisherman into whose boat she has fled that she cannot "read aright, / What hard misfortune" brought her there (III.viii.23). The numerous figures of Busyrane's rout are "hard to read" (III.xii.25). The false Florimell is "so hard . . . to be ared" that all take her for the true Florimell (IV.v.15). Reading, in short, is always difficult business. The narrator, his characters, and his own readers all seem to see through a glass darkly, or, in the Bishops Bible version we cited earlier, they seem to read "through a dark speaking." The covert veils drawn by the fiction over the truth are never easy to penetrate. At times Spenser goes so far as to suggest that right reading is a blessing granted only by God. As in the dedication to *Virgils Gnat*, the "Oedipus" who pierces through the textual riddle must have been granted the "power of some diuining spright." He must have been taught by faith or had his text enlightened by Christ's lamp of heavenly wisdom.

And yet, surprisingly enough, certain kinds of reading seem remarkably easy. Archimago, narrating for Una the "death" of Redcross, which "sad sight . . . [his] eies haue red" (I.vi.36), has little difficulty convincing her that his reading is true. Lechery's ability to dance, sing, tell fortunes, and "read in louing bookes" is particularly effective not only in teaching but also in directly moving his "readers" (I.iv.25). Despair quickly seduces Terwin when he "areeds" strange tidings and adventures (I.ix.28). Mammon "reads" Guyon as rash and heedless of himself (II.vii.7), while Guyon seems strangely blind to what the demon so quickly discerns. Hellenore easily reads the secret meanings in Paridell's glances and the profane message of his spilled wine, while Britomart and Satyrane apparently "read" nothing at all (III.ix.28–30). And Kingdom's Care, in the most obviously dangerous passage of Spenser's political mirror in Book V, reads "high regards and reasons" against Duessa so convincingly that Arthur and Artegall are led to urge against Mercilla's (and Elizabeth's) judgment (V.ix.43). That such blatantly evil characters—with the exception of Kingdom's Care, who is merely overzealous—have no difficulty either in reading themselves or in making their meanings clear to others raises considerable question about man's power to read. Is it indeed a God-given skill or an instrument of the demonic forces? At the very least, Spenser here returns to an issue that he has not resolved satisfactorily: why are *mala carmina* always read plainly and easily when *bona carmina* must be seen "in cyphers"? And why are such *mala carmina* so effective in moving their readers when *bona carmina* seem hardly to move at all? This question obviously addresses the "ending end" of poetry, for if narrative actions are evoked more easily by literal false readings, does reading metaphorically actually hinder ethical action?

Spenser brings such questions to bear upon himself by exploring the power of his own narrator to "read aright," and he discovers some troubling answers. From the simple *humilitas* trope confessing that he is "all too meane" to blazon forth the truth which "the sacred Muse areeds" (I.Pro.1), the narrator grows increasingly less able to read portions of his own text. He cannot read the fruits of the Garden of Proserpina (II.vii.51), the kind of music heard in the Bower of Bliss (II.xii.70), the names or natures of the fantasies attacking "wauering wemens witt" (III.xii.26), what womb bore Lust (IV.vii.7), all the rivers at the wedding of Thames and Medway (IV.xi.40), or even the identity of the fourth Grace to whom his surrogate pipes on Mount Acidale (VI.x.25). It is evident that such confessions go beyond any simple trope of authorial humility. In a world in which "least part to vs is red," the narrator's inability fully to read his own tale is a clear warning against interpretive presumption. In fact, the narrator's confessions of inadequacy are set in striking opposition to the attitudes of the many bad readers in the poem. Archimago never questions his ability to read; nor does Ate, or Sclaunder, or Detraction. It is precisely their arbitrary presumption that defines, in part, the falseness of their several readings. Spenser here forces us, along with the narrator, to concede that all readings are provisional, that too satisfactory an interpretation is likely to prove simply the closure of misreading.

The methodology of Spenser's own narrative enforces this point again and again. After reading of so many false hermits we begin to interpret all hermits as false, only to be confronted by a good one. After witnessing the dangers apparently inherent in all descents into a cave, we begin to read Redcross as exceedingly foolish in his desire to enter yet one more in the Despair episode. We must learn, with him, the necessity of descending at times in order to ascend. We are constantly trapped into misreadings of this sort by Spenser's habit of giving first *mala* and only later *bona* meanings or readings to figures, objects, and events. We are led into imitating the various false speakers in the poem by drawing these passages to premature closure. We must learn that no single item is doomed to literal disparity and that all figures or actions are capable of being opened to metaphoric parity. Here again Spenser defines the mind faithful to such metaphors as one that reads properly: "for good by paragone / Of euill, may more notably be rad" (III.ix.2).

Although our survey of Spenser's "rede" has been selective and rapid, it is clear that he devotes considerable attention to the activities this verb expresses. Equally clear is the fact that Spenser sees these activities as both difficult for the reader and threatening to his own text. At this point, it may be instructive to summarize the distinct kinds of "work" the poem invents out of this crucial infinitive.[13]

1. to decree III.x.44; IV.xii.27; VII.vii.Arg.
2. to divine, prophesy I.viii.21; III.i.16; V. Pro.2
3. to declare, tell I.viii.31; I.ix.29; II.Pro.2
4. to guess, conjecture II.xii.70; III.vii.16; IV.iv.39
5. to interpret, unriddle II.i.7; III.ii.33; IV.v.15
6. to counsel, advise I.Pro.1; I.i.13; I.xii.28
7. to decide, judge II.i.17; V.iii.35; V.xii.9
8. to peruse, inspect I.i.37; I.iv.19; I.xii.25
9. to think, suppose III.viii.47; VI.iii.31; VI.viii.31
10. to understand, proclaim meaning of II.xii.9; III.xii.25; III.xii.26
11. to see, discern I.i.21; V.vi.8; V.xi.39
12. to make out character by outward signs I.vi.11; II.iii.24; II.viii.23
13. to learn I.viii.33; II.ix.2; IV.viii.13
14. to teach I.x.51; I.x.67; IV.xii.2
15. to speak of, name or call I.vii.46; II.vi.9; III.vi.28

Confronted by such an astonishing array of literal textual possibilities, we cannot easily read "to read." Spenser calls into constant question not only our interpretive readings of various figures and events, but also our simplest presumptions about reading itself. The meaning of any given textual "reading" can alternate between thoughtlessly saying and rationally interpreting, between guessing a meaning and knowing one, between falsely presuming an answer and rightly deducing one. Reading can be the action of a speaker or the action of his auditor; it can mean scrutinizing the past or foretelling the future; it can imply having an abstract Idea or assigning a particular name. By reading one receives something, and through reading one proclaims, announces, and gives something. The metaphoric activity "to read," in short, encompasses and accommodates both learning and teaching, both our task and the poet's, and all the ethical activities, both positive and negative, into which these dichotomies can be bodied forth.

Two final instances of Spenser's use of "read" as a noun rather than a verb again underscore the dangers of reading as a moral activity. In the proem to Book V, Spenser addresses his sovereign Queen, whose role as earthly justice he is about to depict. Realizing the personal risks he is taking in broaching so sensitive and political an issue, Spenser tries to safeguard his narrative position by humbly excusing himself:

> Dread Souerayne Goddesse, that doest highest sit
> In seate of iudgement, in th'Almighties stead,
> And with magnificke might and wondrous wit
> Doest to thy people righteous doome aread,
> That furthest Nations filles with awfull dread,
> Pardon the boldnesse of thy basest thrall,
> That dare discourse of so diuine a read.   [V.Pro.11]

Actually, Spenser is not humble at all in these lines: he confronts the political risk directly and, in his own word, boldly. Yet the ambiguities of the final line—both "discourse" and "a-read" can be taken as noun or verb—betray him by revealing his narrative presumptions. He is presumptuous in thinking he can read aright his divine sovereign's discourse, and presumptuous as well in attempting to speak aright about her divine judgment.[14] Right speaking and right reading, simultaneously involved, are equally problematical. Unfortunately, neither the poet nor his reader can hope to escape either problem.

Spenser's acknowledgment of that fact conditions his portrait of the most vicious false-speaker and misreader in the poem, the Blatant Beast. As suggested in the preceding chapter, Spenser comes to realize that it is primarily his own text that has bred the Beast's envious detractions and backbitings, his wrong-speaking and faultfinding. Had he not attempted his own presumptuous "readings" of Justice and Courtesy, the Beast might have remained imprisoned within the fiction. But the Beast is at large again, and in contemporary society where he can attack the poet himself. The poet's "readings" have provided the opportunity for a second reader to abuse his *bona carmina*, an opportunity to turn good speech into bad speaking, "wise rede" into misreading. But as the hermit's healing of Serena and Timias makes clear, reading is also the only cure for the Beast's slanderous bite. Searching the inner wounds of the unfortunate pair, the hermit perceives that instead of surgery they need "to be disciplinde / With holesome reede of sad sobriety" (VI.vi.5). Later, he teaches them the same lesson:

> In vaine therefore it were, with medicine
> To goe about to salue such kynd of sore,
> That rather needes wise read and discipline,
> Than outward salues, that may augment it more.   [VI.vi.13]

We may recall, in connection with these lines, that in the letter to Raleigh,

Spenser argues that his intention is to fashion a gentleman "in vertuous and gentle discipline" by presenting an historical fiction which will be a "delight to read." Here he has come full circle: if discipline must be taught by reading, reading itself must be conducted by discipline.

I have argued elsewhere that the Blatant Beast is the duplicitous double of Spenser's ideal reader, a deliberately contrived misreader whose very challenge calls forth the activity of right reading. If this argument is correct, it helps to explain why Spenser spends so much time on the Beast's origins.[15] Of particular interest in this regard is the simple fact that the Beast is brought into the narrative by the faultfinding hag, Detraction. In Book V, Spenser describes the hag's characteristic actions:

> For what soeuer good by any sayd,
>   Or doen she heard, she would streightwayes inuent,
>   How to depraue, or slaunderously vpbrayd,
>   Or to misconstrue of a mans intent,
>   And turne to ill the thing, that well was ment.
>   Therefore she vsed often to resort,
>   To common haunts, and companies frequent,
>   To hearke what any one did good report,
> To blot the same with blame, or wrest in wicked sort.   [V.xii.34]

Detraction uses the good actions or words she finds as "groundplots" for her own profitable invention. Spenser here portrays, as clearly and as powerfully as he can, a parodic Sidneyan misreading. Again a text is doubtfully misconstrued and misconstructed because the reader has lost faith in the language. Spenser warns us that if we read in this way, we are likely to become metaphoric Blatant Beasts whose *mala carmina* are "plainely to be red."

At the conclusion of his dedicatory epistle, Spenser tells Raleigh that he has summarized the basic scheme of the historical fiction so "that from thence gathering the whole intention of the conceit, ye may, as in a handfull, gripe al the discourse, which otherwise may happily seeme tedious and confused." In the terms of this chapter, we could conclude on the same note. The various narrative readings that seem either tedious or confusing are intended to teach us the constant conceit which lies behind and unifies them. Unless we grasp that conceit, and understand the ways it can be distorted by particular acts of reading, we will never learn the poet's principal lesson, his "wise rede," which is, appropriately enough, how "to read" metaphorically.

Chapter 8. Amor to Amoret: Writing and Reading Book III

In chapter 6, we suggested that Spenser's doubts about his own ability rightly to speak the heart of perfect love was cognate with his fears about the reader's ability rightly to understand that heart. By focusing again on the Sidneyan paradigm behind Book III, we can see how Spenser makes his fears the central dramatic thread of the narrative and how he shapes the book to teach us how to read it.

It may seem odd to conclude our discussion of *The Faerie Queene* with Book III, but the choice is not as arbitrary as it appears. If our earlier argument about the preliminary natures of Books I and II is correct, Book III is Spenser's first full elaboration of the faerie vehicle he will use in the remainder of the poem. The poet's decision to publish the first three books as a completed unit also implies that his essential principles have been sufficiently articulated by Book III to provide the reader with the terms necessary to understand the installment as a whole. Indeed, it can be argued that even the second installment is conditioned upon our having already mastered the lessons of the first: having learned here how to read, the second installment requires only the correct application of the reading principles we have been taught.

The continual presence of a blind, cruel, and errant Cupid in Book III has led logically to the conclusion that the thematic structure of the quest for Chastity is dialectical: Cupid represents the contrary of the sought Virtue, the Vice that must be unmasked and exorcised. Even those scholars who acknowledge that Renaissance mythographers and philosophers saw Cupid as an image of both positive and negative love, of both *vita intellectualis* and *vita voluptuaria*, still read Spenser's god of love in dialectical terms. Armed with arrows and blindfolded, he is Vice; without arms and blindfold, he is Virtue.[1] The difficulty with this approach is that it fails to uncover the subtlety of Spenser's analysis of love and may even veil his major focus. For the issue of Book III is not to find the "true" Cupid among his dialectical doubles, but to locate a proper perspective from which to view all typological Cupids, a semantic site which avoids the disparities Cupid gives rise to and which thus discloses the Idea that Cupid re-presents. The issue, in short, is how Cupid is to be read. By learning how to read him correctly, by remaining faithful to the way he speaks metaphorically, we ought to learn "why and how [his] maker made him."

The first suggestion we might offer, then, is that Spenser's Cupid represents the critical transition between the inception of love and the subsequent action a character takes on the urging of that love. In Sidneyan terms, Cupid is the mimetic model, the metaphoric fore-conceit, by which the Idea of Love is bodied forth in material acts of loving. By situating Cupid in the seam between *causa efficiens* and *causa materialis*, between initial motive and its moral effect, Spenser fundamentally alters the typical Renaissance treatment of the winged god. Rather than a metaphor explaining why the lover acts, Spenser's Cupid explains how the lover acts; and instead of having Cupid act upon the lover, Spenser has the lovers re-acting to Cupid.[2] Cupid, therefore, is not a figure of the lover which is read only by the external observer, but a conceit read by the lover himself. The success or failure of his subsequent loving is a direct result of how he reads Cupid, for Cupid provides the infinitive options which the lover's actions body forth.

This notion of Cupid as a mimetic model, as an activating fore-conceit, can be clarified by looking briefly at another Renaissance allegory of love. Botticelli's *Primavera* is, as Edgar Wind and others have shown, a programmatic allegory based upon the neo-Platonic scheme of love's progress: *emanatio, raptio, remeatio.*[3] The triads of Zephyr-Chloris-Flora and Beauty-Chastity-Passion are set in opposition to each other: the first represents a progressive, descending, productive love; the second, a receding, ascending, converting love. Similarly, Zephyr and Mercury, the outermost figures of the painting, also serve in a dialectical relationship: "To turn away from the world with the detachment of Mercury, to re-enter the world with the impetuosity of Zephyr, these are the two complementary forces of love."[4] But "complementary" implies accommodation, and it is the task of the reader to discover how the literal disparities are brought to complementary resolution.

The most interesting aspect of Botticelli's allegory, therefore, is not its dialectical structures but its motion, defined by Wind as procession, conversion, and reascent. What, it could be asked, sets this movement moving? It cannot be Venus, for she, as the infolded figure out of which all the others evolve, is singularly static and outside the frame of motion. Nor can it logically be Zephyr, even though he "drives" the first triad.[5] The only figure never extensively treated by criticism on the painting is Cupid, whom Wind offhandedly describes as passionate, impetuous, and energetic. Not only does this gloss restrict Cupid's role to the dialectical groundplot of the painting, but it also encourages us to slight his significance by calling him simply "an agent of Venus." Perhaps the reluctance of art historians to explicate Cupid any further is itself a clue, for Cupid does not function here as a figure of the same status or delineation (he is not even in the same spatial plane) as the rest of Botticelli's gods and goddesses, and hence his role is not recoverable by the usual iconographical analyses. Cupid is the first mover of the love Venus represents; he is a motion, not a being. Consequently, the movement of the painting does not begin with Zephyr but with Cupid, the only figure besides the static Venus who plays no part at all in the dialectical semantics of the programme. He is rather the activating principle that allows the dialectical meanings to accrue and the accommodating principle that permits them to resolve. In Sidneyan terms, since Venus represents the Idea of Love and the triadic, dialectical figures the bodied forth, unfolded, matter of that Idea (i.e., "loving"), Cupid represents the action of mimesis, the initial stage in the bodying forth of the Idea, the infinitive "to love." It is precisely in this sense that Spenser's Cupid must be read.

Assuming, then, that Spenser's quest for Cupid, mirrored in Venus's search for her errant "sonne" in Canto vi, is a quest for the activating, infinitive principle of virtuous, heroic love, it is possible to trace the stages of that quest. And since we are not seeking a figure but an action, those steps are visible mainly in the key act of wounding which is repeated throughout the book. Even this fact is significant: we do not see Cupid—are not allowed to read him—until we have witnessed at least seven or eight versions of the major action associated with him.

At the end of Canto i, Britomart is wounded in Castle Joyous by Gardante's "arrow keene"; in Canto ii, she is wounded by Cupid's arrow as she views Artegall's face in her father's mirror. Obviously, the two incidents are related: Gardante's wound clarifies and affirms Cupid's chronologically earlier though narratively later one.[6] Spenser's inverted chronology is a signal to the reader: since the first wound in Book III comes from "seeing," he is encouraged to read all the following wounds as visual perspectives—readings—rather than physical hurts. Having made that point, Spenser goes on to emphasize the interpretive problem posed by Cupid's wound by having Britomart and Glauce attempt to "read" it: they discuss it at length, try various means to cure it, meditate on it, and finally seek redress from it by visiting Merlin. As Britomart continues her journey through faerieland in Canto iv, her very next action involves the wounding of Marinell. This incident is quickly followed by the forester's wounding of Timias; Belphoebe's entrance, chasing a beast she has wounded; and her subsequent heart-wounding of Timias. In Canto vi, as Venus seeks Cupid, she finds only innumerable wounded hearts, and at the end of the Garden of Adonis episode, Scudamour's heart is "launched" with love's cruel wound. After the parodic woundings of Paridell, Hellenore, and Malbecco, the book ends by focusing on Amoret's wounded heart in the Castle of Busyrane and Britomart is again wounded, this time by Busyrane himself.

Certainly Spenser intends this sequence of actions to represent various perspectives on the inception of love; he therefore uses the conventional Petrarchan and neo-Platonic notion of love piercing the lover. Behind these actions, of course, is the hidden archer Cupid, who, though often named and read throughout as the type shaping the various woundings, is himself not seen until the final incident. By keeping Cupid hidden and by continuously altering the narrative focus on the seemingly traditional love-wound, Spenser never allows the reader secure knowledge of what any given wound means. The sequence shows, in fact, that wounds can be formative (Britomart becomes a woman only after being wounded),[7] reformative (Marinell changes from static sea-emblem to man only after being wounded),[8] or deformative (Malbecco degenerates into a literal emblem, a reversal of Marinell's transformation). Indeed, this range of possibilities is precisely Spenser's point. Since the distinctions between wounds which form, reform, or deform consist largely in the terms by which the wound is read, Spenser uses the ambiguity implicit in the various woundings and his own shifting perspective to clarify the metaphoric heart-wound he wants to hold forth as a fit image of human excellence, here the virtue of love or chastity. A closer look at the major incidents of wounding demonstrates how Spenser's refracting mirror finally reveals a portrait of the gentle heart acting in true and regenerating love.

One aspect of Spenser's programme is established by the first two occasions in which the action of wounding is linked to the image of the human heart. When Britomart enters Castle Joyous, she is confronted by a costly arras in which she reads the love of Venus and Adonis. In this initial, *in malo*, version of the Garden of Adonis,[9] Spenser narrates how Venus's "tender heart" is wounded by Adonis's beauty, how she in turn steals his heart away, and finally how she transforms him into a flower when he dies (III.i.34–38). An appropriate narrative for the castle of Male-casta, the myth presents the terms of a deforming love. Adonis is here not made "eterne in mutabilitie," but explicitly destroyed. In fact, the narrative sequence from Adonis to boar to flower represents a clear descent on the scale of being.

Shortly after this passage, Spenser turns aside from his description of Malecasta's attempt to "wound" Britomart by darting glances at her—an action bodying forth the conceit of love revealed in the Venus-Adonis arras—to address the ladies of his audience:

> Faire Ladies, that to loue captiued arre,
>   And chaste desires do nourish in your mind,
>   Let not her fault your sweet affections marre,
>   Ne blot the bounty of all womankind;
>   .   .   .   .
> For loue does alwayes bring forth bounteous deeds,
> And in each gentle heart desire of honour breeds.   [III.i.49]

The narrative parenthesis introduces two important correctives to the terms of the Joyous arras. The first is that true love is productive, forming and reforming; it generates "bounteous deeds," not delimiting choices or deforming stases like that of Adonis. Second, instead of a rankling or a wounded heart, the heart struck by the darts of true love is still—or maybe only then—a "gentle" one. Both points, when seen in the context of the Joyous arras, help identify the kind of action Spenser's quest sets out to find and describe—the gentle heart activating the principles of love in human society. They intimate, moreover, that the "gentle" heart transfixed with Cupid's dart is not "wounded" at all: it is pierced or impregnated so as to bring forth the moral action of reforming love. The heart properly transfixed, in other words, is that of the noble and complete gentleman *The Faerie Queene* intends to fashion.

There are four major instances of wounding in Book III: Britomart's heart-wound before Merlin's magic mirror; Belphoebe's wounding of Timias; the parodic wounds of Hellenore, Paridell, and Malbecco; and Amoret's wounded heart in the castle of Busyrane. In terms of the narrative as a whole, it is clear that Britomart's wound in Canto ii presents the incident which the remaining stories of wounding seek to explicate. For that reason, it is developed carefully and fully along a series of graduated stages. In stanza 23 of Canto ii, as Britomart stands before Merlin's mirror, the narrator lets us read his heroine's thoughts:

> But as it falleth, in the gentlest harts
>   Imperious Loue hath highest set his throne,
>   And tyrannizeth in the bitter smarts
>   Of them, that to him buxome are and prone:
>   So thought this Mayd (as maydens vse to done)
>   Whom fortune for her husband would allot,
>   Not that she lusted after any one;
>   For she pure from blame of sinfull blot,
> Yet wist her life at last must lincke in that same knot.

The ambiguity of line 5 ("So thought" refers back to lines 1–4 and ahead to lines 6–9) is deliberate: Britomart knows she must love and wonders who her husband will be; but she also conceives of love as tyrannical and as a "bitter smart." While acknowledging Britomart's purity and innocence, Spenser also emphasizes the ironic myopia which conditions her "reading" of love and of Cupid's domination. That reading, in turn, conditions Britomart's subsequent reaction to "falling in love".

In stanza 26, Spenser humorously describes that "fall" as Britomart views Artegall for the first time:

> The Damzell well did vew his personage,
>   And liked well, ne further fastned not,

> But went her way; ne her vnguilty age
> Did weene, vnwares, that her vnlucky lot
> Lay hidden in the bottome of the pot;
> Of hurt vnwist most daunger doth redound:
> But the false Archer, which that arrow shot
> So slyly, that she did not feele the wound,
> Did smyle full smoothly at her weetlesse wofull stound.

Spenser's treatment of the narrative perspective here is significant because the narrator is made to adopt Britomart's own view: Cupid is the false archer, the wound is woeful, her lot is unlucky. None of these adjectives is true, of course, but Spenser's strategy forces the reader to give momentary assent to them simply by voicing them through the detached and observing narrator. And the fact that the narrative itself adopts this reading helps to vindicate, even to affirm, Britomart's own subsequent echoes of it. The reader is thus invited to share a perspective Spenser had suggested only three stanzas earlier was naive and distorting.

The next several references to either Britomart's wound or her heart extend the implications of reading Cupid as the false archer. In stanza 29, Britomart's "wearie spright" is overcome with "slombring rest"; but her "feeble nature" is so instantly "opprest" with "dreames, and with fantasticke sight / Of dreadfull things," that she leaps from her bed "As one with vew of ghastly feends affright." Britomart is, in fact, frightened by a ghostly fantasy: she reads Cupid solely as a threatening and destructive force and concludes that the pain she now endures can end only in death (stanza 35). Glauce suggests this may not be the case, for "That blinded God, which hath ye blindly smit / Another arrow hath your louers hart to hit" (stanza 35). But Britomart refuses to accept Glauce's alternative reading: her heart is "launched" with "this wound wyde" and her "bleding bowels" rankle inwardly as "th'vlcer groweth daily more and more" (stanzas 37–39). Again Britomart argues that death is the only cure. As the nurse tries her various charms to salve Britomart's love-longing, the narrator once more underscores the apparent validity of the heroine's perspective:

> But loue, that is in gentle brest begonne,
> No idle charmes so lightly may remoue.   [stanza 51]

The proverb starts to correct the increasingly false terms by which love is being read, for it reminds us that Britomart's heart is not merely wounded but "gentle"; and in the next canto, Spenser sharpens his focus by concentrating on the true meaning of this "gentleness" in his heroine.

Merlin, who provides Britomart with a goal, a future, and a specific task, also corrects the myopic reading to which she subjects her wound. In so do-

ing, he corrects the reader's view of it as well. Spenser prepares carefully for
Merlin's refined reading by reminding us that love, although it may burn
dangerously in living breasts, is still the source and spring of "all noble
deeds" (III.iii.1). His words reiterate the definition of true love given in
Canto i.49, and they lead directly to Merlin's warning to Britomart:

> Most noble Virgin, that by fatall lore
> Hast learn'd to loue, let no whit thee dismay
> The hard begin, that meets thee in the dore,
> And with sharpe fits thy tender hart oppresseth sore.
>
> For so must all things excellent begin,
> And eke enrooted deepe must be that Tree,
> Whose big embodied braunches shall not lin,
> Till they to heauens hight forth stretched bee.   [III.iii.21–22]

Britomart's heart is oppressed, says Merlin, by a "fatall lore," by a false reading through which Britomart has "learn'd to loue." As we know, Merlin is
correct, for the "lore" out of which Britomart has "read" love is the destructive myth of Venus and Adonis. Merlin thus substitutes a new image, Britomart's Tree, which is both familial and communal, and which assures her that
Cupid's wound is neither destructive nor fatal, but a natural and inevitable
beginning for any actively regenerating and reforming love.[10] Love is not,
therefore, a wound to be "rewed" or complained against, but a natural fact to
be accepted as part of the divine scheme. Complaint, suggests Merlin, is the
action generated by misunderstanding, inaccurate perception, and wrong
reading.

This entire narrative sequence, in which first the nurse (parodically) and
then Merlin (correctly) figure as types of Lady Philosophy correcting the
myopia of a lamenting "Boethius," parallels the two passages isolated above
at the very beginning of the book. Love's wounds may be read as producing
pain and death (the deformative view of Britomart), or as generating bounteous and societal deeds (the reformative view of Merlin). The difference,
Spenser implies, is whether the wound is read literally or metaphorically. Literal wounds lead logically to a literal death and are the product of a literal
reading ("fatall lore"); metaphoric wounds give birth to life and result from
reading metaphorically. In the three succeeding incidents Spenser repeats
this paradigmatic heart-wounding with increasingly sharper focus on the issue of how the wound is interpreted. As with Britomart, his central intent is
to clarify the human problem love poses by seeming to deform in order to
reform.

Spenser devotes the whole of Canto v to the various woundings of Timias.
The canto begins with Timias chasing the forester who has himself been pur-

suing Florimell. From ambush, the forester manages to wound Timias in the thigh with his "quiu'ring dart" (stanza 19). Since this action has been depicted several times already, the reader is alert to the potential love metaphor. When Belphoebe-Diana comes running through the woods chasing a beast she has wounded with "her arrowes keene," the narrative has at once prepared to shift its focus from beast to man (a movement ascending the scale of being and therefore seemingly reversing the deforming pattern of love involving Belphoebe's alter-image, Venus, and Adonis). As in the earlier mythological narrative, the first sign of affection occurs when the "goddess's" tender heart is pierced and the hunter turns hunted (stanza 30). The analogue to the Joyous arras could be followed through to the end of the canto: like Venus, Belphoebe's heart is wounded; like Venus, she watches daily over her squire; and again like Venus, the final "cure" involves a specific flower which does not save the lover from death. The parallel is instructive in suggesting how figures normally seen as literal opposites are closed when read metaphorically. Belphoebe-Diana, here surely representing some form of virtuous chastity, ought logically to contrast with the arras Venus, who is more nearly Male-casta. But the striking similarities in the two narratives demonstrate that Spenser is dealing with gradations and shadings, not with opposites. To read aright is to bring the apparently disparate figures into mimetic and metaphoric accommodation. Timias and Adonis, Belphoebe and Venus are all narrative embodiments of the same conceptual infinitive—to love.

As Belphoebe dresses and redresses Timias's wounds, she unwittingly hurts him in the familiar way:

> O foolish Physick, and vnfruitfull paine,
>   That heals vp one and makes another wound:
>   She his hurt thigh to him recur'd againe,
>   But hurt his hart, the which before was sound,
>   Through an vnwary dart, which did rebound
>   From her faire eyes and gracious countenaunce.
>   What bootes it him from death to be vnbound,
>   To be captiued in endlesse duraunce
> Of sorrow and despaire without aleggeaunce?
>
> Still as his wound did gather, and grow hole,
>   So still his hart woxe sore, and health decayd:
>   Madnesse to saue a part, and lose the whole.   [III.v.42–43]

A full narrative taxonomy of wounds is hinted here: Timias's "literal" wound by the forester first turns "metaphoric" (the heart-wound given him by Belphoebe), then re-turns to the "literal" (his subsequent death for love). The double wounding of Timias, like that of Britomart, leads Spenser to ex-

plore the victim's psychological reaction. For five stanzas (44–48), Timias
tries to read his love-wound and to subdue his passion with reason. His complaint against his "lucklesse lot and cruell loue" insistently focuses on what
he, like Britomart earlier, conceives to be his only option—death. Unwilling
to be so "disloyal" as to declare his love to Belphoebe, he chooses instead
to "Dye rather, dye." But this resolve proves merely rhetorical as Timias
quickly succumbs to Cupid's power. Spenser's description of this yielding is
significant in heightening the lover's own distorted perspective:

> Thus warreid he long time against his will,
>> Till that through weaknesse he was forst at last,
>> To yield himselfe vnto the mighty ill:
>> Which as a victour proud, gan ransack fast
>> His inward parts, and all his entrayles wast,
>> That neither bloud in face, nor life in hart
>> It left . . . .   [stanza 48]

Then, in stanzas 49–50, Spenser startles the reader by apparently literalizing
the squire's metaphoric condition:

>> Yet neuer he his hart to her reuealed,
>> But rather chose to dye for sorrow great,
>> Then with dishonorable termes her to entreat.

Whatever else Belphoebe and Timias may represent in the poem,[11] Spenser's focus here is on the Cupidean heart-wound that is unspoken, misread,
and unread. Because Timias reads his heart as wounded, he presumes that
allowing Belphoebe to read it would be to accuse her of cruelty. He decides,
therefore, not to speak of it. Because Belphoebe cannot read his heart, she is
unable to offer the sweet cordial and sovereign salve which could cure the
apparent wound.[12] In this connection, we may recall that Britomart's heart-
wound is "cured" precisely because she allows it to be reread. Timias, having
lost faith in his "reader" by reading her as his antagonist, loses also the opportunity of a corrective reading. By not returning to the squire in the remainder of the canto (indeed in the remainder of Book III), Spenser invites
the reader to presume that Timias actually dies. The irony of deriving a literal
self-destruction from a metaphoric misreading alerts us again to the ethical
effects of not knowing how to read aright. Any reading wrongly derived becomes a "fatall lore."

The third major episode in which Spenser explores the human significance
of love's wound involves the parodic couple, Paridell and Hellenore. Spenser
treats their entire courtship with fairly broad humor, but underneath is yet
another version of Cupid's triumph. Sitting at Malbecco's table, the two cast
secret and telling (the pun is intended) glances at one another:

> she sent at him one firie dart, whose hed
> Empoisned was with priuy lust, and gealous dread.
>
> He from that deadly throw made no defence,
>   But to the wound his weake hart opened wyde;
>   The wicked engine through false influence,
>   Past through his eyes, and secretly did glyde
>   Into his hart, which it did sorely gryde.
>   But nothing new to him was that same paine,
>   Ne paine at all; for he so oft had tryde
>   The powre thereof . . .   [III.ix.28–29]

Unlike Timias, Paridell lets his wound be spoken and consequently read:

> Thenceforth to her he sought to intimate
>   His inward griefe, by meanes to him well knowne:
>   . . . .
>   Or therein write to lett his loue be showne;
>   Which well she red out of the learned line.   [III.ix.30]

All the usual terms of Cupidean love are here: dart, empoisoned, deadly, wound, wicked, false, secret, pain, power, and grief. But to Paridell and Hellenore, the terms are mere deceits: they speak the opposite of what they mean. Ironically, these two professional lovers are better readers of love's language than Spenser's true lovers. At least they understand that the terms cannot be taken literally. Much of the humor of the incident, in fact, resides in the contrast between these would-be lovers' playful perspective on Cupid's wound and Spenser's other lovers, who read their wounds with a fatal or deadly seriousness.

When Britomart learns from Merlin her historical and personal destinies, her reading of the love-wound alters radically. Paridell ironically shares Britomart's historical destiny, for as a descendant of Troy his line crosses hers in the lineage of Troynovant. Yet for Paridell, it is precisely the historical lineage which blinds him and, as it were, reliteralizes his reading. Instead of engendering a reformed society, Paridell's history dooms him literally to repeating Paris's initial rape. Spenser underscores the blasphemous misspeaking and misreading of Paridell by having him use the story of his lineage solely as an instrument of seduction.

By an ingenious shift of his own narrative perspective, Spenser reintroduces the seriousness of Cupid's wound by playing the wanton and irresponsible lovers off against Malbecco, the duped and cuckolded husband. A parody of the quest for Cupid, Malbecco's quest for the errant Hellenore ends when he finds her sated among the Satyrs. Driven by rage and jealousy, he flees over hill and dale:

> Griefe, and despight, and gealosie, and scorne
> Did all the way him follow hard behind,
> And he himselfe himselfe loath'd so forlorne,
> So shamefully forlorne of womankind;
> That as a Snake, still lurked in his wounded mind.   [III.x.55]

Significantly, it is not Malbecco's heart, but his mind, that is wounded, and Spenser immediately goes on to describe the deformation such a wound can occasion as Malbecco transforms himself from a human being into a literary emblem:

> . . . he through priuy griefe, and horrour vaine,
> Is woxen so deform'd, that he has quight
> Forgot he was a man, and *Gealosie* is hight.   [III.x.60]

The narrative strategy here is extremely clever as Spenser, for the first time in the poem, details with precision the process by which wrong reading is capable of deforming a man into a fixed abstraction.[13] It is the same process that might have transformed the erring and errant Redcross into Error had he not expanded his naive and literalizing perspective by adding faith. More important, Spenser's description of Malbecco's deformation reintroduces the image of Cupid's dart by again extending literally the earlier readings which link that dart and the wound it causes with death:

> Ne euer is he wont on ought to feed,
>   But toades and frogs, his pasture poysonous,
>   Which in his cold complexion do breed
>   A filthy bloud, or humour rancorous,
>   Matter of doubt and dread suspitious,
>   That doth with curelesse care consume the hart,
>   Corrupts the stomacke with gall vitious,
>   Croscuts the liuer with internall smart,
> And doth transfixe the soule with deathes eternal dart.   [III.x.59]

The wonderfully incremental rhythm here and the dramatic shift in verb tense force Malbecco's myopic perspective to its logical end. Like all misreaders in *The Faerie Queene*, his initial fault is a loss of faith and a concurrent fall into doubt which results in a "fatall lore." The subtle allusion to the mythic Prometheus[14] implies that Malbecco has transgressed human limits and, as a result, deformed himself, literally killed his humanness by transfixing now his soul with death's dart. As in the narrative of Timias, the transfixing dart, earlier just a metaphor for the piercing heart-wounds of love, here discloses the destructive effects of misreading. If we recall the Renaissance myth that Cupid and Death exchange darts, we can see how Spenser recreates that myth in terms of its human mimesis. Cupid, misread and misinterpreted, becomes Death. As Spenser summarizes in the opening stanza of Canto xi, the "fatall lore" of jealousy, a reading which results from having displaced love's faith by doubt,

> mak'st the louing hart
> With hatefull thoughts to languish and to pine,
> And feed it selfe with selfe-consuming smart.

The problem Spenser is addressing here can be clarified by recalling his earlier use of emblem in the book. Whereas Malbecco begins as a man and ends as an emblem, Marinell begins as an emblem and ends as a man. The wounds that both figures receive offer opportunities to reread their conditions. And the way they learn to read suggests again the stakes that are involved. Malbecco's reading moves increasingly within, into literal enclosure, and finally into death. Marinell, who begins by fearing death, learns to read his wound properly by moving outside himself, by opening his perspective; and he discovers not death, but life.

It is perhaps not unwarranted to suggest that the deadly regression into emblem and the lively progression out of emblem speak metaphorically of the alternative ways of reading *The Faerie Queene* itself. The interpretive quest for a permanent and fixed Idea, for a rigid or naive allegory, is a death of the mimetic process the fiction tries to set in motion. Only by freeing the Idea from its status as emblem can the reader make the transition back to ethical life and human action. Spenser's task is not to define or to emblematize, but to offer the opportunity to invent. And our task, analogously, is not to seek the emblems but to rewrite them, to use them as the groundplots of our own profitable actions.[15]

Spenser's final exploration of the wounded heart in Book III concerns Amoret's torture in the enchanted palace of Busyrane and her subsequent rescue by Britomart.[16] This difficult passage is clarified in part when framed by the sequence of woundings just described. In fact, Spenser may have arranged these four incidents as contrasting pairs, Britomart and Amoret serving as the external, right-reading frame; Timias and Malbecco serving as the internal, wrong-reading one. Both pairs are adumbrations of the reforming / deforming paradigm Spenser sets out at the beginning of the book. Amoret's torture, therefore, takes its meaning not only by its contrast to the two preceding incidents of "fatall lore," but also by its typological link to Britomart's creative story. And, as in Britomart's case, Amoret's reformation is brought about by a shift in psychological perspective which entails a full and knowledgeable reading of the destiny metaphorically spoken in Cupid's wound, a substitution of faith for fear, a faithful reading rather than a doubtful one.

Spenser begins this incident by having Scudamour, "Cupid's man," describe Busyrane's torture of Amoret:

> Whilest deadly torments do her chast brest rend,
> And the sharpe steele doth riue her hart in tway.   [III.xi.11]

Instead of focusing immediately on the wound, however, Spenser leads Britomart and the reader through Busyrane's castle slowly and carefully, paying more attention to images of the steel dart than to the wounded heart. We experience and witness the transfixed heart, in other words, only after experiencing the full terror of the transfixing dart.[17] The rhetorical / narrative strategy is thus parallel to that used in the quest for Cupid himself: we see the action before we are allowed to read the actor. Similarly, the strategy forces the reader to share momentarily the same fears and doubts as the love-struck heroine, for after the "deaths" of Timias and Malbecco there is no longer any question about the destructive potential of Cupid's dart.

The first view of the dart comes in Busyrane's tapestries, which offer another reading of Cupid[18] by depicting his victories over the entire panoply of gods, as well as "Kings Queenes, Lords Ladies, Knights and Damzels gent" (III.xi.46). In Canto xi, stanza 30, Jove feels "the point of his hart-piercing dart"; in stanza 36, Phoebus is struck "with a leaden dart"; in stanza 44, Mars is depicted with "vnwarlike smarts," and "painted full of burning darts, / And many wide woundes launched through his inner parts." Finally, the whole border of the tapestry is shown to consist

> Of broken bowes and arrowes shiuered short,
> And a long bloudy riuer through them rayld,
> So liuely and so like, that liuing sence it fayld.   [xi.46]

The tapestry invites comparison, of course, with the Venus-Adonis arras in Castle Joyous, and a similar tale of deforming love might therefore be anticipated. This itself is a sign of Spenser's larger purposes, since the constant which draws the disparate sites of Joyous and joy-less into mimetic relation is the figure of Cupid presiding over both.

The culmination of the extended descriptive passage is the statue of Cupid himself. Since we have waited eleven cantos to see this figure whom so many have misread, it is initially surprising to find that he is nothing more than a summary of already familiar terms: blindfolded, cruel, a "mortall" bow and arrows. Our second surprise comes upon reflecting that we still have not actually "seen" Cupid; all we see is an icon, a representation or metaphor. Ironically, this is all Cupid has ever been, but we may be a bit frustrated at having that fact so blatantly spelled out to us:

> Blindfold he was, and in his cruell fist
> A mortall bow and arrowes keene did hold,

> With which he shot at randon, when him list,
> Some headed with sad lead, some with pure gold;
> (*Ah man beware, how thou those darts behold*). [III.xi.48, my italics]

Spenser is absolutely precise in this parenthesis: as emphasized throughout Book III, and as the following narrative of Amoret will illustrate once more, the only danger posed by either Cupid or his "deadly" dart is the interpretive one of how they are beheld. Only a reader can make this statue move or the dart strike. Spenser's parenthesis, dramatically breaking the spell of the description, calls us back to the character now called upon to read the statue, Amoret.

As Britomart watches the masque of Cupid, Grief parades by with a pair of pincers:

> With which he pinched people to the hart,
> That from thenceforth a wretched life they lad,
> In wilfull langour and consuming smart,
> Dying each day with inward wounds of dolours dart.   [xii.16]

The hyperbole of this description addresses the reader's cleansed and sharpened perception. Death has become once more metaphoric and hence less terrifying, and the consuming smart is self-inflicted and willful. Then, in the midst of the procession, Spenser allows the first sight of Amoret:

> Her brest all naked, as net iuory,
>   Without adorne of gold or siluer bright,
>   Wherewith the Craftesman wonts it beautify,
>   Of her dew honour was despoyled quight,
>   And a wide wound therein (O ruefull sight)
>   Entrenched deepe with knife accursed keene,
>   Yet freshly bleeding forth her fainting spright,
>   (The worke of cruell hand) was to be seene,
> That dyde in sanguine red her skin all snowy cleene.
>
> At that wide orifice her trembling hart
>   Was drawne forth, and in siluer basin layd,
>   Quite through transfixed with a deadly dart,
>   And in her bloud yet steeming fresh embayd.   [xii.20–21]

The description is at once dramatic and shocking, and the detail with which Spenser loads it is clearly intended to pull the reader up short. Prepared for a metaphorically wounded Amoret, we are given instead a picture that insists upon its own literalness. It is difficult here to adjust our focus sufficiently to see that the bleeding heart is Amoret's own willful perception and not simply ours, that it is a psychological extension of fear and doubt, not a perceptible fact. Again the progression of the narrative demonstrates the sureness of Spenser's art. Although the reader ought to be fully aware of the issues by now (and certainly the two hyperbolic parentheses, along with the cue-word "orifice," ought to make them even clearer), he is once more forced to adopt a reading which is patently false. The ease with which we accept that reading is itself revealing, and our inability to distinguish our perception from Amoret's perspective instructs us that the false view is perfectly natural. In this way, the reader is made to confront his own humanity as he witnesses Amoret discovering hers; he is reading, in short, his own case.[19]

In his second description of the same emblematic picture, Spenser allows the focus to clear somewhat. As Britomart enters Busyrane's chamber, the entire "rude confused rout" of Cupid's masque vanishes, leaving only Amoret and the enchanter:

> And her before the vile Enchaunter sate,
> > Figuring straunge characters of his art,
> > With liuing bloud he those characters wrate,
> > Dreadfully dropping from her dying hart,
> > Seeming transfixed with a cruell dart,
> > And all perforce to make her him to loue.
> > Ah who can loue the worker of her smart?
> > A thousand charmes he formerly did proue;
> Yet thousand charmes could not her stedfast hart remoue.   [xii.31]

Alpers has commented perceptively on the seventh line of this stanza and on its overall effect. "The worker of her smart" is a conventional epithet for the lover, here perhaps for the very one Amoret does in fact love.[20] What seemed at least straightforward torture suddenly turns to stock seduction, a seduction even slightly mocked by the observing narrator. The healing of Amoret's heart and the final cleansing of the reader's perception have already begun in this passage. Like Archimago, Busyrane is the false poet in the process of encouraging a false reading, but his figures are purely figurative, his dart only "seeming" to transfix Amoret's heart, and her "dying" is actually steadfastness and recovering faith. As Britomart leaps forward to defend Amoret, she is herself wounded by Busyrane's "wicked weapon" so that "little drops empurpled her faire brest" (stanza 33). This particular wound serves to reinforce the link between the present incident and Britomart's own love-wound at the opening of the book; it also implies that Britomart's actions in the palace serve as the final cleansing of her perception as well as Amoret's.

Britomart now moves to slay Busyrane but is stopped by Amoret, who pleads that he must live since only he can cure her wound. As Busyrane reads his figures backwards, the charms are removed (thus correcting Britomart's earlier presumptions about this impossibility), perception is cleansed, and Spenser presents the third dramatic portrait of Amoret's heart. It is important to stress the causal relationships here: because the figures are unfigured, reread and thus rewritten, the charms are removed; because the charms are removed, perception is cleansed; because perception is cleansed, the human action can be written and read as such. Without becoming too polemical, it is clear that Spenser is again discussing the problem of how to read his fiction. The human lesson cannot be recognized unless the figures are understood as purely figurative—as emblems, allegories, metaphors, personifications. The rhetorical tropes must be undone before perception can be cleansed or action can be taken. To read the figures as anything other than figurative (as characters to imitate, for example, or as literal ideals of human behavior) is simply to perpetuate the fiction, the charming *carmina*, not to make the shift from fiction to life. We need to focus, therefore, not on the way Spenser creates his figures and especially not on what they should be called, but on the ways he uncreates them, unfigures them for the purpose of moving the reader.[21] To anticipate a bit, we need to see how Spenser's unfiguring of the emblematic Amoret enlists the reader in the same act of love that she has thus far figured in the narrative. We must understand, in other words, how compassion for and recognition of the human problem Amoret re-presents, and affirmation of that problem as human, is the reader's act of faithful loving which crosses over the borders of the fiction, or which shifts the sphere of action out of the containing fiction to the real world.

The third portrait of Amoret's heart is Spenser's richest articulation and reading of the issues he has posed in the book:

> The cruell steele, which thrild her dying hart,
>   Fell softly forth, as of his owne accord,
>   And the wyde wound, which lately did dispart
> Her bleeding brest, and riuen bowels gor'd,
> Was closed vp, as it had not bene bor'd,
> And euery part to safety full sound,
> As she were neuer hurt, was soone restor'd:
> Tho when she felt her selfe to be vnbound,
> And perfect hole, prostrate she fell vnto the ground.   [xii.38]

It is difficult to resist a knowing smile as Cupid's fearful and doubtful dart suddenly loses all force and even identity in the phallic play of the opening lines of this stanza. In fact, it is hard not to read the entire description as simply Amoret's relief that her broken "maidenhead" has nonetheless left her intact. But perhaps this is too insensitive a reaction. Alpers is closer to the tone required here when he tactfully argues that "the meaning of these lines lies in the profoundly erotic sense of relaxation, wonder, and wholeness after the terrors of . . . the preceding stanzas." The healing of Amoret's heart "expresses the resolution of problems with which the whole book is concerned and in which Britomart is fully implicated." [22] Yet "resolution" is not the most appropriate word here; "re-reading" would be better. In the truly gentle heart, love's dart is not cruel at all and the desire it breeds is always activated for productive ends. Cupid's dart, in the gentle heart, serves as an impregnating force (again in Alpers' "profoundly erotic sense") engendering bounteous deeds and heroic actions which are, at the same time, very simply human.

Book III is shaped by the poetic quest for an errant Cupid; its narrative encourages us to expect that by its end Cupid will have been found. But neither Venus in Canto vi nor Spenser in Canto xii can locate him. Failing to find Amor, both questors discover Amoret. And yet, of course, Amoret is the only Amor that could be found, for Cupid was never anything more—nor less— than the infinitive option to love. Only when bodied forth in actual loving— in varieties of amoretti—does Cupid have any tangible existence.

In these terms, we can see the importance of Amoret to Spenser's programme. By reading her the poet can write Cupid, for she is the only character in Book III that remains faithful to the metaphor Cupid is. The conflicting and coequal tensions that define Amoret's condition—hating and loving, fearing and desiring, wounding and healing, binding and unbinding, doubting and having faith—define as well the disparities her actions resolve. Paradoxically, it is not Amoret who is freed in xii.38 but Amor. Freed from the various distorted readings to which men and women subject him, Cupid can now be conceived as the opportunity "to love." And insofar as the reader reads this conceit aright, he too has been freed to create what he has read by following the poet's groundplot to his own profitable invention.

Afterword

One obvious difficulty in writing any study of Spenser's poetry is that his most important poem remains unfinished. But if the terms of this study are valid, then all the poems are essentially unfinished because they are offered only as groundplots for a reader's subsequent invention, as incentives to conversation, rather than completed orations. The critical urge to sum up, to draw the activity of interpretation to a literal close, runs directly counter to Spenser's own refusal to allow such an enterprise. Like the poet, the critic is forced to call his own terms into question.

The term that has been in question throughout this study is metaphor: what does it mean to speak metaphorically, and what are the characteristics of a poetry that tries to do so? I have assumed here a certain perspective on metaphor, but that perspective must find its place among a variety of perspectives, and it must situate its definitions in relation to other conceptions of how to speak about metaphor or of the particular nature of the Spenserian metaphor. Is Spenser's metaphor, for example, a product—a speaking picture, a notable image, an allegorical abstraction—or a process—an activity of imitating? Are such metaphors already constructed and hence ready to be read, or are they constantly being made, fashioned and refashioned, by both poet and reader? One perspective separates the activity of the poet from that of the reader, whereas the other enlists them both in the same creative act. Such discrepancy returns us to the more familiar notion of Spenserian allegory as a continued metaphor or "darke conceit." What, exactly, does "continued" mean here? Does it identify a coherent line or level of meaning external to the text and consequently both unmade and uncontrolled by the poet, or does it point to the unceasing task of making metaphors both within and out of the words of the text?

The two principal metaphors of Spenser's poetry are the Poet and the Reader. As I have tried to show, the metaphor of the poet is something the poet is continually in the process of making at the same time, and by the same principles, as the reader is continually trying to make it out. The reader, no less than the poet, confronts the words of the text in order to express that metaphor. The same process describes the metaphor of the reader. There is no ideal reader external to the text to which the metaphoric vehicles refer and defer; there is only the language of the text out of which the metaphoric reader is constructed and construed. The invention of each metaphor must be the cooperative venture of both poet and reader, neither privileging his own words over the words of the other.

It would not be wrong, I think, to say that all of Spenser's poetry is focused on the writer's and the reader's uses or abuses of the word. My own sense is that this subject was opened to Spenser largely by Sidney's *Apology*, but that is not the important point. More compelling to us may be the ambivalence Spenser has to his language and the feeling he seems to harbor that however skillful his own verses might be, the verbal medium is one that resists all control. It is surely no small matter of interest that one of our three or four greatest English poets seems intent upon exposing the errors into which that language continually leads us.

Throughout this study, I have emphasized Spenser's distrust of literalizing speech, of the false disparities into which speech inevitably traps us. But it is also clear that Spenser distrusts as well a language that speaks metaphorically, that always puts off the definitive word and always defers to an unspeakable and unreadable truth. To have committed himself so completely to the written word while entertaining such doubts about that word was one of Spenser's most heroic endeavors. And the challenge he expresses in the opening book of *The Faerie Queene*—the urge to doubt versus the desire to have faith—would seem to have a direct bearing on his own vocation.

If Spenser thought about his situation as a poet in these terms, did he realize that the disparity between literal and metaphoric language is as false as any he had drawn? How can the written or spoken word be other than literal? The concrete, particular word is there, present and situated in a text or on a page, and therefore to be confronted as a perceptible fact. Yet how can it be merely literal when its meanings derive from words around or outside it? Is not the meaning of every word transferred from the site of its utterance to another site beyond that utterance? To say this is not to concede to a pessimistic model of infinite regression or to plunge us into a Derridean void or absence; it is, rather, to repeat what the Right Poet has always known—that poetry speaks one thing to mean another, that the word means what we can make it mean, that the word is both an opportunity of and an invitation to the making of meaning. That making is always metaphoric and it always follows the principles of mimesis. These are the only strictures within which language and poetry operate.

> So when I thinke to end that I begonne,
> I must begin and neuer bring to end.

Thus the spider-lover of Sonnet 23 describes his desire to bring his suit to fruitful conclusion. But the beloved, a perfect Spenserian reader, refuses to allow such a closure and thereby effaces his presumed distinction between endings and beginnings:

For with one looke she spils that long I sponne,
And with one word my whole years work doth rend.

The conditions which make the success of a narrator's text dependent upon the word or words of a narrative reader are emblematic of not only Spenser's own situation, but of his critic's as well. No less than the poet, the critic wishes "to bring to perfect end," only to discover that the work of reading Spenser, like the work to which his poetry calls us, is always endless and only just begun. Yet Spenser offers a consolation and a lesson: to speak what we can in one place is to open a place for another, and to draw one text to an end is to incite a second to begin. If the present study provides an occasion for further speaking or further reading, I, like the poet, can ask no more, "for that the ground-worke is, and end of all."

Notes

Introduction

1. These terms for false poets and wrong readers are taken from Sidney's *Apology for Poetry*. Although Spenser is thinking of the difficulties such ill-users of poetry present to the serious poet long before he could have seen Sidney's work, it is certain that Sidney's articulation of poetic abuses heightened Spenser's awareness of the subject.

2. All passages of Spenser are taken from *The Works of Edmund Spenser: A Variorum Edition*, ed. E. A. Greenlaw et al. (Baltimore, 1932–1949).

3. All quotations from the *Apology* are taken, with one noted exception and with the silent capitalization of Sidney's Idea, from *Miscellaneous Prose of Sir Philip Sidney*, ed. Katherine Duncan-Jones and Jan Van Dorsten (Oxford, 1973).

4. "Rereading Sidney's *Apology*," *JMRS* 10 (1980): 155–191.

5. "Fore-conceit" occurs only in the crucial paragraph just cited; elsewhere in the *Apology*, Sidney consistently uses the simpler "conceit." His unique "fore" in the early passage indicates merely that this conceit is set in relation to its origin (the Idea) and its end (the work or text).

6. I here alter the punctuation of the Duncan-Jones and Van Dorsten text by adopting the Ponsonby version. For a more detailed argument on this variant, see my "Opening and Closing the Sidneian Text," *Sidney Newsletter* 2 (1981): 3–6; and S. K. Heninger, *Touches of Sweet Harmony* (San Marino, 1974), pp. 307ff., and 323n.

7. We see a clue to this uniting of poet and reader in Spenser's letter to Raleigh, where he uses the same verb—*fashioning*—to define both his own activity of making the text and the reader's activity of remaking his life. A fascinating exploration of further implications of this term can be found in Stephen Greenblatt's *Renaissance Self-Fashioning* (Chicago, 1980).

8. *Commentary on Plato's Symposium*, ed. and tr. Sears Jayne (Columbia, Mo., 1944), p. 175.

9. Ernst Cassirer, *The Individual and the Cosmos in Renaissance Philosophy* (Philadelphia, 1963), pp. 66–67.

10. Henry Holland, *The Historie of Adam, or the foure-fold State of Man* (London, 1606).

11. *Allegorical Imagery* (Princeton, 1966). A recent extension of Tuve's principles, Jonathan Goldberg's *Endlesse Worke: Spenser and the Structures of Discourse* (Baltimore, 1981), appeared after my own study was completed. Although Goldberg's reliance on structuralist models seems to me to distort rather seriously Spenser's depiction of literary characters or figures, it does occasion provocative discussions of Spenserian narrative and, in a general way, supports my own assumptions.

1. *The Shepheardes Calender*

1. See especially *"My Ecchoing Song": Andrew Marvell's Poetry of Criticism* (Princeton, 1970); *The Resources of Kind* (Berkeley, 1973); and *Shakespeare's Living Art* (Princeton, 1974). Other important studies of this topic have been done by E. H. Gombrich, *Meditations on a Hobby Horse* (New York, 1963), and *Norm & Form* (New York, 1966).

2. It must be emphasized that Spenser does not conceive of the genres in the *Calender* in terms of Ideas, fore-conceits, or texts. But he does recognize that genres are metaphors, and his manipulation of generic elements does imply a discrimination between metaphoric levels. To show that those levels correspond to Sidney's three terms merely suggests how close Spenser's early practice is to Sidney's subsequent theory. The issue here is not influence but similarity of Renaissance assumptions.

3. Obviously, I am arguing from a perspective within the pastoral system. Were that perspective enlarged to include other generic possibilities, "Ye goat-herd gods" or any other pastoral poem could be seen as expanding rather than limiting generic potentials. The point, however, is that only by so broadening the generic "fix" or "set" can the poet avoid generic distortion. Hence the urge to write what Colie calls *genera mista* or *mixta*.

4. Compare Claudio Guillen's remarks on genre in *Literature as System* (Princeton, 1971), especially part 2, pp. 71–220.

5. *Spenser, Marvell, and Renaissance Pastoral* (Cambridge, Mass., 1970). As the following analysis reveals, I am much indebted to Cullen's study, though I wish to reinvoke a term he rather carefully avoids. Because he is alert to the fact that both pastoral in general and its Arcadian and Mantuan "strands" can be called "genres," Cullen shies away from this word. More often than not, he calls pastoral a "mode" and its subforms "perspectives." The problem with this solution is that it does not sufficiently address the place of genre in the poetic process. To describe the metaphoric speaking of the *Calender*, I shall use the term "genre" to mean the infinitive fore-conceit (pastoral), and the term "textual genre" to mean any particularized perspective yielding a narrative structure (thus, not only Arcadian and Mantuan, but also the pastoral subforms of fable, debate, song-contest, and so forth).

6. It may also be observed that E. K.'s discussion of the divergent opinions on when the year begins occasions the first of the poem's many debates. The persistence of debate, in fact, encourages us to think more seriously about the double-talk: not only does the term call to mind familiar definitions of metaphor—saying one thing to mean another—but also it identifies the structures within which such debates take place. Compare Cullen: "The comedy in the debates is, therefore, a comedy of character and misperception, of talking at cross-purposes, on different wavelengths . . ." (p. 33).

7. Cullen, p. 1.

8. For a detailed analysis of Spenser's epideictic rhetoric in the *Calender*, see Thomas H. Cain, *Praise in The Faerie Queene* (Lincoln, Neb., 1978), pp. 14–36.

9. See Colie, *Resources of Kind*, pp. 26, 30, 86, and 116, for more on how genres themselves can be used as metaphors.

10. Spenser's generic mixing has also been noted by Wolfgang Iser, *Spensers Arkadien: Fiktion und Geschichte in der englischen Renaissance* (Krefeld, 1970).

11. Although I would agree with the recent studies by James N. Brown and John W. Moore, Jr., that Colin is the failed poet of the *Calender*, Harry Berger proposes a progress in Colin's career that should be taken into account. Berger argues that Colin begins, in the *Calender*, as a simple *persona* in the Greek sense (a fixed posture); he is transformed in *Colin Clout* into a complex creation, half-poet, half-human being; and he ends, on Mount Acidale, as a Boethian *persona*, representing "the inmost reality of the human soul" ("The Prospect of Imagination," *SEL* 1 [1961]: 111–115). While I have no particular quarrel with this outside-to-inside progression, it does not alter Colin's function in the *Calender* itself. See Brown, "'Hence with the Nightingale will I take part': A Virgilian Orphic Allusion in Spenser's 'Avgvst'," *Thoth* 13 (1972–1973): 13–18; and Moore, "Colin Breaks His Pipe: A Reading of the 'January' Eclogue," *ELR* 5 (1975): 2–24.

12. The terms are Guillen's, cited in Colie, *Resources*, p. 7.

13. The notion of tuning occurs frequently in the *Calender*. As evident particularly in E. K.'s epistle, it seems virtually synonymous with framing.

14. In two separate studies, "The Implications of Form of *The Shepheardes Calender*," *SR* 9 (1962): 309–321, and *Touches of Sweet Harmony*, pp. 309–315, Heninger has applied the notions of *discordia concors* and micro-macrocosmic correspondences to the *Calender*. A useful addition—partly corrective—is Harry Berger's "The Spenserian Dynamics," *SEL* 8 (1968): 1–18.

2. "The Ruins of Time"

1. See W. L. Renwick, *Complaints* (London, 1928), p. 189; and Harold Stein, *Studies in Spenser's Complaints* (New York, 1934): "Even a superficial examination reveals the fact that 'The Ruins of Time' is not a finished and workmanlike job, that it is uneven in quality, that its transitions are awkward, and that it consists of four loosely articulated sections" (p. 35).

2. William Nelson, *The Poetry of Edmund Spenser* (New York, 1965), pp. 66–69; Millar Maclure, "Spenser and The Ruins of Time," in *Theatre for Spenserians*, ed. Judith Kennedy (Toronto, 1968), pp. 3–18; Peter Bayley, *Edmund Spenser: Prince of Poets* (London, 1971), pp. 55–58.

3. It might be more accurate to say that the focus on poetry is the principal unifying frame, for another is provided by Spenser's epideictic structure. Since the poem is a praise of an individual,

it follows the rhetorical formulae for *encomia*. The various sections of the poem should be seen therefore as rhetorical *loci* or places of praise. Thomas Wilson, for example, in *The Arte of Rhetorique* (1561), suggests three steps to praising any person: the orator-poet should treat things (i) before his life, (ii) during his life, and (iii) after his death. The first step, Wilson continues, should discuss the man's realm, country, city, ancestors and parents. The second treats the praiseworthy deeds the man himself has done, while the third shows the effects he had on others after his death. In general, Spenser's praise of Sir Philip follows this pattern. The public line of Verulame and the family lineage of the Dudleys conform to Wilson's first stage; the middle of Spenser's poem—lines 274–343—treats Sidney's life; the action of the Countess in becoming Spenser's patron and that of Spenser himself in writing the poem illustrate the effects of Sidney on those who outlive him.

4. Although neither Ponsonby's *Defense* nor Olney's *Apology* appeared until 1595, there can be little doubt that Spenser had seen a copy of his friend's work written some twelve to fifteen years earlier. The two met in 1579, when Spenser was invited to join Sidney in reforming English poetry; and since we know that Spenser had written a treatise on "The English Poet," it is natural to assume he would have been interested in Sidney's critical views. Specific evidence of his knowledge of the *Apology* may be found in the 1589 letter to Raleigh appended to the first installment of *The Faerie Queene*. Discussing, like Sidney, the relation between poetry, history, and philosophy, Spenser repeats both Sidney's language and his meaning when he too uses Xenophon as his literary example: "For this cause is Xenophon preferred before Plato, for that the one in the exquisite depth of his iudgement, formed a Commune welth such as it should be, but the other in the person of Cyrus and the Persians fashioned a gouernement such as might best be: So much more profitable and gratious is doctrine by ensample, then by rule." One of the Commendatory Verses affixed to the first installment summarizes the relations between the two poets more emblematically: "But *Sydney* heard him sing, and knew his voice"; "So *Spencer* was by *Sidney*'s speaches wonne."

5. The shift of speaking voice in these lines is indicated by the confession of mortality (Verlame, as a genius, is not so limited) and by the fact of song (Verlame is not technically singing and certainly not addressing Sidney).

6. Compare Goldberg's conception of "character" or "figure" in *The Faerie Queene*: "throughout book IV, the figures move in groups in ways that resemble the trajectory of some unknown, mapped by an algebraic formula onto a functional grid. In these equations X is the individual, placed and replaced in relational matrices" (*Endlesse Worke*, p. 8; see also pp. 73–121).

7. The *Complaints* is not, of course, Spenser's first fruit, but the dedication to "The Ruins," which speaks of his "first blossoms nipped and quite dead," fictively envisions it as such.

8. Some—not all—of the difficulty we have with Verlame's character is resolved by recalling that she is a distorted imitation of Verulame, not the city itself.

9. Nohrnberg, *The Analogy of The Faerie Queene* (Princeton, 1976), pp. 237–238. Fuller studies of Verlame are: Carl J. Rasmussen, "How Weak Be the Passions of Woefulness," *Spenser Studies* 2 (1981): 159–182; and Andrew Fichter, "And nought of *Rome* in *Rome* perceiu'st at all," *Spenser Studies* 2 (1981): 183–192.

10. It is not necessary to identify Burghley or any other historical figure to see the form of Spenser's argument here, but both Renwick and Stein provide information on probable contemporary allusions. More interesting is the fact that even in this early poem false detractors are singled out as the most dangerous of the poet's antagonists.

11. Again the shift of speaking voice is apparent in the nomination of "this verse" (l. 253) and "my verses" (l. 259): Verlame does not write a poem.

12. Renwick argues that Spenser's two references to Mary Dudley (ll. 260, 274ff.) are awkward and unnecessary (p. 195); but since Mary is the essential transition between the Dudleys and the Sidneys, the two references are inevitable.

13. Spenser cannot state his relationship with the Countess in blatant terms, but he implies it in dedicating the poem to her, in the praise accorded her in lines 317–322, in the fact that both have joined voices to praise Sir Philip, and by the simple strategy of turning to the principle of patronage immediately after defining their oneness in song.

14. For the sources of these and the following six emblems, as well as their possible topical allusions, see Renwick's notes, pp. 200–203, and Rasmussen's essay cited above (n. 9).

3. *Daphnaida* and *Colin Clout*

1. I do not mean to deny that the *Calender* is concerned with right and wrong poets, for Spenser's shepherds are, as we have seen, both readers and writers. Furthermore, as argued earlier, disjunctures between poet and reader, writing and reading, are not ones that Spenser usually allows. Still, it is possible to identify Spenser's general emphasis in the *Calender* as the act of reading; here, it is that of writing.

2. The best study of the relation between the poems is Duncan Harris and Nancy Steffan's "The Other Side of the Garden: An Interpretive Comparison of Chaucer's *Book of the Duchess* and Spenser's *Daphnaida*," *JMRS* 8 (1978): 17–36. See also Thomas W. Nadal, "Spenser's *Daphnaida* and Chaucer's *Book of the Duchess*," *PMLA* 23 (1908): 646–661; and Norman Berlin, "Chaucer's *Book of the Duchess* and Spenser's *Daphnaida*," *Studia Neophilologica* 38 (1966): 282–289.

3. The fullest studies of *Colin Clout* are: Sam Meyer, *An Interpretation of Colin Clout* (Notre Dame, 1969); Thomas R. Edwards, *Imagination and Power* (London, 1971), pp. 48–62; and Nancy Jo Hoffman, *Spenser's Pastorals* (Baltimore, 1977), pp. 119–142.

4. Frank Kermode, *English Pastoral Poetry* (London, 1952): "The first condition of Pastoral is that it is an urban product" (p. 14).

5. See Harris and Steffan, p. 27.

6. *In Defense of Reason*, 3d ed. (Denver, 1947), pp. 22ff.

7. Although Harris and Steffan note the problem the reader faces in the opening stanzas, they do not pursue his options far enough to see that Spenser invites him to become, at least momentarily, the black pilgrim.

8. Renato Poggioli, "The Oaten Flute," *Harvard Library Bulletin* 4 (1957): 165.

9. Harris and Steffan, pp. 30–31.

10. Donald R. Howard, *The Idea of the Canterbury Tales* (Berkeley, 1978), p. 142.

11. Spenser's pastoral, of course, is not unique in abruptly revising its view of death; as A. C. Hamilton reminds me, the revelation of Christian pastoral is usually a sudden, not a growing, awareness. It is helpful, in this light, to consider Daphne as an interpreter, a reader, of the poetic pastoral. In that guise, she directs not only Alcyon but also the poem's external reader to the correct interpretation of her death. Chaucer uses Seys in exactly the same way.

12. Harris and Steffan, p. 32. The conventionality of the "nature reversed" trope also contributes to the ironic affirmation of universal order. See O. B. Hardison, *The Enduring Monument* (Chapel Hill, 1962), pp. 116–117.

13. Harris and Steffan, p. 31.

14. Cf. Harris and Steffan: "When Alcyon discovers that the world is not what it seems, he would have it seem what he thinks it is" (p. 29). Instead of making the poem accommodate experience, Alcyon rewrites experience to fit the poem. For another reading of Alcyon's failure, see William A. Oram, "*Daphnaida* and Spenser's Later Poetry," *Spenser Studies* 2 (1981): 141–158.

15. Hoffman also discusses poetic failure in *Colin Clout*, but she thinks the failure is Spenser's. The poet is unable, because of generic restrictions, "to tell us convincingly *why* Colin Clout has come home" (p. 121); and the poem, she argues, "consists of Spenser's unsuccessful attempts to absorb into the happy [pastoral] formula his personal experience and the contingencies of an individual historical moment" (p. 126). The basis for these judgments is that Spenser, "as Colin, makes a literal journey and speaks about it directly in his own voice" (p. 126). I see no reason to assume that Colin is Spenser in the poem. Even on Mount Acidale, his seemingly brightest moment, Colin is a poet willfully and totally withdrawn from society and the world. This is a curious *in propria persona* for a humanist poet concerned primarily with reforming society. Until we learn to distinguish Colin Clout from Spenser himself, we will never be able to understand fully the poems in which Colin appears or to understand what aspects of his own tasks Spenser is exploring in dramatizing Colin-as-poet.

16. Lines 307–310; cited from my *The Poetics of Orpheus*, Seventeenth-Century Editions and Studies 3 (University Park, Pa., forthcoming).

17. Underlying Spenser's complication of place is the familiar pastoral dichotomy between an active life and contemplative withdrawal. On Mount Acidale, for example, we may see Colin in

such contemplation, but here the mental journey does not seem to motivate Colin's return home. Even were Colin's retreat preparatory to reentry into the courtly world or to his becoming a Right Poet, his use of the *locus amoenus* is questionable. On the contradictory classical advice on pastoral withdrawal, see Vida, *Art of Poetry*, 1.489ff.; Quintilian, *Institutes* 10.3.22; and the discussion of these two passages in Nohrnberg, *The Analogy*, pp. 672, 724.

18. The differences between the Shepheard of the Ocean and Colin Clout force a reconsideration of what Richard Helgerson argues are Spenser's principal poetic options. To Helgerson, Spenser can be private shepherd or public knight ("The New Poet Presents Himself: Spenser and the Idea of a Literary Career," *PMLA* 93 [1978]: 893–911). *Colin Clout*, and even Book VI of *The Faerie Queene*, which Helgerson takes as his test case, suggest that the choices are more complex. Both the pastoral and the epic stances, for example, can be public or private in orientation. In fact, only when we recognize the complexity of the possible stances, and the ways in which any one "speaks metaphorically" of the other, can we appreciate the success of Spenser's accommodations of generic perspectives, such as the public pastoral, as is the case with the Shepheard of the Ocean, or the private epic, as the case with Calidore and the poet-narrator in Book VI.

19. Compare Edwards' treatment of the songs in *Imagination and Power*, pp. 49ff.

20. Hoffman perceptively notes the tension created in the poem by the persistent questions raised by Corydon, Cuddy, Alexis, and the rest, but she draws what seems to me an untenable conclusion: that the naiveté of the questions implies that it is good sometimes to stand as far apart from society as possible (p. 138).

21. Colin's error, and Spenser's disclosure of that error, are clarified by Berger, who, while denying Colin's failure in the poem, nonetheless pinpoints exactly his motivation: "The mind may visualize the condition to which it aspires as a perfect place—heaven, paradise, utopia, fairyland, arcadia—but this *locus amoenus* may be designed primarily as a mental hideout from one or another set of earthly imperfections. It is in dealing with dangers and temptations of precisely this sort that the techniques of fiction—fiction *as such*—reveal their usefulness" ("The Renaissance Imagination: Second World and Green World," *Centennial Review* 9 [1965]: 40). For another reading of place in *Colin Clout*—one which also tries to draw Spenser's poem into relation with Sidney's theories—see Terry Comito, "The Lady in a Landscape and the Poetics of Elizabethan Pastoral," *UTQ* 41 (1972): 200–218.

22. See the provocative study by Daniel Javitch, *Poetry and Courtliness in Renaissance England* (Princeton, 1978), for a fuller exploration of the complexities involving Castiglione's dissembling and poetic feigning, deceits and conceits.

4. *The Amoretti*

1. The critical studies of the *Amoretti* I have found most useful are: P. M. Cummings, "Spenser's *Amoretti* as an Allegory of Love," *TSLL* 12 (1970): 163–179; O. B. Hardison, "*Amoretti* and the Dolce Stil Nuovo," *ELR* 2 (1972): 208–216; William C. Johnson, "Amor and Spenser's *Amoretti*," *ES* 54 (1973): 217–226; Louis Martz, "The *Amoretti*: 'Most Goodly Temperature'," in *Form and Convention in the Poetry of Edmund Spenser*, ed. William Nelson (New York, 1961), pp. 146–168; J. W. Lever, *The Elizabethan Love Sonnet* (London, 1956); Hallett Smith, *Elizabethan Poetry* (Cambridge, Mass., 1966); and Alexander Dunlop, "The Unity of Spenser's *Amoretti*," in *Silent Poetry*, ed. Alastair Fowler (London, 1970), pp. 153–169.

2. The difficulties of actually naming or classifying such sonnet groups are immense, for not only do the groupings range from as few as two to as many as seventeen poems, but they are also developed by different means. Some groups are imagistic (variations on eye conceits or hair conceits), some rhetorical (varieties of blazon or *carpe diem* poems), some thematic (pride sonnets, cruel mistress sonnets), some structural (calendric sonnets) and so on. The problem is even more complicated when we realize how Spenser interlaces motifs. Thus a quatrain from a sonnet in group A may be expanded into a full sonnet belonging to group B. Despite the risks, however, a full study of such groupings would demonstrate the complexity of Spenser's *entrelacement* and act as a positive corrective to presumptions that we can understand this sequence by means of a few numerological keys.

3. A more comprehensive discussion of these three divisions and the contexts they create can

be found in Hardison's "*Amoretti* and the Dolce Stil Nuovo." Hardison's argument seems strongest on the Petrarchan context of the first division.

4. The only study of Spenser's use of the Song of Songs is Israel Baroway's "The Imagery of Spenser and the Song of Songs," *JEGP* 33 (1934): 23–45. In the light of more recent studies of the Song, such as Stanley Stewart's *The Enclosed Garden* (Madison, 1966), a reexamination of the sequence in terms of its biblical—rather than liturgical—imagery is long overdue.

5. Cited from *The Geneva Bible: A Facsimile*, ed. Lloyd Berry (Madison, 1969), p. 281.

6. The problem can be posed in linguistic terms by seeing the conventional "devotion" of Sonnet 22 as the signifier and the Christian devotion of Sonnet 68 as the signified. But as in all linguistic signs, signifier and signified can be reversed. The interpretive problem is the same as that defined by Tzvetan Todorov's discussion of *La Quest de Sanct Graile*: "For us . . . combat must occur either in the material world or else in the world of ideas; it is earthly or celestial, but not both at once. If it is two ideas which are in combat, Bors's blood cannot be shed, only his mind is concerned. To maintain the contrary is to infringe upon one of the fundamental laws of our logic, which is the law of the excluded middle. X and its contrary cannot be true at the same time, says the logic of ordinary discourse. The Quest of the Holy Grail says exactly the contrary. Every event has a literal meaning *and* an allegorical meaning." See *The Poetics of Prose*, tr. Richard Howard (Ithaca, 1977), pp. 128–129. In Spenser's terms, the spiritual can as easily be the signifier of the material as the material can be the signifier of the spiritual. The sign-system of love thus depends upon a recognition that all forms are *significant*, revelatory of the signified truth.

7. It may be noted, especially in light of the paradigm linking Maker and maker we observed in the Introduction, that only God can figure forth without reduction, hence without the need for metaphor. Christ's act is a literal bodying forth of the divine Idea, but it neither distorts nor limits that Idea and it does not cease to participate directly in the Idea.

8. *Annotations upon the Five Bookes of Moses, the Booke of the Psalms, and the Song of Songs, or Canticles* (London, 1627), p. 34.

9. *The Conversion of Salomon* (London, 1613), p. 148.

10. *Enchiridion*, in *Ausgewählte Werke*, ed. Hajo and Annemarie Holborn (Munich, 1964), p. 96.

11. Sidney's *Astrophel and Stella* (1582, pub. 1591) may be taken as the standard Elizabethan model in this regard.

12. I am following the Variorum numbers here, hence Sonnets 35 and 83, although identical, are retained.

13. Cf. Spenser's descriptions of the Blatant Beast, *FQ* VI.i.8; VI.xii.27–28.

14. For a fuller analysis of the "venemous toung," see my "'Who now does follow the foule Blatant Beast': Spenser's Self-Effacing Fictions," *Renaissance Papers 1978* (1979), pp. 11–21.

15. Carol V. Kaske, "Spenser's *Amoretti* and *Epithalamion* of 1595: Structure, Genre, and Numerology," *ELR* 8 (1978): 271–295, also argues a qualification on the lovers' success in the concluding sonnets. But Kaske sees the failure here as occasioned by the period of sexual frustration following their betrothal and preceding the marriage. Such literal terms seem to me to limit the process of loving that Spenser is exploring here.

16. Cited from *The Book of Common Prayer 1559*, ed. John E. Booty (Charlottesville, 1976), p. 296.

17. I am indebted to Professor John N. Wall for first suggesting this point to me.

5. *The Fowre Hymnes*

1. *The Poetry of Edmund Spenser*, p. 99.

2. On the neo-Platonic scheme of the *Hymnes*, see Josephine W. Bennett, "The Theme of Spenser's *Fowre Hymnes*," *SP* 28 (1931): 18–57; Bennett, "Spenser's *Fowre Hymnes*: Addenda," *SP* 32 (1935): 131–157; James T. Stewart, "Renaissance Psychology and the Ladder of Love in Castiglione and Spenser," *JEGP* 56 (1957): 225–230; and Enid Welsford, *Spenser: Fowre Hymnes & Epithalamion* (Oxford, 1967), pp. 36–63. The mystical schemes are treated by Nelson, p. 108; Jefferson B. Fletcher, "A Study in Renaissance Mysticism: Spenser's *Fowre*

Hymnes," *PMLA* 26 (1911): 452–475; and Joseph B. Collins, *Christian Mysticism in the Eliza-bethan Age* (Baltimore, 1940), pp. 203–230. Robert Kellogg and Oliver Steele, *Books I and II of The Faerie Queene* (New York, 1965), see a dialectical structure of passion versus reason in the work (pp. 484–487).

3. See Joseph Moreau, "Introduction à la lecture des Hymnes de Spenser," *RPT* 14 (1964): 65–83; James E. Phillips, "Spenser's Syncretistic Religious Imagery," *ELH* 36 (1969): 110–130; John Mulryan, "Spenser as Mythologist," *MLS* 1 (1971): 13–16; and Welsford, pp. 36–63.

4. I realize that the issue of whether the work is four separate poems, two contrasting pairs, or a single long poem is still not settled. I have tried to address this question in "Spenserian Medita-tion: 'The Hymne of Heavenly Beauty'," *American Benedictine Review* 25 (1974): 317–334, and shall here presume that Spenser intends the work as a single unit.

5. My count is a rough one, based on occurrences of the words flame, fire, light, lamp, heat, and illumine. Obviously, other terms—bright, blaze, beam, and so on—might be included to increase these numbers. Also obvious is the fact that this cluster is perfectly conventional for Renaissance treatments of love and beauty, especially for religious treatments. See Stewart, pp. 226–229; Nelson, p. 98; and Sears Jayne, "Ficino and the Platonism of the English Renais-sance," *CL* 4 (1952): 225–228.

6. Spenser uses "illuminate" rather than "enlighten," but until we clarify the movement of his light imagery, the latter is the more practical term.

7. It is not accurate, however, to speak of first and second lamps: for Spenser, the lamps exist only in a continuum descending from and ascending to the one true Lamp, Christ. The imagery, therefore, is not dialectical but unfolding.

8. Although I would not want to argue a source for this particular verbal paradigm, it may be noted that Augustine uses the same constellation of terms in *De Trinitate*, Book 15: ". . . the creature that was formable shall be formed so that nothing shall be wanting to that form at which it ought to arrive, yet it will not be made equal to that simplicity, where nothing formable is either formed or reformed, but where there is only form; and since it is neither unformed nor formed, itself is an eternal and unchangeable substance." See *The Trinity*, tr. Stephen McKenna (Washington, 1963), p. 491. More to the point, however, is that while the paradigm has ap-peared occasionally in modern criticism—see A. Bartlett Giamatti's "Marlowe: The Arts of Illu-sion," *Yale Review* 61 (1972): 530–543—we have not always observed its Renaissance currency. See the Henry Holland citation given in the Introduction from *The Historie of Adam* (1606), where man is "well formed in his creation, deformed in his corruption, and reformed in Grace." For a more expanded example, and one which relates the paradigm, as Spenser does, to the Sid-neyan model, see Ficino, "De Vita Coelitus Comparanda": ". . . because the soul of the world possesses, through divine influence, the seminal reasons of things—as many ideas as are in the divine mind; by means of which reasons it fashions just as many species in matter. Wherefore each individual species properly answers to an idea through the appropriate seminal reason: and often it can easily accept through this middle something from that place. When, indeed, it is effected through this middle from there, and if on that account it degenerates from proper *form*, it can be *formed* afresh by this middle nearest to itself, through which middle it is easily *reformed*. And certainly [this is so] if you correctly concentrate on the species of a thing, rather than the individuals of it—which are scattered—*conforming* to the image of the idea" (my italics). The passage is cited in Nohrnberg, *The Analogy*, p. 551.

9. Ficino discusses such illumination in terms reminiscent of Sidney's statements in the *Apol-ogy*: "Finally [Plato] adds that in the mind thus affected the light of truth is lit not slowly in the manner of human love, but suddenly. But from where? From the fire, i.e. from God, which shoots forth and emits sparks. By sparks he designates the Ideas . . . and he also thus designates the impressions of these Ideas innate in us, which, formerly benumbed by lack to use, are kin-dled by the breeze of teaching, and they are brightened by the Ideas just as the rays emitted by the eyes [are] by starlight." Cited in Erwin Panofsky, *Idea: A Concept in Art Theory* (Columbia, S.C., 1968), p. 57.

10. Kellogg and Steele note Spenser's allusion to the conventional meditative pattern, but they do not suggest that the poem actually reproduces such a meditation (pp. 512–513).

11. In "Spenserian Meditation," I have drawn the potential parallels between the fourth hymn and the *Itinerarium* more comprehensively.

12. *The Soul's Journey into God*, tr. Ewert Cousins (New York, 1978), pp. 55, 54.

13. It will be noted that I have avoided the idea of a dramatic speaker in the *Hymnes* and thus distinguished it from each of the other poems treated so far. It would be possible, I suppose, to argue the presence of such a speaker at the opening of the third hymn and perhaps even at the conclusions of the first two hymns, but I do not think this would alter the fact that this poem *is* unique in Spenser's canon. The mere fact that the *Hymnes* is a contemplative meditation sets it apart from the poet's other, more dramatic, works. And the poet's insistence on the reader's own performance of the poem-as-meditation also precludes his use of an individualized speaker. The poetic voice, that is, must here be kept vague or neutral enough to represent the reader's own contemplative process.

6. "Writing" the Proems

1. In her recent study of *The Language of Allegory* (Ithaca, 1979), Maureen Quilligan argues that the abuse of language is the real subject of all allegories (p. 86). Whatever weaknesses such a sweeping thesis might have, it does locate one apparently central focus in a number of widely divergent literary texts and Quilligan's own analyses would seem generally to support her notion.

2. By examining the proems from this perspective, I am also suggesting that they serve as both the first commentary on and the first criticism of the poet's own text. Or, more precisely, I would argue that what we have always accepted as one function of the proems—commentary— is in fact explicit self-criticism. This too is a defensive maneuver: the poet defuses potential criticism by having already criticized himself.

3. In the broadest of terms, the progression Spenser suggests here is the one he follows in the romance as a whole. What the poet does not see, at the moment, is that his narrative problems will increase the closer he approaches that historical present.

4. A representative treatment of the Virgilian echo is Douglas Brooks-Davies, *Spenser's Faerie Queene: A Critical Commentary* (Manchester, 1977), p. 11. See also the comments of Jonathan Goldberg, *Endlesse Worke*, pp. 14–18.

5. Brooks-Davies. See also Thomas H. Cain, "Spenser and the Renaissance Orpheus," *UTQ* 41 (1972): 34; and A. C. Hamilton's gloss on the lines in his recent edition of *The Faerie Queene* (London, 1977).

6. A. Bartlett Giamatti, *Play of Double Senses* (Englewood Cliffs, 1975), especially chapter 2.

7. I am in fundamental disagreement, therefore, with Alpers, who, if I understand him correctly, denies that the reader's memory of a given passage extends far beyond a single canto (*The Poetry of The Faerie Queene* [Princeton, 1967], p. 125). My own sense is that the reader is asked to remember everything he has read and that this is a major motive for Spenser's repetitions throughout the poem. Further, I would argue that memory itself is a constant theme of the work and that it is precisely the reader's remembrance of incidents that guides his evaluation and his experience of the various narrative actions.

8. See Giamatti's provocative study of Archimago in *Play of Double Senses*.

9. *The Analogy*, p. 105.

10. *The Analogy*, pp. 116–119.

11. For a brilliant discussion of narrative generating itself out of conflict with its own internal antagonists and its own urge to conclude, see Todorov, "The Quest of Narrative," in *The Poetics of Prose*. Todorov's essay raises a number of important questions which bear on Spenser's narrative art in *The Faerie Queene*. Although he uses Roland Barthes rather than Todorov, Goldberg has equally important things to say on Spenser's narrative strategies in *Endlesse Worke*, especially pp. 1–72.

12. It is Erasmus, perhaps, who makes the strongest humanist case for the dependence of conversion upon conversation. In her study of Erasmus's intentions in his 1519 translation of the New Testament, Marjorie O. Boyle writes: "The discriminating scholarship which altered [Jerome's] *verbum* to *sermo* was not a dry grammatical exercise but an incentive to conversation, and so, to renaissance. Erasmus plotted a conversational network which extended from the Father's utterance of his speech into creation; through the patrimonial words of men of classical

and Christian antiquity, foreshadowing or witnessing the *Logos* in the world; to himself conversing with them, the reader joining in, and reader speaking with reader in a ring around the continent" (*Erasmus on Language and Method in Theology* [Toronto, 1977], p. 129).

13. Douglas Waters, *Duessa as Theological Satire* (Columbia, Mo., 1970); and *The Analogy*, p. 206.

14. What has been said about Archimago's false dream intruding upon Redcross and Una in Canto xii is equally true of Duessa's false tale. In fact, it could be argued that only the specific terms of her story teach us one important metaphoric meaning of the couple's betrothal. The "dearest Lord" that Duessa purports to seek, and whose cruelly slain "blessed body" has been hidden from her, is the Christ who calls all lovers into Him on the "spousall" day. Moreover, if Spenser intends the union of Redcross and Una to represent the emergence of the true Church, then it is precisely their recovery and reconstitution of this "blessed body" that both nominates and ensures the full glory of their wedding. As with Archimago's dream, the presence of Duessa's fable in Canto xii opens the literal narrative betrothal to further metaphoric extension.

15. Despair's principal connection to Archimago lies in his doubtful doubling of feigned truth: like his poetic forbear, he dis-pairs the wholeness of Christian doctrine by severing Old Testament justice from New Testament mercy. See Quilligan, pp. 36–37.

16. While no one would object to the notion that Archimago parodies Redcross, the assertion that Fidelia parodies Archimago is less acceptable. But if we allow parody to carry positive as well as negative meanings, then it is useful in defining the mimesis of figural or typological representations. In such a positive sense, parody would be a rhetorical analogue to Sidneyan imitation, a mimetic strategy leading us away from inadequate or distorted embodiments of a given Idea to more accurate conceits of that Idea. For discussions of a positive rhetorical parody, see Rosemary Freeman, "Parody as a Literary Form," *EIC* 13 (1963): 307–322; and Edmund Reiss, "Chaucer's Parodies of Love," in *Chaucer the Love Poet*, ed. Jerome Mitchell and William Provost (Athens, Ga., 1973), pp. 27–44.

17. *Books I and II*, pp. 44–46; *The Analogy*, chapter 2.

18. Actually, this is not quite what happens. Una does come forth, unveiled, but the reader is not permitted to see her. As Spenser begins to describe her, he suddenly stops, pleading that his "ragged rhymes are all too rude and base" to portray her accurately. Emphasizing the reader's exclusion from the scene, he then tells us that Redcross had never seen her looking so beautiful and "did wonder much at her celestial sight" (I.xii.23).

19. Nohrnberg sees the "light-heartedness" and the "joco-serious" undertone as getting the better of the narrative here. Trying to make some sense of this tone, he suggests that Spenser's point may be that Redcross is regaining his generic (and fun-loving?) childhood. See *The Analogy*, pp. 196–197.

20. As Nohrnberg reminds us, Book II is not the first instance of the poet's peculiar relation to veiled truth: "the poet in Book I might seem to be working at an obtuse angle to his subject, if not precisely at cross-purposes: he is veiling the very truths that religion unveils" (*The Analogy*, p. 759).

21. This is the reading proposed by Brooks-Davies, pp. 117–118.

22. *The Language of Allegory*, chapter 2.

23. Harry Berger, Jr., *The Allegorical Temper* (New Haven, 1957), pp. 89–119.

24. Berger, *Allegorical Temper*, p. 111. See also Madelon S. Gohlke, "Embattled Allegory: Book II of *The Faerie Queene*," *ELR* 8 (1978): 123–140. I am in general agreement with this essay, although Gohlke seems to shy away from the logical conclusion of her argument—that Guyon is not human. She does hint at such a conclusion in an isolated footnote (p. 135).

25. Compare Berger: "The Britons—Arthur, Redcross, Britomart, and Artegall—are relatively complicated, ambiguous, continu illy changing and developing figures whose destinies lie beyond Faerie in the historical world. Elfins and Faeries, on the other hand, are restricted to Spenser's fairyland. They are ideal not only because they are exemplary, but also because they may personify aspects of human nature" ("The Spenserian Dynamics," p. 17). Or again: "Spenser's distinction between Elfin and Briton temperaments is concisely stated in the opening stanzas of Canto ii [of Book II]: some knights have it all by nature, others have to work hard to get it" ("The Prospect of Imagination," pp. 17–18).

26. See Thomas E. Maresca, *Three English Epics* (Lincoln, Neb., 1979), p. 42.

27. The parody is noted by Hamilton, *The Faerie Queene*, p. 216.

28. Compare Colie's discussion of this phrase in *Shakespeare's Living Art*, pp. 3–30; 351–361.

29. For a fuller discussion of why the text is inevitably a distortion, or marring, of both Idea and conceit, see my "Rereading Sidney's *Apology*," pp. 165–180. Nohrnberg directs us to another Renaissance statement of this fear of textual distortion: Hooker's worry, in *Ecclesiastical Polity* I.xiii.2, of "what hazard truth is in when it passeth through the hands of report, how maimed and deformed it becometh" (*The Analogy*, p. 695).

30. *The Allegorical Temper*, pp. 133–149. See also Alpers' treatment of Belphoebe, pp. 186–195; 387–395.

31. *The Faerie Queene*, p. 197.

32. On the general relations between these two characters, see Thomas P. Roche, *The Kindly Flame* (Princeton, 1964), pp. 96–150.

33. Kathleen Williams, *Spenser's Faerie Queene: The World of Glass* (London, 1966), pp. 93ff.

34. Compare Berger's discussion of the triad Belphoebe, Florimell, and Amoret: "They personify determined or deterministic functions of feminine life. Because of this they do not undergo interior development, but appear fixed and childlike and are always described as perfect. Their trouble is that they are perfect in too limited a manner, or limited because too perfect" ("The Spenserian Dynamics," p. 17). Although this description seems to me inappropriate regarding Amoret and distorted regarding Florimell's change after she emerges from Proteus's underworld, it defines exactly Belphoebe's fictional distortion. Obviously, I am concerned with only one aspect of Belphoebe's character; her typological relation to Elizabeth would not, I think, be affected by this interpretation.

35. Berger also senses a change in Spenser's understanding of his own narrative problems in this proem. He relates the change, rightly I think, to Spenser's "new sense of the poem as a poem, a fiction produced under circumstances influenced by the poet's social and political environment" ("The Prospect of Imagination," p. 98). This change and its enunciation in the proem of Book IV is also explored by Goldberg, *Endlesse Worke*.

36. Compare again the provocative essay by Helgerson, "The New Poet Presents Himself." While I do not agree with Helgerson's formulation of Spenser's choices in assuming a poetic stance, he has clearly opened a subject here which demands more careful attention.

37. Giamatti, *Play of Double Senses*, pp. 121–133; Gorden Braden, "Riverrun: An Epic Catalogue in *The Faerie Queene*," *ELR* 5 (1975): 25–48; and Goldberg, *Endlesse Worke*, pp. 70–72; 134–144.

38. Compare Nohrnberg: "But Marinell has fallen in love with 'mortall creatures seed,' and it is really the surrender of a precariously maintained state of privacy and perfection—a state of arrested development—that will humanize his character" (*The Analogy*, p. 646).

39. See Graham Hough, *A Preface to The Faerie Queene* (London, 1962), pp. 191–200; Williams, pp. 151–188; and Judith H. Anderson, *The Growth of a Personal Voice* (New Haven, 1976), pp. 154–197.

40. The failure to see how the merely human constantly judges and qualifies the mythic seems to me a major flaw in Jane Aptekar's *Icons of Justice* (New York, 1969), and, to a much lesser extent, in Angus Fletcher's *The Prophetic Moment* (Chicago, 1971).

41. See Nohrnberg, *The Analogy*, p. 408. Sidney, it might be noted, suggests a similar definition of Justice in the *Apology* (p. 84), and in the concluding trial of the *Old Arcadia*.

42. C. A. Patrides discusses the theory of accommodation in *Milton and the Christian Tradition* (Oxford, 1966), pp. 9ff.; see also his "*Paradise Lost* and the Theory of Accommodation," *TSLL* 5 (1963): 58–63.

43. Although he is not talking about Arthur in particular, Berger has accurately noted the problem here: "The subject of Book V is reflected in its style, which reveals two opposed stances of the imagination: one fixed on its interior world, the other directed outward. In the characters, a tension is produced between their status as persons and as personifications" ("The Prospect of Imagination," p. 100).

44. Compare Giamatti's discussion of Bon Font in *Play of Double Senses*, pp. 116–117.

45. Interestingly, Spenser's narrative of justice leading to reform inverts his own scheme of political renewal. In *A View of the Present State of Ireland*, he writes: ". . . everye daie we per-

ceave the trowbles growinge more vppon us, and one evill growinge on another, in soe muche as theare is no parte now sounde or ascerteined, but all have their eares uprighte waytinge when the watche worde shall Come That they shoulde all ryse generallye into Rebellion and Caste awaye the Englishe subjeccion . . . and therefore where ye thinke that good and sounde lawes mighte amende and reforme thinges theare amisse, ye thinke surelie amisse. For it is vaine to prescribe lawes wheare no man carethe for kepinge them nor fearethe the daunger for breakinge them. But all the Realme is firste to be reformed and lawes are afterwardes to be made for kepinge" (*Variorum*, p. 147). In other words, Spenser has Artegall attempt the very scheme he here labels as vain and useless.

46. Berger argues that the Beast is "the culminating *social form* of all previous evils" (my italics), and that it has "penetrated to the domain of words and names, thought and culture" ("The Prospect of Imagination," p. 107). The "social" extension of the poet, I would add, is the reader, who has now not only penetrated but also been made the guardian of the poetic words and names.

47. The relation between the Beast's origins in Envy and Detraction and its end as a public misreader finds a provocative gloss in Marlowe's *Doctor Faustus*. In II.ii, as Lucifer and Mephistophilis attempt to humor Faustus with a "diversion" of the Seven Deadly Sins, Envy crosses the stage with these words: "I am Envy, begotten of a Chimney-sweeper and an oyster-wife. I cannot read and therefore wish all books burned" (ll. 127–128). Cited from Irving Ribner, ed., *The Complete Plays of Christopher Marlowe* (New York, 1963).

48. The two best studies of this self-examination are Richard Neuse, "Book VI as Conclusion to *The Faerie Queene*," *ELH* 35 (1968): 329–353; and Humphrey Tonkin, *Spenser's Courteous Pastoral* (Oxford, 1972). Tonkin, by the way, is one of the few critics who has thought seriously about the proems, and he has anticipated some of my remarks on that to Book VI.

49. See Helgerson's discussion of Spenser's self-analysis in "The New Poet Presents Himself."

50. *The Analogy*, p. 658.

51. See Gerald Snare's description of this cyclic movement in "The Poetics of Vision: Patterns of Grace and Courtesy in *The Faerie Queene*, VI," *Renaissance Papers 1973* (1974), pp. 1–8.

52. See also Nohrnberg, pp. 661 and 700; and Maresca, p. 58.

53. *Allegory of Love* (New York, 1958), pp. 351–352.

54. On the more personal stance of the poet in Book VI, see Berger, "The Prospect of Imagination," pp. 93–94; and Anderson, pp. 184ff.

55. See the Berger passage cited earlier (note 46): "because the enemy has penetrated to the domain of words and names, thought and culture, the field of battle becomes, once again, the soul—but now it is the soul of the poet rather than that of the hero." It should be remembered, however, that the very passage in which Spenser has the beast attacking him in person is itself an adaptation of Ovid. In the famous envoy to Book I of the *Ars Amatoria*, Ovid affirms his poetic immortality even in the face of "gnawing Envy" (I.xv.1). Spenser's adaptation is the more striking for its pointed refusal to urge the eternity of the poem. It, like all else, is subject to "envious and calumniating time."

56. "Who now does follow the foule Blatant Beast'," *Renaissance Papers 1978*.

57. Compare Berger: "Fiction can fulfill itself only by going beyond itself and invading life. It does this through open gestures of self-limitation, as when, by revealing itself as mere make-believe, it seals off its image, breaks the transference, releases the audience and consigns the fate of its rounded image to their wills" ("The Renaissance Imagination," p. 75).

7. The Poem's "Wise Rede"

1. If Gay Clifford is correct when she argues that "to write allegorically is not merely to create a particular kind of literature, but also to make assumptions about its functions and about a particular way of reading," then we ought to expect Spenser to focus on the reading process. See Clifford's *The Transformation of Allegory* (London, 1974), p. 36.

2. The importance of this descriptive choice is noted by Quilligan, *The Language of Allegory*, p. 260, and by Nohrnberg, *The Analogy*, pp. 99–100.

3. Nohrnberg, pp. 99–100.

4. Quilligan, pp. 258–261, also observes the etymological play on rœd / rede / read, but does little with the observation.

5. In addition to the Helgerson essay cited earlier, see also his "The Elizabethan Laureate: Self-Presentation and the Literary System," *ELH* 46 (1979): 193–220. The issue of self-presentation is an extremely important one and intimately connected with the defenses I am suggesting Spenser marshals in his own behalf.

6. Spenser makes the priest an unwitting satirist himself of contemporary clerical abuses when he preaches a "ghostly sermon" to the Ape and the Fox on the painlessness of the religious life. With hindsight, we can see that the priest avoids doctrinal squabbles because he is more interested in keeping his life free for play than in reading obscure texts. He is obviously well read in the ways of the world.

7. Although several recent studies have addressed the problematics of reading in *The Faerie Queene*, none has studied the particular uses to which Spenser puts the verb *read* itself. The fact that the verb occurs over one hundred and thirty times in the poem is a clear measure of the constancy of Spenser's focus on the problem it names. Among the critical works I have found most useful on this issue are: Alpers, *The Poetry of The Faerie Queene*; Jerome S. Dees, "The Narrator of *The Faerie Queene*: Patterns of Response," *TSLL* 12 (1971): 537–568; Giamatti, *Play of Double Senses*; Mark Rose, *Spenser's Art* (Cambridge, Mass., 1975); and Alpers' important response to Dees, "Narration in *The Faerie Queene*," *ELH* 44 (1977): 19–39.

8. As my first example will indicate, there are "readings" in Books I and II that do involve moral commitment, but the majority of them do not. It must be added, of course, that I am not discussing implicit acts of reading—such as Redcross's difficulties in understanding figures bearing foreign names—but instances in which Spenser explicitly calls the interpretive act a "reading."

9. As before, I am treating only explicit acts of reading which are signaled by Spenser's narrative use of the verb.

10. Obviously, Spenser uses many strategies and devices to make his readers conscious of their own acts of reading. My contention here is that those which make use of the verb *read* serve as the rhetorical foundation for the others.

11. See chapter 6, note 7 above.

12. See also the useful treatments of this passage by Giamatti, pp. 121–133; Braden, pp. 25–48; and Nohrnberg, pp. 569–578, 643–645. For a much larger version of an external reading-text, see Goldberg's fascinating study of Spenser's use of Chaucer's Squire's Tale in Book IV (*Endlesse Worke*, pp. 31–72).

13. The definitions are cited from the *Oxford English Dictionary*. I have given only a sampling of the Spenser passages that might be aligned with these definitions, and I have selected only those meanings that Spenser unquestionably uses. It should also be noted that the OED cites Spenser as the Elizabethan example for several of these meanings.

14. This passage is the more striking because Elizabeth is, at least fictively, the one true reader for whom the poem is intended. For more on the problem of the poet's relationship to Elizabeth-as-reader, see Cain, *Praise in The Faerie Queene*.

15. Not only is the Beast a product of various misreading false-speakers, but as a "babbler" the Beast is also the final perverse double in the poem of the poet himself. In this regard, the Beast's movement through Book VI exactly reverses the symbolic topography of Spenser's own Virgilian progress: from court and city, the Beast regresses through farms to the pastoral core. Such a "progress," ironically parodying the poet's own return to the pastoral in Book VI, would seem to make the Beast an anticivilizing poet. See Nohrnberg, p. 664, and my " 'Who now does follow the foule Blatant Beast?' "

8. Amor to Amoret

1. Although this dialectic is not always on the surface of the text, it does seem to underlie most studies of Book III: Alpers, *The Poetry of The Faerie Queene*; A. C. Hamilton, *The Structure of Allegory in The Faerie Queene* (Oxford, 1961); Nohrnberg, *The Analogy of The Faerie Queene*; Isabel G. MacCaffrey, *Spenser's Allegory* (Princeton, 1976); Roche, *The Kindly Flame*; Mark

Rose, *Heroic Love* (Cambridge, Mass., 1968); and Williams, *Spenser's Faerie Queene*. The most extensive treatment of Cupid in Book III is William V. Nestrick's "Spenser and the Renaissance Mythology of Love," *Literary Monographs* 6 (1975): 37–50. For broader studies in the dialectics of Cupid, see Erwin Panofsky, *Studies in Iconology* (Oxford, 1939; reprt. New York, 1962), pp. 95–128; and Edgar Wind, *Pagan Mysteries in the Renaissance* (New York, 1968), pp. 53–80; 141–170.

2. Compare Nestrick: "In shifting the interest in mythology from *Gnosis* to *Praxis* . . . Spenser necessarily concentrate[s] on the concrete dramatization of myths. The emphasis on the moral level and human embodiment results in a corresponding de-emphasis on the mythological abstraction, the allegorical personification, and renders any four-fold exegesis ludicrous" (p. 69). Unfortunately, Nestrick does not pursue this shift to *praxis* to its appropriate conclusions regarding Cupid.

3. Wind's analysis, summarized here, appears in *Pagan Mysteries*, pp. 113–127. See also E. H. Gombrich, *Symbolic Icons* (London, 1972), pp. 31–63.

4. Wind, p. 125.

5. Although Wind is vague on this point, he seems to imply that Zephyr is the initiator of the painting's motion (p. 125).

6. Rose argues that Gardante is "an allegorical projection of Cupid in one of his aspects" (*Heroic Love*, pp. 92–93).

7. Compare Rose: "we have witnessed the growth of Britomart from a young girl . . . into a great lady" (*Heroic Love*, pp. 100, 103).

8. See Roche, pp. 190–191; and Williams, pp. 118–119.

9. C. S. Lewis's early remarks on the dialectics of love in the Bower of Bliss, the Joyous arras, and the Garden of Adonis are still worth careful examination (*Allegory of Love*, pp. 330–333). It is important, of course, that Britomart's first conceit of Cupid is occasioned by the destructive love figured in Malecasta's arras.

10. Compare Berger's treatment of this passage in "The Structure of Merlin's Chronicle in *The Faerie Queene* III (iii)," *SEL* 9 (1969): 42.

11. See Michael O'Connell, *Mirror and Veil* (Chapel Hill, 1977), pp. 99–124.

12. The anatomical imagery of the final stanzas of Canto v should be seen as leading first to the description of the *mons veneris* in the Garden of Adonis (III.vi.43–49), and second to the erotic description of Amoret's healed heart in III.xii.38. Although this thread of sexuality runs through Book III, one must be careful not to overstate it, as Nohrnberg does when he focuses on Amoret's fears of "a traumatic thrust" (p. 475), or on Malecasta's "suppressed impulse toward self-excitement" (p. 477).

13. For an excellent analysis of Malbecco's transformation, see Alpers, pp. 215–228.

14. Commenting on the phrase, "that rockes fall," in the preceding stanza (III.x.58), Alpers is led to identify the rock which threatens to fall on Malbecco as one of Tantalus's punishments in hell. This identification may be correct, but it leads me to suggest a slightly different alignment: "that rockes fall" alludes to Sisyphus; "Ne euer is he wont on ought to feed" in the present stanza alludes to Tantalus; and "Croscuts the liuer" suggests Prometheus. This triad, often depicted as a group by Renaissance mythographers and poets, clarifies the nature of Malbecco's transgression.

15. I hope it is clear by now that my broader conceptions of Spenser's allegory, and hence of the methods for reading it, are heavily dependent upon Rosemond Tuve's *Allegorical Imagery* (Princeton, 1966).

16. There have been a number of studies of this episode, but all take Roche's analysis as their starting point: Busyrane is a psychic projection of Amoret's fear of male domination and the incident as a whole depicts the Triumph of Chastity succeeding the Triumph of Cupid dramatized in Cupid's masque (pp. 72–87). My own reading of the incident is anticipated by Quilligan: Busyrane, she notes, has "been allowed within his castle 'so cruelly to *pen*' Amoret (3.11.10–11). With the pun on 'pen,' meaning both to imprison and to write, Spenser literalizes the dangers of Petrarchism; penned in passivity, suffering the torments of passion, Amoret is imprisoned in a metaphysical way of talking about love where one is always dying but never really free of torment in a real death. Caught in a web of pernicious metaphor, neither she nor

Scudamour can escape from the abuse of language literalized by Busyrane's bloody versus, until Britomart breaks the 'spell' and makes Busyrane those same bloody lines reverse. With the pun on 'verse' Spenser completes the process of redemption and signals to his reader that the real subject of Britomart's adventures has been the terms in which one can define love. Only if one understands the power of language to corrupt love, only when one understands how to speak of love honestly, literally, and boldly, as Britomart learns to do, will the providential design behind human sexuality be revealed" (*The Language of Allegory*, pp. 84–85). Despite some misleading usage of the terms literal and metaphoric, this sense of the incident is very close to my own.

17. The most useful study of the reader's involvement in the Busyrane episode, and the first serious challenge to Roche's analysis of the scene, is Alpers, pp. 15–20, 398–405.

18. See Nestrick, p. 60.

19. The oft-noted upbringing of Amoret in the Garden of Adonis is important to the Busyrane episode in precisely this way: Amoret has been raised as a divine, as a creature set apart; here she learns that she is human.

20. Alpers, p. 18.

21. Compare Nohrnberg's provocative thoughts on this issue in the final chapter of *The Analogy*, pp. 757–793.

22. Alpers, pp. 17–18. The function of Britomart in the Busyrane section has still not been sufficiently explicated. One point in particular needs considerably more attention: that both Britomart and Amoret are made to confront the condition of the opposite sex in the act of love which Cupid represents. The fact that Britomart is dressed as a male, therefore, may be the real clue to the lesson which each damsel learns. Britomart sees the feminine terror through her now-masculine eyes; and Amoret sees masculine power through her feminine eyes. Once more a potential disparity is thus resolved into the accommodation which leads, in the first version of the installment, to the hermaphroditic union at its end. And in these terms, one might wish to return to Britomart's own beginning and reconsider the significance that her first encounter is with *Male*-casta.

Index

A. Leigh DeNeef is Associate Professor of English, Duke University. He is the author of *"This Poetick Liturgie": Robert Herrick's Ceremonial Mode* (Duke University Press), as well as numerous articles.

Books of related interest

"This Poetick Liturgie"
Robert Herrick's Ceremonial Mode
A. Leigh DeNeef

Kinde Pitty and Brave Scorn
John Donne's Satyres
M. Thomas Hester

Gentle Flame
The Life and Verse of Dudley Fourth Lord North
Dale B. J. Randall

Jonson's Gypsies Unmasked
Background and Theme of "The Gypsies Metamorphos'd"
Dale B. J. Randall